The Hebrew Republic

ALSO BY BERNARD AVISHAI

The Tragedy of Zionism
A New Israel

The Hebrew Republic

How Secular Democracy
and Global Enterprise
Will Bring Israel Peace at Last

Bernard Avishai

Harcourt, Inc.
Orlando Austin New York San Diego London

Requests for permission to make copies of any part of the work
should be submitted online at www.harcourt.com/contact or
mailed to the following address: Permissions Department,
Houghton Mifflin Harcourt Publishing Company,
6277 Sea Harbor Drive, Orlando, Florida 32887-6777.

www.HarcourtBooks.com

Parts of this book have appeared, in somewhat different form, in
Harper's, Slate, Barron's, Prospect, and *Forward.*

Library of Congress Cataloging-in-Publication Data
Avishai, Bernard.
The Hebrew republic: how secular democracy and global enterprise
will bring Israel peace at last / Bernard Avishai.
p.   cm.
Includes bibliographical references and index.
1. National characteristics, Israeli.   2. Israel—Social conditions—
21st century.   3. Israel—Economic conditions—21st century.
4. Israel—Politics and government—21st century.
5. Civil society—Israel.   6. Arab-Israeli conflict—1993— I. Title.
DS113.3.A95 2007
956.9405—dc22   2007034413
ISBN 978-0-15-101452-1

Text set in Spectrum
Designed by Lydia D'moch

Printed in the United States of America
First edition
A C E G I K J H F D B

For Sidra

At the fringe of the sky, at the edge of the desert,
There's a faraway place, full of wildflowers.
A small place—forlorn and deranged—
A small place for worry.

All-that-will-be is spoken of,
And all-that-has-happened is thought,
God sits there and shudders, guarding all He has created.

"You are forbidden to pick the flowers of the garden—
You are forbidden to pick the flowers of the garden!"

And He's worried. Awfully worried.

—Yonatan Gefen,
from Matti Caspi's hit album,
Side A Side B, 1978

CONTENTS

The Hebrew Republic

PROLOGUE

The Situation

Jerusalem's a place where everyone remembers
he's forgotten something
but doesn't remember what it is.

—YEHUDA AMICHAI,
Songs of Zion the Beautiful

Six years ago, I moved to Jerusalem for the third time, to join my new wife, a professor of literature at the Hebrew University, and to teach at an Israeli business school. This was the winter of 2002 and not the best of times to move to Israel, for the Al-Aqsa Intifada had become a scatter of suicide bombings, and Ariel Sharon's government was preparing the first of its fierce responses in Operation Defensive Shield. When I met one old friend, she put her hand to the back of my head and started feeling around through my hair. "I'm looking for the hole," she said. I had spent the best part of the 1970s living in Israel, and the better part of the 1980s visiting and writing about the country, so the new disturbances, and little ironic gestures of solidarity, were not unfamiliar. But something had changed, certainly among my graying friends, a sadder but wiser air, a sense of being unlucky—a barely suppressed hunger to speak in big categories about formative years.

There have been dramatic turns since then, which raised spirits for a time, the way shock treatments are said to cure for a time: the fall of

Saddam, the Saudi peace plan, Arafat's succession by Fatah's Mahmoud Abbas, Sharon's blitz evacuation of Gaza, the launching of the centrist Kadima party. Hamas then won a majority in the Palestinian parliament, refusing recognition of Israel, and Israelis elected a government sworn to unilaterally erecting permanent borders—each vote a relapse into the logic of vendetta.

Then there was war again in Southern Lebanon, which took nearly all Israelis by surprise, though in a way that seemed to vindicate the working hypothesis. My wife noticed that even educated Israelis had begun to refer to the *matzav,* the "situation," no longer to the "conflict." And that is still the case. As I write, the Israeli Defense Force (IDF) exchanges periodic fire with Hamas-controlled Gaza, Tony Blair has assumed the post of Middle East envoy, and Secretary of State Condoleezza Rice has convened a peace summit in Annapolis for later in the fall. If, by the time these words are published, peace talks are not in the headlines, then the consequences of their failure will be. But you listen to the talk shows, or have dinner with a colleague, and there is little about possible diplomatic openings. The conversation is rather about managing a chronic condition, like cancer, or earthquakes.

Not that Israelis are stoic about people they think are insufficiently worried about them. During the Lebanon fighting, in July of 2006, I got in touch with an old friend who has lived in and around Tel Aviv since the 1970s. His parents' big Hungarian family had been decimated by the Holocaust; I have known (and dearly loved) him since we were children in Montréal. I happened to be out of Israel at the time of the war, and I had called to express my concern. But I also wanted to share misgivings about the Israeli Air Force bombing Lebanese ports, oil refineries, and southern towns in response to Hezbollah provocations—not just instinctive misgivings about the deaths of so many Lebanese civilians (among them, children), but the fear that, by bombing in this way, Israel could only alienate the Beirut middle classes and inadvertently strengthen the prestige of insurgent groups it could not destroy. And how long before scenes of bloody rubble, broadcast on Al Jazeera, would prompt demonstrations in Cairo that the Mubarak regime would be unable to contain?

These were not particularly shrewd misgivings. The Winograd Commission, later appointed by the government to look into the conduct of the war, restated most of them as if they were self-evident.[1] But by the time I reached my friend that summer, Hezbollah missiles were falling by the hundreds on Northern Israeli towns, and our conversation grew fraught. I had missed, he told me, the "robust consensus" that had spontaneously developed in the country. He e-mailed the next day:

> I believe that you are profoundly out of touch with the realities of dealing with our neighbors; that you mirror the ideas which have made the left increasingly irrelevant to the great Israeli debate of how to disengage from the settlements and the Palestinians, on the way to rescuing Israel as a Jewish and democratic state, and finding some workable formula first for co-existence, and later for peace. The brutal and reactionary nature of the regimes and ruling élites involved, and the imperialistic interventionism of regional powers (now it's Iran's turn), continue as in the past to sabotage the effort to move us in a constructive direction. The new factor, which did not exist before, is an Islamic, jihadist imperialism with global aspirations and the mega-trillions of oil revenues to back it. I'm well aware of its non-homogeneous nature, internal contradictions and weaknesses. And I contend that to belittle or underestimate it is suicidal folly . . .
>
> I'm writing to confirm what my red line is, even though you know it very well. It's the commitment to the *two*-state framework. It's because I know how deeply you care about Israel, and about the Jewish people, that I can handle anything you say, no

matter how much I may disagree. What I can't do is accommodate people like Meron Benvenisti, whom I respect, or Tony Judt (less so), who have concluded that the Jewish state is a lost cause. I don't need to question their good intentions or integrity, and I don't. But being under attack for merely existing is radicalizing, which makes middle grounds and moderate positions increasingly untenable . . . [No peace plan] has a chance if we don't demonstrate once again that we have the will to exercise the force necessary to defeat attempts to undo 1948 . . .

What I'm wondering is where *your* red line runs. We have been like brothers for the vast majority of our lives, over 50 years. I won't repeat my earlier comments about the polarizing effects of such conflicts. I want to believe, as I always have, that nothing could ever come between us, no matter how much we might disagree about anything. But this is too deep, too central to my entire life and being, too critical for my system of meaning, for it not to be a threat. It's not an intellectual difference. It's absolutely about who we are, in our deepest essence.

There are many claims in my friend's letter that might seem true to the situation: that naïveté about Arab intentions has marginalized the old Israeli peace movement; that a measure of this naïveté is the refusal to recognize how national power derives from military power (or the credible threat of military power), and that Jews have no excuse for believing otherwise; that older Arab regimes are more or less reactionary and positioning themselves for regional hegemony; that they pander to Islamist fundamentalists, who have Israel's destruction (but not only Israel's) in their sights; that Israelis, in contrast, have always stood ready to offer reasonable terms for peace, while the regime in Iran, bound to acquire nuclear weapons, would have no compunctions about exterminating Israel; that last summer's war was the moment to draw "red lines."

These claims are arguable. Anyway, you don't have to be Thucydides to notice how, in a time of war, people will see immediate threats and apparent loyalties, and fail to see their own past provocations or, indeed, the absurd violence historians see. But the most revealing moment in his letter comes in the second paragraph, a barely noticeable elision he assumes I will understand, the slide from an analysis of Arab intentions, which raises the question of Israel's preparedness, to a demand that I endorse a Jewish state, which raises the question of Israel's legitimacy. What is the connection, really, between Israel's need to defend itself against its enemies and his need to hear that Israel is a just cause? The answer is not as obvious as it seems.

PERHAPS THE HARDEST THING for people not living in Israel to grasp is that for most Israelis, talk about how to deal with the Palestinian militants, Islamists, and others is just foreground. In the background is a contest over what kind of state Israel must be. It is not just thinking about war that makes the situation demoralizing. Thinking about peace is also demoralizing, though in a different way. For Israel would not come out of a sustained war the same country it was when it went in, but nobody expects it to come out of a peace process the same country, either. What leaks into nearly every conversation these days is uncertainty about Israel's future boundaries. I don't just mean geographic boundaries. I mean legal, institutional, and cultural limits. Most people in the country will insist that Israel is and must remain Jewish and democratic. Almost nobody can tell you what this means.

Obviously, Israel cannot maintain an occupation, denying a great many people political rights, and remain democratic in any ordinary sense. But there is an even more disturbing problem, which (my friend knows) calls Israel itself into question. Can a state for world Jewry be a republic of citizens, many of whom are not Jews? The question is troubling enough as it is, but it also has immediate consequences for the ways Israelis imagine their fight. "Look," most Israelis will tell you, "we might have to push the Arab states around, or make them believe that we can—and we have to be able to do this with the blessing of Western democracies." If you ask them, "But isn't preemption and lethal force making your neighbors more determined to fight you?" they answer, "Our neighbors hate us anyway, and, sadly, most of our own Arab citizens do, too. It is naïve to believe that they won't, given the kind of state we are."

Israelis of my own generation do not commonly see a way out of this bleak reasoning. And younger Israelis are certainly no more confident about their neighbors. A former student, who saw hard action in Lebanon, now goes on about the clash of civilizations. Yet another student, a Herzliya entrepreneur, wryly told me just after Sharon was hospitalized, "It is my friends and I who've lapsed into a coma. We've tried thinking and it doesn't work."

THIS BOOK ARGUES that there *is* a way out, and an emerging Israeli élite quite capable of leading the country to it. But Israelis, especially members of this élite, first have to see how much better things are than what they commonly imagine, and worse than they commonly fear.

Better, because Israel's democracy—indeed, its survival—does not simply depend on how its military does against jihadist threats in Israel's immediate neighborhood. Israelis live in a wider world and have already met the more daunting challenge: building a vibrant Hebrew culture and an exacting economic engine, qualifying themselves to be included among advanced, global players. The challenge of the old industrial world was national self-sufficiency—some called this self-determination—which Israel's socialist and military leaders of the 1960s were reasonably good at. The challenge of the new economy is integration into global markets, corporations, and universities, which today's Israelis are *really* good at. Israel's technology entrepreneurs, scientists, designers, and artists provide their country with a staying power more impressive than anything the Israeli armed forces could ever achieve for it. This cosmopolitan economic and intellectual power reduces to insignificance any fight over tracts of land. It should also reduce anxieties about Jewish cultural survival in Israel's immediate vicinity.

Some call success at globalization a soft form of power. This is shortsighted. The ultimate aim of realpolitik today is to gain the capability of participating in the knowledge economy—the power to create wealth, cultivate human capital over time, develop technologies into entrepreneurial innovations—the power to attract, rather than the power to deter. There can be no winners in war now, only rival claims to make the other side suffer more. Israelis could anchor regional development and contribute in myriad ways to the future prospects of their neighbors—and their neighbors know it. America lost the Vietnam War, but who if not America is winning the Vietnam peace? In my capacity as a consultant for a global strategy firm, I have personally trained dozens of Libyan managers and entrepreneurs who are impatient for openings to the West—even to Israel, should peace be possible.

Besides, the global economy depends on political institutions that portend a global commonwealth. The European Union, with which Israel enjoys free trade, is the most impressive diplomatic fact of my generation. But there is also NATO, the Group of Eight, the Organisation for Economic Co-operation and Development (OECD, which Israel just joined), the span of world corporations, international peacekeeping protocols, the political pressure of twenty-four-hour newscasts and blogs—changes that define much of democratic life today and that make the political language of Israel's majority (indeed, phrases like *Jewish majority*) seem unexamined.

The great achievement of Zionism, the creation of the Hebrew-speaking nation, is a settled fact. The country that serves as its homeland might now adapt to any number of international political arrangements, while preserving its cultural distinction. The bloodshed between Israelis and Palestinians may not end anytime soon. Yet Greater Israel has a rival in global Israel. Palestinians, Israeli Arabs, even the vast majority of Jews removed from settlements could do worse than find themselves in the gravitational pull of Greater Tel-Aviv.

AND YET THINGS are also worse because Israel's Arab citizens, a fifth of the population, are threatening a shock to Israel's civil society, which the state apparatus has no means to absorb. Talk about Israeli vulnerability is usually focused on Gaza and the West Bank, or on Iran's long-term nuclear ambitions. But even if the occupied territories just disappeared, and if things were somehow to revert to the status quo ante 1967, the country would face, soon, another intifada, this time from within—not an uprising like Gaza's, perhaps, but something far worse than Watts in 1965, or the suburbs of Paris in 2005.

Sure, Israeli Arabs are the children and grandchildren of Palestinians who were led by reckless strongmen at the end of the British Mandate. They were wrong to reject partition in 1947. Ethnic cleansing happened on both sides during the 1948–49 war. And, also true, Israeli democracy has been a kind of liberation for many Arab intellectuals; Israeli Arab workers earn, on average, about seven times the average income in the territories. None of this changes the fact that the vast majority of Israeli Arabs are now third-generation Israelis. They cannot be told that Israel is a haven in a heartless world. Nor is their resentment of Israel just natural; polls show that about two-thirds of Israeli Arabs accept their country as "Jewish and democratic," enigmatic as this term is.[2] Rather, their country has evolved into an advanced, global, multicultural state, and its democratic flaws have therefore become insufferable to them.

Arabs believe, and their experience confirms, that no matter how well they perform as citizens they cannot aspire to live as equals or even live where they please. Their resentment is toward a pervasive legal structure that discriminates in favor of Jews as individuals.

Make no mistake: The danger of alienating a million and a quarter Arab citizens is imminent and very serious. This danger is exacerbated by the spectacular increase in the population of Israel's ultra Orthodox Jews, whose legal privileges encourage them to wonder why Arabs fit in their state at all. And what's going wrong with the country threatens to destroy what's going right. Israeli élites cannot hope to have an economy like Singapore's and a nationalities war like Serbia's. Israel will have to grow at an unprecedented rate, not only to absorb this large Arab minority into a Hebrew urban society, but also to mitigate growing inequalities in the Jewish population itself; globalization has left many undereducated Israeli Jews behind. If civil disturbances break out, the economy will go south, and Israel's brightest children will go west.

This danger is lodged in the back of every Israeli's mind, but most here still treat it lethargically, or brush it aside while stewing over Iran, or Israel's image abroad, or the latest political scandal—most, that is, except for Jewish settlers and rightist politicians who exaggerate the Otherness of Arab citizens and just assume a fight to the finish.

AT THE HEART of my argument is a tribute to democratic standards of the most ordinary kind—not just to a fair electoral system but, as V. S. Naipaul writes, to a certain kind of society, a certain kind of awakened spirit: "the idea of the individual, responsibility, choice, the life of the intellect, the idea of vocation and perfectibility and achievement. It is an immense human idea. It cannot be reduced to a fixed system." He might have added other attitudes embedded in this idea: scientific doubt, a utilitarian approach to property, the idiosyncrasy of religious imagination, the hybridity of national identity.[3] We are all born adorable little fascists, Naipaul implies, so the question is: What laws, norms, experiences, etc., in our social milieu will prepare us for tolerance, "the individual, responsibility, choice"?

Democracy, in this sense, cannot just be something that happens after a peace process. It is itself a peace process. And even if it cannot be reduced to a "fixed system," we have nevertheless seen democratic movements succeed because they pursued radical principles without quite knowing where these would lead. They fixed on the dignity of individuals, openness to federal power sharing, racial integration, collective security. Think of the early development of the European Community, or the American civil rights movement, or Québec's Quiet Revolution, or the newly minted peace in Ireland. Are Israeli leaders approaching their problems with anything like these precedents in mind?

Still, the Israel envisioned by this book will be a republic in which the Hebrew language predominates, partly through established legal protections, but also naturally, because the commercial hegemony of Israel's Jews will make Hebrew the language of work. It is a country already largely in existence. This Israel—this Hebrew republic—would be patently the state of the Jewish people, with voluntary links to Jews around the world, but it would be organized in a way that does not presume to straighten the crooked timber. Nor, I should emphasize, would it presume to replace Jews with Hebrews. A language is an ambience, not an indoctrination. Hebrew will provide a distinctly Israeli context in which its citizens—mainly Jews, but also Arabs, and others—work out their own lives.

No doubt, some of Israel's most prominent defenders—in the Israeli diplomatic corps, or American Jewish organizations—will rush to say here that Israel is already a fine democracy, or that exceptional circumstances make full democracy impossible, or that Israel's democracy is much better than anything its neighbors have produced, or that Israeli

Arabs are actually cavalier about democratic values—or all of these claims at once. And it is true that Israeli democracy is, at times, wildly underestimated.

But these people are missing the most interesting paradox here. Israel's deficiencies as a democratic state have always been most transparent to Israel's Arab citizens. Yet its promise as a Jewish state is also most transparent to them. I do not mean that Israeli Arabs want this state more than Jews do. They just envision it more clearly than Jews do, especially Jews of a certain generation. Israel's Arab citizens contend with its promise every day in the ambient pressure to integrate into Israeli civil society. It is a pressure exerted by the force and grandeur of secular Hebrew culture.

ISRAELIS TAKE IT personally—the arguments, the hyperbole, the history. Needless to say, I do, too, though I have followed debates about what is Jewish and democratic with a particular fascination since my return to Jerusalem. More than twenty years ago, I published a book, *The Tragedy of Zionism,* which explored the uncertain influence of democratic ideas on classical Zionist theories and, in turn, the influence of Zionist institutions on Israeli democracy. I tried to show that the residual Zionism of the state after 1949, and the settlements in occupied territory after 1967, were one problem. I'd often wondered if I had not been too rash or elliptical in making the case. (I'd learned from many subsequent years of business consulting that being called "ahead of your time" was no real compliment.)

The book, obviously enough, did not make friends among people for whom any criticism of Israeli democracy was seen as a comfort to Israel's enemies. ("Jew Against Zion," the *New Republic* cover declared.) But even people I admired—people who were otherwise quite prepared to entertain public criticism of Israeli government policies—were surprisingly hostile. One colleague at the Hebrew University publicly accused me of "liberal theology." Over the years, close friends in Jerusalem, people active in the peace movement for decades, insisted that my focus on the performance of Israeli democracy was putting the cart before the horse, that one first had to get to a two-state solution, and then deal with the internal problems of democracy—which would become more tractable, presumably, once the peace process succeeded. I returned to Israel in 2002 still wondering if they had had the bigger part of the truth.

By now it is clear that democratic principles are no cart, and the old peace movement's tactical sequence—first, a two-state solution, then, everything else—has not worked out as planned. Consider, if nothing else, the skeptical reaction of even moderate Palestinian leaders, in advance of the Annapolis meeting, to the proposition that Israel be recognized as a Jewish state. Would that not mean, they say, recognizing discriminatory practices against Israel's Arab minority? If they are wrong, do Israeli Jews really understand why? For even if a peace treaty were signed tomorrow, it would take many years for peace to take root. Peace will never take root unless Israeli Jews reform the ways they approach their future with Arab citizens. Recent decisions of Israel's supreme court suggest how far-reaching those reforms will have to be.

But this book has another task—which *The Tragedy of Zionism* could not have anticipated; namely, to create an intellectual bridge between Israel's veteran peace activists and Israeli entrepreneurs. There are exceptions, of course, but most people who've worked for peace over the years, in and out of Israel, have backgrounds in left-wing movements. One way or another, they've deplored international capitalism; the idea that Israel's entrepreneurial élite has itself become a natural peace camp seems to them strange, even vaguely cunning. I shall not explore all the ways the knowledge economy has transformed capitalism in our lifetime, spreading what often seems a magical egalitarianism on the job along with dreadful inequalities in society at large. What I shall do is connect the dots between Israel's economic and democratic prospects. There are novel pressures building on Israel's politicians, themselves increasingly members of a global professional class. Indeed, Israel's room for maneuvering has narrowed as its economic horizons have widened. Western diplomats should particularly take note of these novel pressures on Israeli leaders. Israel and Palestine cannot make peace alone.

A FINAL WORD about the book's title. I first heard the term *Hebrew republic* from Hillel Kook, a minor Zionist celebrity, whom I met in 1975. I was a young political scientist living in Jerusalem and had written a series of articles on Israeli affairs for the *New York Review of Books.* Kook had read them and decided I needed some mentoring.

He was then a man in his sixties, still robust and almost always accompanied by (and in what seemed intimate conversation with) his striking new wife. He sported a gray goatee, tweed jacket, and had a lean aspect—a modern Jewish aristocrat, I thought, with an air of precise, perpetual disappointment. He was the nephew of Jewish Palestine's first chief rabbi, Abraham Isaac Kook, and had been an aide to Revisionist leader Vladimir Jabotinsky. In the 1940s, under the pseudonym Peter H. Bergson, he organized the New York–based Emergency Committee to Save the Jewish People of Europe, the first American group to organize against the Nazi horrors then unfolding.

Kook became a member of the first Knesset in Menachem Begin's Herut party—which he left in disgust after one term. Israel, he began to warn, was heading for a fall because it had not shaken free of its revolutionary Zionism. It had failed to enact a written constitution. It was still in the thrall of old socialist Zionist institutions. It was being blackmailed by rabbis. It was completely lost regarding its own minorities. It had failed to redeem the real promise of Zionism, which was to create a "Hebrew republic." These ideas struck a chord, but there was something so familiar, so *material,* about Kook's liberalism that I could not quite believe it applied to the bloodied, noisy, metaphysical Israel emerging around me after the Yom Kippur War. He died near Tel Aviv in 2001, and I had not been in touch with him for years.

But more and more I've been thinking about him, and how he personified Gramsci's famous dictum that the pessimism of the intellect should be coupled with the optimism of the will. So let us say, willingly, that it will take another generation to implement a Palestinian peace and, with it, slowly realize the vision of a Hebrew republic, which is actually a return to the most original Zionist vision. Fresh arguments will have to be made for this inspired vision, in Israel and in Western democracies. And fresh arguments, coming at a dark moment, have to pass a plausibility test that standard arguments, however stale and improbable, do not. Then again, a generation or more is not too much to ask. That is the time it took all of us to create the disaster we will now have to unmake.

PART ONE

Jewish and Democratic

The phrase *Jewish and democratic* is not simply a slogan. It appears in something like constitutional law in Israel and has become as iconic as *life, liberty, and the pursuit of happiness.* I say *like* constitutional law because the Knesset never actually enacted a constitution. It enacted fourteen Basic Laws since 1949 (three of which have been repealed), which govern the operations of the state apparatus, elections, public lands, and so forth. Bundled together with the 1950 Law of Return—which accords immediate citizenship to any Jew who immigrates to the country—and with the (partly informal) Status Quo Agreement, establishing the Orthodox rabbinate as officials of the state, the Basic Laws amount to the so-called small constitution.

Which brings us back to the phrase *Jewish and democratic.* The most important law to be passed in recent years, the Basic Law on Human Dignity and Liberty, took final shape in 1994, and is the closest thing Israelis have to a bill of rights. It was enacted—so the text states—to advance the "values of the State of Israel as a Jewish and democratic state." Since that time, virtually all Israeli leaders assume the justice of the phrase. They speak it unreflectively, as if it needs no explanation.

Of course it does. For there are no definitions of *Jewish* or *Judaism* in any of the Basic Laws. Nor were there any in Israel's Declaration of Independence, read, memorably, by David Ben-Gurion on May 14, 1948, as Arab armies prepared to invade—only some euphemistic references to the Book of Books and the Rock of Israel, to "freedom, justice and peace as envisaged by the prophets of Israel." Democracy, for its part, was not mentioned at all in the declaration, though, intriguingly, the document made a commitment to "the complete equality of social and political rights to all its inhabitants irrespective of religion, race or sex" and to "freedom of religion, conscience, language, education and culture." Sadly, these liberal norms were never incorporated into the Basic Laws. They are even less pervasive in Israel's comparatively large and diverse population today than they were in the small, pioneering community that brought the state into being, just after the fight against fascism had been won.

The Basic Law on Human Dignity and Liberty, for example, guarantees the protection of life, body, dignity, property, privacy, and (touchingly) "intimacy." No citizen of a Western country would be embarrassed by its language. But unlike some other Basic Laws, this one can be revoked by a simple majority of the Knesset. Although liberal norms are fixed in the hearts of élite Israelis—journalists, scientists, business professionals, and scholars accustomed to working in the West and performing by its standards—the Basic Law on Human Dignity and Liberty falls well short of the European Union's Charter of Fundamental Rights, or Israel's Declaration of Independence, for that matter. There is still no civil marriage in Israel, no separation of religion and state, and no universal (or, for most, secular) standard for earning Israeli nationality. There is weak protection against being held without charge for "security" offenses, and very weak protection against discrimination on racial or ethnic grounds. One could go on.

No wonder, then, that a 1999 poll of the Israel Democracy Institute exposed a fascinating anomaly: 96 percent of Israeli Jews wanted a "democratic" state, and 85 percent wanted it "Jewish." Yet where democratic freedom and Jewish law clashed, only 54 percent said they would protect democratic freedoms. Thirty-eight percent said they wanted a state at least partly based on Jewish law, or Halakha. A 2003 IDI poll revealed that some 56 percent of Israelis agreed with the statement "A few strong leaders would do more good than all the discussions and laws," which makes you wonder what more than half of the 96 percent of Israeli Jews who approved of democracy were really thinking.

Speak of these holes in Israel's democracy, and hardliners will tell you that Israeli Jews must naturally treat their Arab minority with suspicion—hence, without full equality. Peace activists, in contrast, will say that it is Israel's occupation of Palestinian territories since 1967 that has coarsened democratic attitudes in everyone. Few on either side seem prepared to discuss the questionable legal construction the state has always put on Jews and Arabs alike, irrespective of enemy encirclement or the occupation. The simple fact is that Israeli Jews call their state Jewish and democratic, but the laws have engendered premodern notions of Jewish and partial ideas about democracy. Why?

THE ANSWER IS that Israel came into being, in effect, as two states, not one. Israel was established so successfully after 1948 because a revolutionary Zionist national home—populated by Hebrew-speaking worker-citizens—had succeeded in establishing a pioneering state within the larger colonial state administered by the British Mandate. This informal Jewish state, recognized by the United Nations after the Holocaust, had many sources of power: a land bank for settling Jewish collective farms (the Jewish National Fund); dozens of exclusively union-owned industrial enterprises; a system of self-government, with competing Zionist parties; a world organization to represent, and raise funds for, Palestinian Jews (the Jewish Agency); a Jewish health fund; a British-sanctioned Orthodox rabbinate to perform Jewish marriages and funerals; a Jewish defense force; and Labor Zionist schools, theaters, newspapers, cultural institutions, and much more.

Ben-Gurion originally thought this Zionist state would be a kind of scaffolding to be dismantled when the Israeli state was built. Alas, it proved more resilient than that. Israel's new leadership incorporated into their fledgling democracy most of the institutions, improvisations, regulations, etc., that had worked so well in settling Jews for the previous fifty years. Presumably, Israel would need them to ingather exiles for the next fifty.

So Israel is inarguably Jewish and democratic, but this really means that Israel is a democratic state encasing an older, heroic state, made up of residual Zionist institutions and an officially sanctioned rabbinate. Israelis share a public realm of democratic law and judicial protection, assuring the equality of all citizens, including the minority Arab population. But Israeli Jews share an inner state, in both senses of the term, focused on the material and spiritual needs of Jews alone.

This odd architecture has produced three crises. Israelis readily acknowledge them but rarely see the common root. First, the institutions designed to advance the heroic Zionist state have become unworkable for the democratic one. Laws alone did not create either the "situation" or the predicament of Arab citizens, but far-reaching legal reform will be needed to get beyond both. Second, settlements in occupied territory after 1967 were a true, if twisted, product of Israel's residual Zionism. A rollback of settlements, even for obvious security reasons, will be especially painful to a large number of Israelis; it will prompt them to rethink Israel from its inception—its culture heroes, the deeper claims of democracy, the price of love for the Land of Israel, and the prestige of Jewish religious Orthodoxy. Third, the legal status quo maintained for the Orthodox rabbinate has not maintained a social status quo. It has engendered a community whose political power is growing along with a burgeoning population—a power that threatens to sink the democratic part of Israel, irrespective of Israeli Arabs or the occupation.

Israel can emerge from these crises a stronger, better place. But today, one quarter of Israeli first graders are Arab and one quarter are ultra-Orthodox Jews. Many critical institutions are anachronistic; the laws are a muddle. You don't have to be a prophet to see where the children of Israel are heading.

CHAPTER 1

Basic Laws

What geniuses you are! What strategists! Don't you get it? Don't you see that our principle of "territorial compromise" means "as much land as possible, and as few Arabs as possible"?

—YITZHAK NAVON,
Labor leader, and former president of the State of Israel
(from a speech before a jeering audience in Yoqneam,
a Likud stronghold, during the 1984 election campaign)

Israel is an open society: Palestinians will be the first to tell you this, often with a hint of envy. Most Jewish Israelis, 81 percent according to reliable polls, also think "equality before the law" is essential, regardless of "political opinion."[1] And the judiciary is pretty much with them. Under the tenure of its recently retired president, Aharon Barak, Israel's High Court of Justice (its Supreme Court) broadly applied the Basic Laws to protect a wide array of civil liberties. Barak's court, for example, overturned the military censor's effort to ban Mohammed Bakri's 2002 film, *Jenin Jenin,* which charged (on thin evidence) that élite IDF combat units intentionally caused civilian casualties during Operation Defensive Shield. The court also rejected government efforts to ban Arab political parties.

Actually, when people speak of Israeli freedoms they usually mean speech. Hundreds of foreign reporters, including reporters from Al

Jazeera, are permanently posted to Jerusalem. Government politicians are notorious for their efforts to manage the broadcast news at Channel One, which is state owned[2]; but this did not stop veteran news anchor Haim Yavin from broadcasting (on the rival, and commercial, Channel Two) an independent documentary, filmed with his own video camera over a couple of years, exposing the extremist views of many West Bank settlers. In a country about the size and scale of Massachusetts, there are three fiercely independent Hebrew newspapers that together sell about a million papers a day (the more impressive when you realize that the mother tongue of a million citizens is Arabic, and the mother tongue of another million citizens is Russian).

John Stuart Mill wrote that the majority-but-one had no more right to silence the one than the one had the right to silence the majority. Israelis might have added that the one also had the right to jump into everybody else's sentences. Television talk shows are nicknamed *tarshe lee*—"allow me"—shows, as in "Allow me to finish." Former Knesset speaker Reuven Rivlin used to call out warnings to disorderly members the way a basketball referee calls fouls; three get you expelled from a session. He had to ban cell phones from the chamber.

But then, cell phones are themselves an infrastructure of expression. Roughly 100 percent of Israeli households have one. Most of the Israeli high-tech business community has acquired the libertarian feistiness of Silicon Valley. Israelis are adopting high-speed Internet access at twice the rate of Americans. Over 180,000 students are enrolled in five major universities and nearly fifty colleges and institutes. More than 30 percent have over thirteen years of schooling. Israelis publish more scientific papers per capita than any other country. Typically, about twenty political parties organize for elections. Gays march proudly in Tel Aviv. If their society is not exactly civil, silencing Israelis, including Arab Israelis, seems almost unimaginable.

———

YET ISRAEL IS A society where institutional discrimination against individuals for an accident of birth or a profession of faith has been so routine it is hardly noticed—not, at least, by Jews. The real contradiction in Israeli democracy is not between people who claim the right to dissent and people who would stop them, but in the conflicting impulses of officials, even in the judiciary, to realize democratic standards and yet protect the extraordinary mission of Israel as a state that ingathers, but cannot quite define, Jews. The most widely embraced Zionist principle is the justice of Jewish settlement. The most conspicuous inequality is, everywhere, preferential residency.

Start with population figures. There were about 180,000 Israeli Arabs in 1949, and they lived under military government until 1966. Now as then, Israeli Arabs constitute about a fifth of the country's population, roughly 1.2 million people. Of the 15 percent of Israelis who are Muslim, bedouins account for just under 3 percent. Druze and Circassians account for about 2 percent of Israelis, and Christians about 3 percent. (Incidentally, many now prefer to be called, not "Israeli Arabs," but "Palestinian citizens of Israel." The latter term is more fashionably defiant, but implies the very tribal concept of nation that Arab citizens normally try to break down. It is also more clumsy, creating a confusion with Palestinians across the Green Line, the internationally recognized border prior to 1967; will *they* be called "Palestinian citizens of Palestine"? In common Hebrew parlance, Arab citizens are called Arviyei Midinat Yisrael—"the Arabs of the State of Israel." I'll just continue saying Israeli Arabs.)

So the Israeli Arab population has grown by a factor of six since the founding of the state, pretty much the same rate as the Jewish population. Arabs are disproportionately engaged in farming. Remarkably, however, land available to Arab municipalities has meanwhile declined by 50 percent, to just under 3 percent of land within the Green Line. When you include privately held land outside their towns and villages, Israeli Arabs own just under 4 percent of their country.[3]

This segregated pattern of settlement is not the result of normal market forces. It results from the fact that some 92 percent of Israeli territory is public land, in effect, closed to Arab residency since 1949. The Knesset, not the municipalities, controlled public land from the start; in 1960 it handed over custodianship to the Israel Lands Administration (ILA), a state agency it created through a Basic Law. There were three kinds of land to administer, moreover. First and foremost was the land of the Jewish National Fund, the JNF or Keren Kayemet, including all properties originally purchased by Diaspora Jews during the time of the British Mandate. Today, JNF land is about a sixth of public holdings. The second parcel belonged to Israel's Development Authority, perhaps another sixth of the total. The remainder was said to be "state land," eventually to also include Jordanian publicly administered lands captured in 1967.

All of this would seem innocent enough if one could think of the ILA as an impartial state agency, considering development projects on their merits. Now and then, the ILA has behaved in just this way, allowing Arab towns to expand. But on the whole, the ILA has acted like the continuation of the JNF by other means. Official government brochures still justify the foundation of the ILA by adverting to "the special relationship between the People of Israel and the Land of Israel and its redemption."[4] This language, and mission, were borrowed directly from the JNF. The ILA did not formally adopt pre-state JNF regulations, which had stipulated that land could not be alienated to non-Jews. But until very recently, when it was challenged in the courts, the ILA strictly enforced JNF regulations on lands it had inherited from that old Zionist body.

Just to be clear, the JNF owned about half the territory assigned to Jews at the time of the UN's partition proposals—disproportionately arable land, on which most of the veteran settlements had been built. A majority of Jews still live on what does, or did, belong to the JNF. Nor

did the JNF remain a mere land bank, funded by Western Jews for pioneering settlement. After 1948, once the War of Independence was won,
the Knesset swelled JNF holdings with land no Jew had ever paid for.
The Knesset passed a series of laws to confiscate "abandoned" Arab
property, that is, the homes of Arabs who had either fled or were driven
from war zones. While the UN pressed Israel to allow the refugees to return—or at least to compensate them—the Israeli government simply
assigned their land to the JNF, tripling its holdings.[5] Of the 370 settlements established in Israel between 1948 and 1953, 350 were established
on formerly Arab property.[6] All of this land, too, was closed to Arabs.

There were desperate Jewish refugees as well, of course, as Israel
emptied out displaced-persons camps in Germany, Cyprus, etc. The
new Jewish state soon offered homes to refugees from Iraq, which
dispossessed its Jews in 1950–51. As the historian Howard Sachar wrote
of the 1949 turmoil, "Two hundred thousand Jewish immigrants pre-
empted 80,000 Arab rooms." But nothing can change the fact that Israel
simply extended JNF regulations to vast stretches of land forcibly confiscated from Arabs, and the ILA pretty much took over from there. JNF
regulations wound up being applied even to "internal refugees," Arabs
who never actually left the country at all, but may have fled short distances to escape the fighting, for example, the several hundred yards
from the new city of Acre to the walled Old City. Some 40 percent of
lands belonging to legal Arab residents of Israel found their way into
JNF ownership. (These residents were ultimately compensated for only
a small portion of the value of their lands.)

"THE MOMENT ONE of the people took one of the truths to himself,"
Sherwood Anderson writes in *Winesburg, Ohio*, "[the moment he] called
it his truth, and tried to live his life by it, he became a grotesque, and the
truth he embraced became a falsehood." This might have been written
about Israelis who swore by the JNF, or took the work of the ILA

for granted. Today, few outside observers are able to penetrate the ILA's convoluted leasing arrangements, for instance, with the Jewish Agency's mortgage companies, or preferred contractors, or the large and secretive JNF holding company, Himanuta, which has had particular responsibility for extending the reach of Jewish settlers into occupied territory. Government planning commissions may include one or two Arab mayors, but many representatives of old Zionist agencies, including the JNF. The JNF itself remains a quasigovernmental institution, presiding over a $150 million budget, and raising funds among Jewish communities of the Diaspora.

The result of these arrangements is serious material discrimination in favor of Jewish citizens, or planning policies in which the Arab presence in the land is simply effaced. Recently, the JNF, Ministry of Tourism, and Mount Hebron Regional Council published a brochure inviting visitors to the region of the Hebron Hills—partly in Israel, partly in the West Bank—in which the Green Line was not even acknowledged. But ignore, for now, settlements in occupied territory. Israeli politicians still speak urgently of *yehud hagalil,* literally, the "Judaization of the Galilee." Just after the evacuation of Gaza, the then vice premier Shimon Peres announced a plan to put ten thousand housing units in the Galilee for Jewish families from the center of the country. The housing ministry, the Israel Lands Administration, and the Jewish Agency also announced a plan to bring 250,000 Jewish residents to the Negev.[7] "The ILA has obviously followed a 'Zionist' policy since its founding," David Kretzmer, a Hebrew University legal expert on land policy, told me; "it has aimed for Jewish control of the land, through settlements, hilltop outposts, and so forth, and governments never considered any of this secret or embarrassing."[8]

In 2000, before the recession caused by the Al-Aqsa Intifada, about 100 million shekels were slated for Arab communities, about 5 percent of the development budget. In 2002, this was cut to under 70 million shekels, or 3 percent. That same year, the ministry budgeted over 11,000 shekels per resident in the booming Jewish border town of Modi'in. Arab localities, in contrast, were budgeted about 100 shekels per resident. An investigation launched by *Haaretz* revealed that of the 104 northern communities offered various incentives to grow, only four of them were Arab or Druze towns.[9] Recently, the Arab town of Sakhnin—which has a population of 25,000 and provides services to a large rural area in the eastern Lower Galilee—petitioned the interior ministry to extend its own municipal boundaries to include some 8,400 dunams, to account for natural growth. The government approved 1,700. The Jewish Misgav Regional Council opposed expansion. The amount of municipal land per Jewish inhabitant in Misgav will come to thirty-six times the amount of land per Arab inhabitant in Sakhnin.

Finally, some of the most important forms of discrimination are indirect. The government traditionally provides subsidized mortgages to young men and women who've completed their army service. Only Jews and Druze are conscripted—and Arab youth are not provided a comparable national service option—so the subsidy has greatly favored Jews. For their part, Jewish immigrants still get preferred mortgages from the Jewish Agency.

Serious people will tell you that Israel is a young democracy, as if more time and heat will, by some political alchemy, burn things down to a democratic residue. But if democracies can be said to age gracefully, Israel's has not. Its essentially segregated nature has only gotten more extreme over the last sixty years, as Israeli Jews moved away from agriculture and into large cities. Arab farmers and Jewish collectives once lived side by side, albeit distrustfully, and more or less at the same standard of living. But today well over a million Israeli Arabs live in townships in the Galilee or in strings of towns to the east of—and removed from—the Jewish urban mainstream on the coastal plain. In towns like Lod and Ramle, drug gangs control the streets.[10] Towns like

Tira, Taibe, and Umm el-Fahm are prosperous in the way 1950s Jewish towns were prosperous.

No wonder that even as Hezbollah missiles fell on their towns, more than a third of Israeli Arabs refused to back either side during the 2006 Lebanon war, while a small number, about 18 percent, actually backed Hezbollah over Israel. (Instructively, more than 65 percent of Jewish Israelis assumed that a majority of Israeli Arabs backed Hezbollah.[11]) Another recent poll revealed that 68 percent of Israeli Jews would refuse to live in the same apartment building as an Israeli Arab, 46 percent would refuse to allow an Arab to visit their home, and 63 percent agree with the statement that Arabs are "a demographic and security threat."[12]

THE SEGREGATION does not go unchallenged. Israel's High Court of Justice has, almost single-handedly, tried to reverse it, addressing Arab inequality much the same way the Warren Court began to change the face of the South with *Brown v. Board of Education.* The court unanimously struck down one government development plan for towns in the Galilee as "racially biased."[13] In 2002, in a landmark decision, the court used the Basic Law on Human Dignity and Liberty to rule that JNF ownership regulations could not be used to keep an Arab citizen—in this case, Adel Ka'adan, a surgical nurse from Baqa al-Garbiya—from building a new home for his family in the neighboring village of Katzir. ("All I want is to give my family better living conditions, my daughters a better education. That's all I'm interested in," he said.[14]) In 2007, Israel's attorney general, Manny Mazuz, extended the Katzir decision, advising the ILA that the JNF's restrictive regulations could not be used to deny Arabs from participating in its land auctions around Carmiel.[15] Civil rights experts like Kretzmer have been heartened by such decisions. "No way could they uphold a policy of not leasing public land to Arabs," he told me.

Yet as American civil rights workers learned during the 1960s, court decisions have little tooth in the absence of an executive authority willing to enforce them. As of this writing, Ka'adan has still not moved into Katzir. The land auction around Carmiel has been delayed pending appeal. In Israeli cities, most landlords will simply not rent or sell to Arabs. The justice ministry ignores such cases. In towns that have grown from farming collectives (like Katzir), residents get around the High Court's decision by forming "acceptance committees" whose criteria are vague.

Nor have Israel's elected governments been supportive of the judiciary in such cases. When the court decided Katzir, Tzipi Livni, then the justice minister under Sharon, stated that the ILA was "not obligated to the principle of equality" when selling lands.[16] The Sharon government immediately voted 17–2 to support a law overturning the court decision (a law never brought to the Knesset, where it would almost certainly have passed). At the time of Aharon Barak's retirement, polls showed that only a narrow majority of Israelis expressed confidence in the High Court as an institution. One reader of the polls, the Olmert government's justice minister, Daniel Friedmann, has proposed reforms that could, says Barak, "annul the High Court of Justice, [or] the subordination of the army to the civilian authorities" with a simple majority vote of the Knesset. Other polls reported that over two-thirds of Israeli Jews opposed allocating lands owned by the JNF to Arabs, and the JNF threatened to withdraw its land holdings from administration by the ILA.[17] In July 2007, the Knesset voted on the first reading of a law that would overturn the High Court's decision and permit the JNF to continue its policy. The vote was 64–16 in favor.

Even officials sincerely intending to apply court decisions betray ambivalence. When the showdown between the High Court and the JNF first came to a head, Attorney General Mazuz suggested, grotesquely, that the ILA should compensate the JNF from state lands for every parcel sold to non-Jews. In June 2005, he presided over an agreement that finessed the problem: The JNF would transfer its urban holdings to the state in exchange for an equal area of unpopulated rural land to the JNF, so that residency requirements would become moot. Pleading for a "non-discriminatory" standard, and against the proposed Knesset law of July 2007, legal scholar and former education minister Amnon Rubinstein suggested that the JNF should be able to keep its Jews-only policy if it returned to the ILA the land taken from Arabs by force in the War of Independence. The JNF, he said, should be able to manage the 900,000 dunams (approximately 225,000 acres) purchased long ago by Diaspora Jews "in line with national interests," such as building homes for demobilized soldiers. But imagine the Anti-Defamation League's response if an Arab Muslim trust had once bought up most of the attractive land in Brooklyn with Saudi money and then forbade non-Muslims to buy it or live on it.[18]

So the message to Arabs has remained pretty much what it always was. If you intend to live in the big cities, you're taking your chances on finding a willing landlord. If you intend to live in veteran towns and settlements, you had better be prepared to go to court. If you intend to apply for new housing, in developments populating Jerusalem, the Negev, or the Galilee, you had better forget about it. The message is unlikely to change without widespread privatization of public land.

"Just look at the Jewish Agency's settlement activities on either side of the Green Line," educator and entrepreneur David Harman told me. "A buying group, usually affiliated with a political movement, but in any case constituted as a kind of Jewish collective, will petition the Jewish Agency for funds to start a housing project. Then they may get some infrastructure money from the agency, or land from the Jewish National Fund, or mortgages for new immigrants, or parks and playgrounds, or connection to the water system—all 'philanthropic' projects. Then they constitute an 'acceptance committee.'"

Could Arabs expect to become part of the housing project? I asked.

"Don't bother applying," Harman said. The government might formally have to allow this, since the court has decided against discrimination, but the deal is structured in a way that makes legal formalities moot. Harman was the director of the Jewish Agency's now-defunct Joint Authority for Jewish-Zionist Education for eight years during the 1990s. He knows the ropes. Nor is the politicization of the Jewish Agency relevant only to what goes on within the Green Line.

"If the government, say, wants to invest money beyond the Green Line, it just walks over to the Jewish Agency—which is barred from such investments by American tax laws—and tells them: 'If, by using *your* money, we don't have to invest within the Green Line then we can invest *across* the line'—the money is fungible, you see, that's the way it works."

WHO IS A JEW? Here we come to the other knot in Israel's legal tangle. From its inception, the Israeli state apparatus recognized, in effect, two categories of personal status: *ezrahut*, most commonly understood as "citizenship"; and *le'om*, which means "nationality" or "peoplehood." Virtually all residents of Mandate Palestine who remained within Israel's international boundary at the end of the 1948–49 war, including the 180,000 Arabs, qualified for citizenship. They enjoyed equality in the new civil society, including the right to vote. However, people legally designated *yehudim*, "Jewish nationals"—people with Jewish origins, whether coming from Mandate Palestine or the Diaspora—had other material privileges, accorded by the core Zionist apparatus: residency rights in Jewish settlements, subsidized mortgages, and so forth.

The Law of Return defined as Jewish any "child or grandchild of a Jew, the spouse of a Jew, the spouse of a child of a Jew and the spouse of a grandchild of a Jew." This was not the standard of traditional Halakha, which deemed a Jew to be anyone born of a Jewish mother, but the new state—so it was thought—should accord Israeli citizenship to anybody who would have died as a Jew during the Second World War. (In fact, the Law of Return's standard mirrors the 1935 Nazi Nuremberg Laws.) Jewish immigrants were entitled under the law to immediate citizenship—a right extended to no other nationality. They also were also granted a package of *zekhuyot,* "economic rights"—tax breaks for a period of time, or the right to import cars and household goods without tariffs.

During those stirring days, if you could claim any kind of Jewish relative and wanted to come to the young state of Israel, you were welcome as a Jewish national. Under the Law of Return, hundreds of thousands of Holocaust survivors came to the country, making strict criteria for legal status seem tactless. Israel needed immigrants to fight the Arab siege. Western sympathizers took this all for granted. Nowhere in the 640 pages of Leon Uris's *Exodus* do Ari Ben Canaan and his English girlfriend, Kitty, speak about her conversion.

But what legal standard should apply for the long run and ordinary times? We usually think of nationals as people who have grown up and been naturalized in a particular national language and culture. Most Jews of the Diaspora still see themselves as nationals of their native lands—Americans, French, and so forth—and see their identities as Jews formed largely in private or congregational terms. They are Jews by virtue of Orthodox practice, or spiritual affiliation, or family saga, or even literary stereotype. (The writer Jonathan Miller famously quipped that he was not a Jew, but Jew*ish.*)

Obviously, the term *Jewish national* was reasonably applied to the children of the original Zionist settlers at the time the Law of Return was promulgated. These were people (like Moshe Dayan or Yitzhak Rabin) who had grown up in the Hebrew national home. But how to apply the term to immigrants coming from a dispersed Jewish people (some of whom had had no connection to Judaism), speaking many foreign languages? Many of these people had survived the Nazis, and fiercely wished to become Jewish nationals, by learning Hebrew and fighting for the national project. Yet they were not returning to their homeland except in the mythic sense, heightened by the conviction that Europe had been a killing ground. They were coming to something very new—a mobilized, compelling, parched workers' state—which Palestine's Jewish nationals had prepared for them. Novelists from S. Y. Agnon to Yoram Kaniuk and Aharon Appelfeld have written affectingly about the shock.

Early Zionists, it must be said, had never been terribly refined about these terms. Israelis still speak casually of Diaspora Jews as nationals because Israeli grandparents and great-grandparents presumed the simplifications of a workable ideology. Yiddish-speaking Eastern European Jews had lived in small, secluded, rabbi-dominated communities in the Pale of Settlement, where Zionist passions (if not Zionist organizing) got their start. Zionists called these Jews "nationals" the way Marxists called workers "proletarians," supposing that crisis would make the potential actual. After the pogroms of 1881, when over four million Jews began moving westward, Zionist ideas attracted a small, rapt minority of Jews—people who had come to enlightened places like Odessa, Vienna, or Bialystok—but who rejected assimilation. Zionists counted on gentile majorities to make Jewish minorities feel, if not illegal, then vaguely unwelcome. Since the era of the death camps, Israelis have spoken of European anti-Semitism as if it were simply natural. "We see the spread of the wildest anti-Semitism," Ariel Sharon lectured French Jews in 2004; they must come to Israel "immediately," he said. Israeli friends mocked Sharon, but many later told me—with the perverse satisfaction of a subtle doctor whose grave diagnosis has been vindicated—about traveling to Europe and encountering anti-Israel headlines, "which could only be explained as anti-Semitism." Many Israeli academics will tell you that threatened boycotts are simply anti-Semitic. Even civil rights lawyers in the U.S. and Canada warn about the "new" anti-Semitism in Arab lands. Publishers will tell you about the steady sales in Egypt, Japan, and other countries of *The Protocols of the Elders of Zion*. If you mention, in this context, how televised scenes of occupation over a period of forty years have affected the minds of new generations, they tell you how much worse things were with, say, the Dutch in Indonesia, "which nobody complains about."

I AM NOT SUGGESTING, clearly, that anti-Semitism is tolerable. My point is that there is vigilance against anti-Semitism that serves a kind of dialectical purpose for Israelis: namely, to make any Diaspora Jew seem to be a Jewish national, no matter how far removed he or she is from Hebrew culture. Sartre once speculated that anti-Semitism, more than anything else, made the Jews a people. That was simplistic, but anti-Semitism does seem to make any positive definition of "Jewish national" seem superfluous in Israeli law. In any case, no democratic state can assume that bigotry against nationals outside its borders will obviate the need for a reasonable path to naturalized citizenship inside. What is worse, Israel's pliable standard for Jewish nationality has, in the absence of a constitution, become susceptible to being shaped by all kinds of rabbinic pressures.

Consider only the most important precedents. In 1960, the Israeli High Court refused to grant the status of Jewish national to a Carmelite monk, Brother Daniel Rufeisen, who had been born Jewish, survived the Holocaust, and converted to Christianity after the war. He had lived in Israel for over a decade and insisted that he had cast his lot with his nation. Remarkably, the court decided that a Jew who voluntarily left Judaism might still claim citizenship under the Law of Return— you cannot leave your genealogy—but could *not* claim the legal privileges that went along with being a Jewish national.

Nor was this the end of it. The ministry in those years was run more or less continuously by leaders of the old National Religious Party, eager to reassert the halakhic standard for defining who is a Jew. The case of Brother Daniel emboldened them. Faced with scores of Jewish refugees who had brought their non-Jewish wives to Israel, ministry officials adopted the practice of registering the offspring of mixed marriages as, in effect, Jewish.[19] But after the case of Brother Daniel, the ministry adopted a new, more stringent regulation. It declared that to become a Jew, the child of a mixed marriage in which the wife was not Jewish must convert to Judaism according to Halakha—that is, by an Orthodox rabbinic panel and complex ritual procedures. In practice, the child would require at least a year of study and training, during which time rabbis would judge the child's seriousness and piety.

This ruling set the stage for an even more important case, that of Benjamin Shalit, an Israeli naval officer, who had married a Scottish woman while abroad. The Shalits returned to Israel during the early 1960s. They then had two children. As native-born Israelis with a Jewish father who was a citizen, the children were automatically counted as Israeli citizens, too. But were they Jewish nationals? The Shalits, declaring themselves both atheists and yet a part of the Jewish nation through naturalization, attempted to register their children as Jews. The Ministry of Interior refused. The children, they said, were not born to a Jewish mother. Paradoxically, had the same children been born to a non-Jewish mother outside of Israel, knowing no Hebrew or how to find Tel Aviv on a map, they would have qualified as Jewish nationals under the Law of Return. But a child born and raised in Israel could not qualify.

Shalit went to the High Court of Justice to challenge this bizarre regulation. In 1970, the court finally ruled in his favor, five against four, implying that cultural naturalization might indeed become a path to Jewish nationality. The response of the National Religious Party was ferocious. An anchor of Golda Meir's government, the party immediately introduced legislation to amend the Population Registry Law:

Any individual registering as Jewish by nationality, the amended law said, must be a "person who was born of a Jewish mother or who has converted to Judaism"—purely the halakhic standard. Ms. Meir wanted to avoid a confrontation that would undermine her hold on power. The law passed. In 1972, when the Shalits attempted to register their third child as a Jew, the High Court was forced to refer to this amended law and denied the request.

Remarkably, the Shalit decisions still stand. There are no ordinary processes of naturalization other than through rabbinic courts. In consequence, the children of foreign workers—educated in Israeli schools since they were tots—have been routinely deported unless they convert to Judaism. Their plight became so obvious in recent years that Israeli civil rights groups finally brought suit on their behalf in 2005. One such child, whose parents are from Colombia, told Israeli television in perfect, idiomatic Hebrew: "My parents didn't ask me whether I wanted to come here; I want to go to university here, go to the army, marry here."[20]

To its credit, and as a sign of how embarrassing this system has become, the Olmert government has recently approved new criteria: The children of guest workers could stay if they were under fourteen when entering Israel and had stayed uninterruptedly for at least six years. They also had to prove that their parents had held valid work permits and that they themselves were fluent in Hebrew. Yet when these reared-in-Hebrew children become citizens, they will not become Jewish nationals. They will become something like biblical *gerim*—"strangers who dwell in your midst"—people subject to equal protection, but legally anomalous.

SO IF YOU ARE born in Israel to a Jewish mother, then you are a Jewish national and a citizen. You are also a Jewish national if you are an immigrant who has not renounced the Jewish faith and are descended from at least one Jewish grandparent—a grandparent, that is, who was born to a Jewish mother who had not renounced her faith. You can become a citizen of Israel the moment you land. But if you are born in Israel to a Jewish father only, then you are a citizen—but can only become a Jewish national by sincerely converting to Judaism. A non-Jew can also become a Jewish national by converting, like the child born in Israel to a non-Jewish mother, but unlike that child, cannot be a citizen without converting. An Arab Muslim can never become a Jewish national and, if born outside the country, can forget about becoming a citizen. Then again, the interior minister can just make you a citizen. Clear?

I hasten to add that getting the state to recognize unorthodox forms of conversion to Judaism is of no help here. Many Israeli liberals claimed a victory in 2002 when the High Court ruled that conversions to Judaism performed by Reform movement rabbis must be recognized by the Ministry of Interior. (The decision was meant to smooth the way to Jewish nationality for Russian immigrants, whose children serve in the army but who generally detest the Orthodox rabbinate.[21]) In March 2005, the court also ruled that people already residing in Israel who go overseas for a final Reform conversion ceremony must also be recognized as Jews.

But the question, surely, is not whether the Reform movement should have the right to declare a Jewish convert qualified for state privileges. Recognition of Reform authority may do something for pluralism within Jewish religious life but nothing for constitutional pluralism within Israeli democracy. The question is how to square privileges for Jews with the equality presumed by democratic law. The High Court's decisions only made a discriminatory standard somewhat more inclusive. It did nothing to integrate Israeli Arabs, or for that matter, the Filipinas who tend to Jewish grandparents, or the Thais who build Jewish housing.

"Israelis do not really have a familiarity with the concepts of democracy," says Rafi Cohen-Almagor, the director of democratic studies at

Haifa University. "They know the mechanisms, so when you ask them about democracy they will say something about majority rule, or balance of powers. But these mechanisms are not principles of democracy—like liberty, fallibility, equality, tolerance. They are merely functions. Israeli kids hardly study principles."

Haven't schools taught these principles? "We had two educational committees in recent years," Cohen-Almagor told me; "one to study democracy, one Judaic studies. The latter is the one the government cared about. So kids study the role of the government, the role of the Knesset—all the boring stuff. When there is a math exam, citizenship studies get shunted aside. But when you speak about the relation of Judaism and democracy, you find a democracy under stress. We can't take for granted this is going to last forever—not with all the generals we have coming into the government, the power of the rabbinate, and the enemy that we have around us, the security budget. We don't even have a shared raison d'être with 20 percent of the population—Arabs, who are increasingly alienated from the symbols of the state, the flag, the currency, and everything else. And then there is another 25 percent Orthodox or ultra-Orthodox, who'd be happy to replace democracy with theocracy, and who are just looking for the right opportunity. On top of that, we have another 20 percent, immigrants from the Soviet Union, who know nothing about what democracy is all about, who are suspicious about government and have never lived under democracy.

"It is becoming increasingly difficult," Cohen-Almagor summed things up, "to define a state that invites something in common. What we need to address is pluralism and multiculturalism, not Zionism. We have a severe problem of racism in this country, not just about Arabs— prejudice against Russians, against Ethiopians—it starts with the jokes, and ends with anxiety about property values. And we have no constitution to balance the scales."

THINGS DID NOT have to turn out this way. Israel's first national election, in January 1949, was supposed to convene a constitutional assembly that would define the terms of Israeli nationality and pass a bill of rights. It did not. The problem was not the failure to come up with a suitable draft.

"I was a runner in Jerusalem during the 1948 War," the writer Amos Elon told me, "and one mission was to bring a message to the head of the Haganah in the Jewish Agency building in Jerusalem. I arrived one dark evening at the building in the middle of an artillery barrage, with *boom-boom* everywhere, and the place was gloomy and deserted—except for a light in one office, where I found Dr. Leo Kohn, the legal advisor to the Jewish Agency, curled over his desk, writing. 'What are you doing here?' he asked. I told him I was looking for the Haganah headquarters. He pointed me to the basement. I was young and a little brash, so I could not resist. I asked him, 'What are *you* doing here?' He answered almost nonchalantly, in a heavy German accent, 'I am writing the constitution of the Jewish state.'"

Which is exactly what Kohn did. His draft began by defining the character, official language, and citizenship of Israel. It also, in his words, affirmed "the principle of the complete equality of all citizens."[22] In the chapter on human rights, he tried to embody "some of the characteristic spiritual traditions of the Jewish people." And so the sanctity of human life and the dignity of man "were postulated as major objects of the State's solicitude." The death penalty was to be abolished; habeas corpus was to be guaranteed. Preventive detention by executive order was to be prohibited, except when authorized by specific legislation in time of war or national emergency.

The draft embodied, Kohn continued, guarantees of "the inviolability of dwelling and private correspondence." Provisions were designed to safeguard the freedom of conscience and "the free exercise of all forms of religious worship as well as the rights of all communities in their holy places and the administration of their religious properties." It prohibited the extradition of any person to a foreign country where he or she was liable to be deprived of the fundamental rights guaranteed in the Israeli constitution. The draft also included a number of economic and social rights, such as the right of workers to form trade unions, to enter into collective contracts, and to strike in defense of their economic interests. There were, Kohn concluded, "the traditional guarantees of the freedom of speech, assembly and association, but these were not to extend to publications, assemblies and associations aiming at the suppression of human rights and the subversion of the democratic form of government."

DAVID BEN-GURION was supposed to submit the Kohn draft to the elected assembly for ratification. But secular and Orthodox Jews soon wrangled over how Judaism might be privileged. Kohn's draft, for all of its guarantees of equal rights, reserved the largely ceremonial post of president for Jews. Ben-Gurion's own Mapai party, and the Marxist Mapam party—both of which represented most of the left-wing kibbutzim—actually opposed this relatively minor provision, fearing that it would be regarded in the West as racist.[23] For their part, the Orthodox parties were clear that formal privileges for Jews would be just fine with them.

Ben-Gurion quickly realized that that this dispute was an augury of a larger Kulturkampf, which he wanted to avoid. He also saw the possibility of appeasing the Orthodox and governing, in effect, without powerful coalition partners. So he made perhaps his most shortsighted decision and let the moment pass. He mustered a majority, combining his ruling Mapai and the Orthodox parties, and transformed the constitutional assembly into the first Knesset, which would leave the writing of a constitution to "future generations." This was no time, he said, to divide the Jewish people in the young state. It didn't hurt that the decision buttressed his personal power.

"He didn't want to take Mapam into the government; Mapam were philo-Soviet," Elon said. "He didn't want Begin's Herut, which he considered fascist and recently terrorist. He didn't want liberals, who would demand concessions from the Histadrut [the Jewish labor federation] for a freer market. He liked the idea of ruling without real opposition. So Ben-Gurion did the deal with the Orthodox, whose world didn't touch him and therefore didn't threaten him. He himself was a complete nonbeliever. His son had married a non-Jewish woman in London, and he thought nothing of it. It just never occurred to him that these Orthodox rabbis could eventually constitute a danger. He thought 'future generations' might well secure basic rights."

Besides, would not secular life and Jewish-Arab integration be a natural byproduct of working-class solidarity? Socialist Zionist leaders—so we learn from Tom Segev's indispensable book, *1949: The First Israelis*—had hoped that the convergent interests of workers would create a kind of de facto integration in a new Israeli nation. Pinchas Lavon, head of the Histadrut then, advocated bringing Israeli Arabs into the army, which would provide "a national and social" education: "For the first time we will be a majority living with a minority," he wrote, "and we shall be called upon to provide an example and prove how Jews live with a minority." But as the 1948 war raged on, Lavon grew wary of the anticipated results of the escalation, warning of the "Israeli-born generation with its crude and primitive nationalism," and of the Sephardi communities, "with their historical and natural urge to avenge the years of humiliation and oppression they suffered in Arab countries."[24]

BEN-GURION'S SURRENDER of the Kohn constitution was the first instance of what would become a recurrent legal ricochet. Arabs lost a path to full citizenship—to a legal standard where nationality and citizenship just merged—but the most salient obstacle was not a stand-off between Israeli liberals and authoritarian nationalists over the rights of Arabs. Rather, the standoff was between secular and Orthodox Jews over the privileges of Judaism. On the other hand, had Jews opted for a secular solution for themselves, this would have given Arabs an opening. The writer Yitzhak Laor puts it this way: "Israelis have ascribed the absence of opposition to the 'religious' to the absence of a written constitution. They forget that a constitution is impossible because the State of Israel, that unenlightened enlightened state, does not want to open the constitution with a declaration of full equality for all its citizens, and particularly not regarding property rights."[25]

In any case, Israeli Arabs' second-class citizenship does not simply mean getting less official status than they would like from the majority. It means getting less material support from the state than the majority. The Israeli government devotes about 8 percent of its infrastructural investments to Arab towns, less than half per capita of what it invests in the Jewish sector. It is the same with the health ministry's budget. The Arab school system has been underfunded for many years and at all levels. Arab children constitute 30 percent of all children, from newborn to four years old, in Israel, but account for only about 7 percent of the children enrolled in institutional and home-based day-care facilities. About half of non-Jewish Israelis age fifteen and over do not have a high school education, compared with one-fifth of Jews. The proportion of Jewish youngsters who go on to higher education is double that of non-Jews.

Roads and bridges are no better. They are notorious in Arab towns, themselves mostly made up of rambling (and, on the surface, quite handsome) family compounds, which have grown without proper zoning, plumbing, or electricity. Ilan Katz, an engineering consultant and civil rights activist, told me that his own town of Zichron Yaacov has been getting as much as thirty times more land and municipal support per capita than the neighboring town of Faradis. Another nearby town, Ein Hud, is in even worse shape: "The Arab town of Ein Hud, much of which was displaced by what has become the lovely artists' colony at Ein Hod, was declared a municipality in 1994," Katz says. "They are still waiting for roads, sewers, and electricity. Drive there; suddenly you hit a dirt road."

Can't some of this neglect be accounted for by Arab hostility? "Yes, but does the outbreak of fire justify pouring gasoline on it? The Shin Bet [the general security service] has been asked by a succession of governments to determine if Israeli Arabs are a security threat," Katz continued. "I know for a fact that those governments have been provided a series of reports, at least fifteen, insisting that Israeli Arabs are not a threat, but that ignoring and underinvesting in Israeli Arabs is creating a security threat. All of these warnings have been ignored."

Today, average GDP per capita is three times higher among Jews than Arabs, about $21,000 compared with about $7,000. An Arab family is three times more likely to live under the poverty line than a Jewish family. Some 209,000 students in the Arab school system are at the bottom rungs of the scholastic achievement ladder in all elementary grades. By 2003, Arab fifth graders were almost as proficient as Jews in English—not surprising since both spend time watching American television programs and playing with Internet sites. But Arab fifth graders were about half as likely to have mastered written Hebrew.

Not surprisingly, therefore, the rate of participation in the workforce among Arabs aged fifteen and over is about 40 percent, compared with 57 percent among Jews. Currently, about 40 percent of Arab men between the ages of forty-five and fifty-four are not in the workforce at all.[26] About half of all working Arabs are employed in industrial and construction jobs or as unskilled labor, compared with about a fifth of Jews who work in these categories. Hebrew University sociologist Aziz Haidar observes that gaining the requisite educational credentials is hardly sufficient to assure an Arab equal access to a job in an élite profession. Nearly one-third of the Arabs in Israel who hold master's degrees are employed as skilled workers in industry and construction. Medical schools used to base acceptance solely on the psychometric exams, like the American SAT. Today, virtually all medical schools are reducing the number of Arab candidates by including an interview process.

Finally, less than 20 percent of Arab women participate in the workforce, compared with over 50 percent of Jewish women. Most Israeli Jews will tell you that Israeli Arabs like things this way, that Arab women are trapped in backwardness. ("Their brothers still kill them for holding hands," one friend told me.) But Israeli Arab women are actually adapting to Israeli civil society at about the same rate that North African Jews are. Where opportunities exist for Israeli Arab families, women seize them. According to Aziz Haidar, the birthrate is falling palpably among educated Arabs.[27] For women with a college education, the participation rates in the labor force for Arab and Jewish women are similar, about 75 percent.[28] Frustration with the educational system is only accelerating birthrates—about 50 percent higher among Arabs than Israeli Jews. Then again, all poorer families in Israeli society, bedouin, Arab, and ultra-Orthodox, have had strong incentives to raise many children over the past two generations, owing to generous welfare benefits for families with five or more children.

"THE ARABS IN ISRAEL are the true Jews," says Salem Jubran, a Nazareth journalist and educator. "They understand that education is the only necessary capital. A national minority has two choices: to be fanatic and insular or to be pragmatic. The Arabs in Israel feel they live in an achievement-oriented society, but that the world is less open to them."[29] The novelist Sayed Kashua, author of the Hebrew novel *Dancing Arabs,* is more blunt. His childhood friends are feeling hemmed in and enraged, he told me, their towns in commercial despair, many coming under the threat of young toughs.

Attitudes are hardening. According to a 2007 poll, 60 percent of Israeli Arabs say they fear a mass expulsion.[30] More than 68 percent of Israeli Jews fear a civil uprising in behalf of Israeli Arabs, and 63 percent say they won't enter Arab towns in Israel. "When these towns blow," Kashua told me, "Israeli Jews will say it is for intractable political reasons. But if the government would give us two meters for development, we'd all be volunteering for the army. Every time there is a suicide bombing I think two things: Thank god my daughter is not among the victims, and I hope there is an Arab Israeli among the victims, so they won't blame my daughter."

In this atmosphere, exacerbated by the collapse of the Oslo process, tensions become explosive. The first weeks of the Al-Aqsa Intifada inadvertently brought Israel to the brink. The streets of Israeli Arab towns erupted with demonstrations of solidarity for Palestinian self-determination and calls to end the occupation, culminating in a general strike to protest the visit by then opposition leader Ariel Sharon to the Haram al-Sharif, the Temple Mount. And as if on cue, Israeli police responded with a violence that would not have been unleashed against Jews. In two cases, in Nazareth and Umm el-Fahm, police opened fire with tear gas, rubber bullets, and live ammunition at youths throwing stones and burning tires. In the end, thirteen young people were killed—an incident eerily reminiscent of Land Day in March 1976, when six Israeli Arab youths were killed in a general strike protesting the confiscation of land in the Galilee.

After the violence subsided, Ehud Barak's government appointed a commission of inquiry, led by Justice Theodor Or, and including Professor Shimon Shamir, the highly respected expert on Arab affairs, who wound up becoming the primary author of the report. The commission met for twelve months and heard 349 witnesses; their report, published in September 2003, pointed to glaring inequalities in land rights and infrastructural budgets, and also cast doubt on areas thought to be moving toward equality, employment, and education. Nevertheless, the justice ministry's Police Investigations Unit went on to exonerate the police officers charged with using excessive force. Shamir responded, "A situation where 13 people are killed and no one is indicted is one that is hard to grasp."[31] Not coincidentally, only about half of Israeli Arabs subsequently voted in the March 2006 election.

Alas, the social blasting caps may also be deliberate. Some Israeli Arabs have colluded in acts of terrorism coming from the West Bank. The Israeli press tends to play down the arrests of Israeli accomplices but they are becoming too frequent to ignore. And Jews incite violence as well. During the week before the Gaza disengagement, a sad, fanatic youth by the name of Eden Natan-Zada, who had deserted the Israeli Army and drawn close to followers of the late Rabbi Meir Kahane at the settlement of Tapuach, boarded a bus in the Israeli Arab town of Shfaram and opened fire with an automatic rifle, killing four people and injuring more than a dozen others. He was then beaten to death by the mob that surrounded the bus.

"The hands were the hands of Natan-Zada," Ali Haidar, leader of the nonprofit organization Sikkuy, told me at the time; "but the voice was the voice of many. In recent years we have heard all kinds of statements and incitements in the media, from politicians, rabbis—public people— calling us everything from a cancer in the state to worms, snakes to fifth column. When you keep insisting you need a Jewish majority, the answer is decrease, or expel, or oppress, or in Natan-Zada's case, even kill, the Arab minority." (Haidar—ironically, revealingly—determined responsibility for Natan-Zada's crime by adapting Isaac's famous outburst in Genesis: "The hands are the hands of Esau, but the voice is the voice of Jacob.")

THE REALLY HARD QUESTION here is whether the Israeli state could do much to make young Arab citizens less disaffected. Is alienation not built into the status of the Arab minority? I decided to put the question to the hardest test I could think of and sat down with Azmi Bishara, the head of Israel's Balad party. When I spoke with him, in the summer of 2005, he was still a member of the Knesset, as he had been since 1996. But he had already traveled to Syria and met with some of Israel's avowed enemies. I knew of Bishara's reputation, which was precisely what drew me to him. What exactly was he calling for? If one could imagine how Israeli Jews might respond to his demands, could not any Israeli Arab be made a partner in the Israeli enterprise?

After our interview, Bishara traveled to an Arab book fair in Beirut and proclaimed to loud cheers (according to the Lebanese newspaper *As-Safir*) that Israeli Arabs "are like all Arabs, only with Israeli citizenship forced upon them." ("Return Palestine to us," he scolded Israeli Jews, "and take your democracy with you."[32]) After the 2006 Lebanon war, Bishara showed up in the smashed-up Hezbollah strongholds of Southern Beirut, where he exhorted Arab resistance groups "to keep the pressure on Israel." He virtually dared Israeli officials to prosecute him for breaking laws prohibiting this kind of travel and these kinds of contacts. Which, in April 2007, is exactly what Israel did. The secret service, the Shabak, prepared a case of sedition against him, accusing him of aiding Israel's enemies in wartime—also of taking hundreds of thousands of dollars from enemy sources. Bishara then fled the country, resigning from the Knesset, pledging that he would eventually return.

But the man I found in 2005 gave no hint of these dramas to come. He seemed a wry, soft-spoken thinker—a man brimming with formulations, eager to be understood and, like most public intellectuals, at a loss to understand why he is not. If the charges against him prove true, then the unguarded thoughts he shared with me before the war seem all the more poignant. In a strange way, it was clear that there was something about Israel—the experience, if not the state—that he loved.

"We naturally insist on the separation of religion and state, on Israel as a state of its citizens," Bishara told me in his overstuffed Knesset office, "but we are also for recognition of the collective right of the Arab minority, consistent with liberal principles." And what, in this case, is the application of such principles? "You know, most Arab intellectuals in the nineteenth century based nationality on language, like Herder did. They thought the pillar of national identity is language. Mine is Arabic."

Like Québec, I asked? "Say we develop multiple identities," he continued, "and intellectuals have many cultural identities—still, national identity is the cultural identity you need to politicize. I have often used the model of Québec here, and I have even met Québec's foreign minister once—though I'm not sure what foreign relations Québec has, other than to stay in touch with France or Gabon—anyway, this model of Québec is not accepted here. I think the more problematic and richer model is Belgium, a federation of Flemish and Walloons—problematic because we don't know if it will hold. Some say the only real Belgians there are the Jews, since they're the only ones who want this country to continue. Whatever model might have developed here, it is clear that two national identities have crystallized here."

So why, I asked him, choose to politicize, of all things, Israeli Arab identity as a separate nationality? Why not either join Palestine or integrate into Israel, without surrendering ethnic distinction, as Jews have done in countries where *they* were the minority? I could not have been the first person to ask him this, but he curiously had no prepared answer. What he had was a list of grievances against Israel. Consider the educational system, he said, which provides the Arabs a certain autonomy to run their own Arabic schools: "Their problem is with the content," Bishara insisted; "Arabs have autonomy . . . but the curriculum is controlled by the center, and it forces us to teach our children about the justice of Zionism as a settler state. Obviously, this is not an appropriate basis for Arab education, and it requires a collective response."

I had often heard Bishara described as an extreme Arab nationalist. But this was clearly an oversimplification. His nationalism was a kind of surprise to himself. A former Communist, Bishara had spent his salad days in East Berlin parsing Marx's thought. He had been cavalier about the claims of personal identity in the face of "material forces." Then he discovered liberal democratic claims—what Rubashov, the hero of Arthur Koestler's *Darkness at Noon,* called the "first person singular." He also belatedly discovered—so he told me—the claims of national identity, the subtle ways language shapes identity and groups shape interests—the very things he had missed as a frustrated cosmopolitan. In fact, Bishara had taken up the cause of Israel's Arabs with the self-conscious pride of one who had studied Zionism deeply. He reminded me of no one so much as old Marxist Zionists like Nachman Syrkin, who in 1898 wrote about why Jewish Marxists had underestimated the national question.

Bishara saw democracy emerging only slowly in the Arab world, outside of Israel, where the development of a "bourgeois" middle class will have to precede it. One could not "build democracy without democrats, without large middle classes committed to the issue, without liberal democratic forces committed to the ideal of a liberal democracy," he said. The danger in Iraq, for example, was a "confusion of sectarian conflicts with pluralism."[33] So Bishara was looking for financial redress from the national government's budgeting process and affirmative action in higher education. He wanted, he told me, an Israeli Arab technical university. "Our problem was not that four hundred villages were destroyed," Bishara said. "We publicly emphasize this loss because of folkloric consciousness. The real problem was that our urban centers were destroyed and what remained were villages without a center." Again, one could not build much without a middle class.

And into the breach created by this destruction stepped Israeli state planning councils, dominated by representatives of the Zionist agencies: "The whole planning process is in Jewish hands. Arab villages should be called slums—slums around Jewish cities—they are not villages anymore. They supply workers, a proletariat. If you do not deal with a collective Arab leadership to reverse this, then all you have is the market, which has been skewed by the state to put Jews at the center, with the continuous marginalization of Arabs."

WE HAD COME to the heart of the matter. "Planning is ideological," Bishara said, "and is still in the hands of people who believe that you need not only a Jewish majority in this country but a Jewish majority in *every part* of this country. The market does not come into play here; the state does. Even municipal planning is done by the state and Zionist organizations, motivated by ideological goals. I can shout in the Knesset—in fact, I am conceding in advance the legitimacy of Israeli democracy just by coming here, to the Knesset, something many of the people who voted for me would not concede—but then people tell me here: 'We don't plan.' This is done at the level of planning commissions in districts and subdistricts."

Who sits on the planning councils at the level of the districts and subdistricts? "You find the romanticism of the past," Bishara insisted, "Jews longing to be in ancient places, or believing that settling the border areas brings security. There is the *tokhnit av*, the master plan for twenty years, developed by the districts; it goes back to the National Commission on Planning and Zoning, and then the plan, which can be six or seven volumes, goes back down to the districts. These commissions—all of them—have representatives of the Zionist organizations, the Jewish National Fund, Keren Hayesod, the Jewish Agency, the government, and communities—so on the national committee, for instance, which has thirty-nine members, you may get one or two Arab mayors, speaking in the name only of their own villages. The same is true at the local level."

Zionist groups are not always discriminating in favor of Jews. Just after the Shfaram murders, the Jewish Agency announced that it was giving the families of Natan-Zada's victims a total of 100,000 NIS (one U.S. dollar = 4 NIS) from a fund it had established to compensate Jewish victims of Palestinian terror. But even this welcome gesture raised the obvious question of why the Jewish Agency existed at all, especially if it was nothing more than an extension of the state apparatus.[34] The only way to reconcile the existence of the Jewish Agency with the workings of a democratic state, David Harman had told me, was to reconfigure it as a huge NGO—"Let it take its $350 million annual working budget, which it gets from the Diaspora and holdings in Israel, and do what it wants, within property law, and without a connection to the political structure."

This was not the kind of residual Zionist institution Bishara could even contemplate. "When Zionist planners look twenty years ahead, they see beyond whole Arab villages. Is there is an Arab village here? The plan does not recognize it! I have heard this again and again. You have this odd category: unrecognized villages. You wind up having to support illegal construction in a village because the village does not exist in the plan. Or look at the Barbur neighborhood in Acco. For fifty-three years, it has been without services. When does it show up in the plan? When it was decided to build a neighborhood for ten thousand Jews on top of it. Talk about using a liberal democracy to make liberal rights illegal."

WHICH BRINGS ME, finally, to a curious petition. In December 2003, thirty-eight signatories—most of them Jews, a number of them Arabs (including Adel Ka'adan)—asked the High Court to order the Ministry of the Interior to inscribe their nationality as Israeli in the population registry. There were businesspeople, professors, entertainers, writers, jurists—including former Minister of Education Shulamit Aloni, and former Commander of the Israeli Air Force Benny Peled (who has since died). On the surface, Israelis asking the court to make them Israeli may seem frivolous. The petition was anything but that.

The petitioners were asking the court to recognize an inclusive, earned form of nationality, like French nationality. This, too, was tried back in the early 1970s, when George Tamarin, a Jewish Israeli, petitioned the High Court unsuccessfully to have the official registration of his nationality changed from Jewish to Israeli. But the High Court ruled that "there is no Israeli nation separate from the Jewish nation . . . composed not only of those residing in Israel but also of Diaspora Jewry." The then president of the High Court, Shimon Agranat, explained that acknowledging a uniform Israeli nationality "would negate the very foundation upon which the State of Israel was formed."[35] In effect, Agranat said that Israeli identity would undermine the cohesion of the Jewish people at a time of crisis, and that anyway, such an identity did not exist yet.

The new petitioners believed that fifty-five years after the state's founding, when a significant majority of citizens have been born in the country, the experience of Israel itself was now determinative of national identity. They were not denying the importance of nationality; the UN charter recognizes this to be a crucial matter of personal identity and choice. Yet they wanted to close the door on discrimination against people on religious or racial grounds, which is especially important for the state's Arab minority: "I am no Canaanite," the petitioners' lead counsel, Yoella Har-Shefi, insisted, referring to the cultural movement from the 1950s that sought to distance Israelis from Diaspora

Jews. "I have staked my life on the moral and cultural power of the Jewish people. But you can't say 'everybody is equal here, it's just that a Jew is valued differently'—and if there is international or internal protest, well, that's proof that the whole world is against us."

Har-Shefi is an unlikely Thurgood Marshall. A solid, handsome, articulate woman in her midsixties, she is in many ways the embodiment of what people who *do* assume Israel should value Jews differently point to. She was spirited out of the Warsaw ghetto on the night before the uprising; her parents were murdered in Treblinka. She was then smuggled to Palestine in 1946 on a Haganah ship—"the charming little girl I. F. Stone immortalized in his book *Underground to Palestine,*" she told me. When I first met her in the early 1980s, she was a military correspondent for the mass-circulation daily *Yediot Aharonot,* and had covered the Yom Kippur War firsthand. She was the author of a book on Arab citizens and, in her student days, had spent an hour a week studying Talmud with National Religious Party Knesset leader Zerach Warhaftig. Law school came later.

Har-Shefi does not doubt how gravely the political atmosphere has been poisoned by over a hundred suicide bombings, and how numbed Israelis have become to their own retaliations. She is well aware of the hazy, tribal, and dogmatic religious ideas on both sides, following generations of war. But then, even if the Law of Return were entirely retired, why should Israel not continue to legislate a preference for any Jewish immigrant who is a refugee from persecution? "They could come here, spend a few years, learn the language and the political system, and then become naturalized citizens," Har-Shefi says. "But why should a Jew from Borough Park get off the plane, know nothing about this place, and immediately vote my future?" (She might have added politicians like Russian billionaire Arcadi Gaydamak, an arms dealer and fugitive, who buys votes with flamboyant giveaways, and knows virtually no

Hebrew.) Har-Shefi's petition deliberately steers clear of the contro-
versial question of "Who is a Jew?" according to Halakha; the state
should "not be subservient to any rabbinic decision about this, in any
case," she says.

THE STATE'S ATTORNEY has so far responded to Har-Shefi's petition
predictably enough, arguing that the petition will divide the Jewish
people; that it "undermines the very principles under which the State
of Israel was created." The state also argued a technical matter, that the
issue should anyway be decided in district courts, under whose jurisdiction the inscription of nationality ordinarily takes place. As of this writing, the High Court has not ruled definitively. Justice Barak, who at
first signaled that he might himself join a panel ruling on the matter,
withdrew from the matter, and then retired. A less imposing panel, led
by Justice Michael Cheshin (who had been widely perceived as Barak's
somewhat more conservative judicial rival, and who also subsequently
retired) accepted the state's technical objection and sent the case back
down to the district courts. In response, over a dozen people then sent
requests to be inscribed as Israeli nationals to the Tel Aviv court. All of
these were rejected.

"When he heard the case," Har-Shefi told me, "Justice Cheshin
stated tantalizingly that the Tamarin decision might have been 'in
error.' He heaped praise on the petitioners. He told us we were raising
the most basic issues. He suggested that the lower court might be more
appropriate than the High Court to hear the expert opinion the petitioners brought forward. He implied the High Court might well declare the Tamarin decision unsustainable once the technical issue was
resolved. But he also sent the petition back to where it has become
stalled, and to where we are most likely to run out of resources."

In May 2006, Barak's court in effect answered the petition, with a ruling in an entirely different case. The suit in question challenged army

deferrals for ultra-Orthodox students—a clear case of inequality. Barak declared, rather clumsily, that "there is room for the idea that a law or Basic Law that denies Israel's character as a Jewish or democratic state is unconstitutional." Many experts interpreted this to mean that the High Court could abolish a law, or even a Basic Law, if it impairs Israel's Jewish character, even if equality is at stake. ("The service deferral law," Barak conceded, "deals a severe blow to human dignity."[36]) Indeed, to protect the Jewishness of Israel, the Knesset could do pretty much what it wanted.

Anyway, whatever the eventual verdict or the fate of the High Court's purview, Har-Shefi's petitioners are clearly justified in seeing the matter as urgent. As one petitioner, former education minister Aloni, recently put it,

> The central question is whether Israel's Arab citizens—as individuals or collectively as a community—should be denied the same rights accorded to ultra-Orthodox Jews, Druze and Circassians simply because of their numbers and their special relationship with the residents of the West Bank and the Gaza Strip, who have been living under Israeli occupation for the past 40 years? The denial of basic rights would mean that, instead of being a democracy, Israel would be reduced to an Orthodox Jewish ethnic group with a strong army, compulsory military service, detention centers and prisons, tremendous greed for the land of the natives—and immense fear.[37]

As a consequence of their marginalization, Aloni knows, Israeli Arabs are already beginning to float constitutional ideas that strike at the heart of the Israeli center. Recently, the Adalah (Justice of God) advocacy center, a nonprofit representing mainstream Israeli Arabs, published a proposed draft constitution for Israel. It abrogated the Jewish

Law of Return, which awards immediate citizenship to any Jew who wants to immigrate. But it also called for (among other things) a state that recognizes "its responsibility for past injustices suffered by the Palestinian people;" coequal and separate education systems; and national symbols "determined either by a Knesset committee, half of whose members will be Arab, or by agreement of 75 percent of Arab MKs." If their lives must be lived apart, they seem to be saying, then why not a separatist equality?

Then again, if Israel cannot, or will not, transform itself in this way, can Arab enmity ever be appeased—and why, given the intractability of Islamist forces, try such appeasement? Har-Shefi, for her part, remains adamant. Israel's real challenge over the coming generation is not only to get back into a peace process, but to shore this up with a parallel revolution in civil rights: "If we don't give Arab citizens this chance to become Israelis, the country will come apart. We are sitting on the edge of a volcano. Because Israel is the only country on earth that does not recognize itself."

CHAPTER 2

West Bank Settler

Our Brothers who fought in the War of Independence: We have not abandoned your dream, not forgotten the lesson you taught us . . . We have returned to the mount, to the cradle of the nation's history, to the land of our forefathers, the land of the Judges, and to the fortress of David's dynasty. We have returned to Hebron, to Shechem, to Bethlehem, to Anatoth, to Jericho . . . We know that to give life to Jerusalem we must station the soldiers and armor of the IDF on the Shechem mountains, and on the bridges over the Jordan.

—MOSHE DAYAN,
minister of defense,
speech on Mount of Olives, August 3, 1967

During the mid-1960s, a new generation of Israeli leaders might well have curtailed their Zionist state-within-a-state by ordinary democratic processes. Zionism was in the doldrums. The wave of North African immigration was spent, and no other Jews seemed eager to come. Eichmann had been executed. The economy was in recession, and old Labor organizations had come to seem inefficient and vaguely corrupt. Military rule of Israeli Arab towns ended; some avant-garde writers and activists professed to be Canaanites. Youthful Israelis—tested by IDF meritocracy, and focused on all kinds of internal reforms—had begun to dismiss the word *Zionism* as slang for hollow patriotism.

But Zionist ideas and institutions were spectacularly revived in 1967, bursting their boundaries in the aftermath of an unexpected war. New settlements were put down in occupied territory. Accordingly, no Israeli government has ever been able to entertain withdrawals without inviting an uncomfortable debate about the current viability of Zionism, hence the legitimacy of Israel's residual legal structure. As for the settlers themselves, most have not been fanatics. More chilling in a way—and as my own story reveals—settlers were rather simple conformists. They thought they were doing the state's bidding and rectifying a world-historical wrong. They still do.

ARTHUR KOESTLER ONCE wrote that becoming a Communist was an affair of the heart; in the summer of 1931, in Berlin, he fell in love with the Five Year Plan. In the summer of 1967, I fell in love with the Jewish National Fund. I was eighteen and had just finished my first year at McGill University. In what still seems to me an exhilarating rush of events, I arrived in Israel about a week after the end of the Six-Day War and wound up volunteering to work on Kfar Yehoshua, the moshav (farming cooperative) of an indomitable couple, Chanan and Esther Shiloh, whose close friend and neighbor had been killed in the Sinai early in the war. They were now working his widow's dairy farm in addition to their own, so they needed an extra hand—a volunteer like myself, Chanan took pains to explain to me, since members of the moshav had always refused to hire wage laborers, certainly not Arabs, whom they refused to "exploit." Chanan did not quite rub it in, but he and Esther made it plain that Israel's collectives, unlike Diaspora Jewish communities, enjoyed a certain authentic self-reliance. The vanguard of the state lived, like them, in the *hityashvut ha-ovedet*—literally, the "working settlement"—from which the word *moshav* derived. The old Hebrew motto of Labor Zionism was *kibbush ha-avodah*, "The conquest of labor," where the real thing to be conquered was a Diaspora Jew's civilized sluggishness.

And what had made it all possible was the Jewish National Fund, the Keren Kayemet, the jewel in the crown of historic Zionism, whose green logo was still painted on the sign to Kfar Yehoshua, and on all the collectives in the lush Valley of Jezreel. Members did not own their land, my friends explained; the land had been leased in perpetuity from the Keren Kayemet, which had raised money abroad, penny by penny, then bought Arab estates in the 1920s, '30s, and '40s, eventually distributing parcels to socialist *halutzim,* Zionism's pioneers, that is, their parents.

As a child, I had myself slipped nickels and pennies into the Keren Kayemet's little blue tin collection boxes. I can still taste the sweet, leaf-shaped stamps, which I bought for a couple of cents and stuck onto a cartoonlike tree. When I had filled up the branches with leaves, the tree was "planted." For the fund kept on raising money for reforestation and other projects after the state was founded in 1948, after Israel could have expropriated land as easily as have the Zionist fund buy it—and, again, large tracts were expropriated after the 1948 War, effacing some four hundred Arab villages. Anyway, we were now done with wars, and Kfar Yehoshua's land remained the "inalienable property of the Jewish people"—that is, mine. I worked until I dropped. After about a month of this I was smitten: the warmth of welcome, the élan of revolution, the conviction that just war had brought lasting peace—that Israelis had won the former, and Jews deserved the latter—the pleasingly triangular smell of cow's milk, cow's feed, and cow's shit rising into Hebrew air.

THIS WAS NOT exactly love at first sight. My father had been a socialist Zionist scout in Bialystok in the 1920s, a member of the Shomer Hatzair, and later, more grandly, a Zionist Organization leader in immigrant Jewish Montréal. (His socialism faded with the success of his children's apparel business in the 1950s, as his claim to leadership faded with the general failure of his real-estate investments in the 1960s.) I had never really thought much about what his Zionism meant, except that it covered the bases for "modern" Jews, which Montréalers were not quite. I understood, vaguely, that Zionism meant Jews could have orange trees, fighter jets, a tan.

Most vivid was the prestige of the Hebrew language, which I had suspected since childhood contained a world worth knowing. As a pupil at Montréal's Talmud Torah school, half my class's day had been devoted to general studies and the other half to Hebrew studies, beginning in the second grade with readings from Breishit, the book of Genesis. While the ABCs conjured scrubbed little boys watching girls play with kittens, the *aleph bet* conjured up families torn up by arbitrary fathers, jealous mothers, and rival brothers, all devoted to enigmatic things like "sacrifice" and "birthright," or stirred by the promise of mysterious power. I knew immediately where to find a plausible version of my own benighted family. Hebrew stories seemed absolute, and talking about them seemed a kind of responsibility. Actually, I sang in Hebrew more than talked, first in synagogue services, then at summer camp, then playing my father's LPs of Israeli folksingers—Shoshana Damari, the Oz Group; songs about Negev battles; verses lifted from the mild erotica of the Song of Songs—until I knew every tambourine tap by heart. Pete Seeger, after all, sang these songs, too.

Zionism's personal (or, if you were at McGill, "ideological") requirement, that Jews should go and live in Israel, had always been finessed in my family circle. My father's line, which I never quite bought, was that sending one's money was "as Zionist" as sending oneself, though he often lamented that his "big mistake" was not joining his own pioneering group, which had founded Kibbutz Kfar Menachem in 1938. I never pressed the point, since his mistake had resulted in, among other things, my birth. But I understood that his Zionism was a part of what he meant when he once declared that he "had not been put on earth to make little girls' dresses."

There was an edge of daring to his Jewishness. There had been cousins lost in "European" camps, and I had seen pictures of piles of corpses, though these were usually hidden away with other forms of nakedness. My father at times seemed more triumphant than humbled by all of this sorrow, like someone who had been proven right by events so terrible they made all Zionist prescience seem exalted. With Israel's wars periodically in the headlines, he spoke about commanders like Dayan the way teachers in general studies spoke about generals Wolfe and Montcalm. Because of Zionism, he said, Jews had made it back into history. I concluded from this that Israel had put Jews in a league where winning or losing was somehow less important than playing. One of the first grown-up jokes my father had told me, after the 1956 Suez War, was a cheerless pun that "Hitler had swum to Egypt and become *nasser,*" that is, "wet," in Yiddish. Dayan, my father once said, was "our answer to Arcand"—Adrien Arcand, the Jew-baiting leader of Québec's fascist L'Action Français—and Father Coughlin. I never told him that Dayan also made most young Montréal Jewish boys vaguely ashamed of our fathers in ways Arcand and Father Coughlin could not.[1]

So in May 1967, after the CBC reported that Israel was being encircled—"strangled," my father said—by Egypt's blockade of the Straits of Tiran, he sat me down at the kitchen table and sketched a map on a paper napkin, explaining how Israel, whose reserves had been mobilized, would soon have to attack in Gaza ("with a pincer's movement," he added, with a certain bravado). I became fixed on the vain fantasy I had had as a child, that were I to be lined up to board a cattle car, I would charge the guards in an ecstatic rage rather than get on the train. That is what "Israelis" would do. My warm, unstable mother, who had long been estranged from my father, had died suddenly just a few months before this, so I was anyway in the grip of a rather apocalyptic sensibility. At the same time, I now had the body of a strong young man and told myself coldly that I could not just see it all—Israel, "history"—end. I quit my job at Expo 67 and determined to fly to Israel as soon as I could get there. My father finally went along with the plan, but to his relief (and mine), the war was over before I could leave.

NOTHING HAD PREPARED me for the atmosphere of the country when I arrived. It seemed that an entire people had done spontaneously what every human being should do deliberately—defend one's life, touch one's roots, spread progress, show magnanimity. The tokens of Israeli exceptionalism were everywhere. Overnight, cousins became brothers and sisters. Conversations with new acquaintances almost immediately turned intimate, exuberant. And if relief was palpable, the humor was black. Much was made of the inept Hebrew broadcast of Egypt's state radio, which had intended to say at the beginning of the battle that its troops were advancing "*be-khol ha-khazitot,*" that is, "on all fronts," but said instead "*be-khol ha-haziyot,*" "in all the brassieres." I laughed and laughed. How many gears in an Egyptian tank? Five—one forward, four reverse. We were living out the miracles of the Passover Haggadah, it seemed, where Egyptians were drowned in the sea, and rabbis fantasized about the multiplications and varieties of plagues.

The radio played jingoistic songs: "Nasser is waiting for Rabin, ay-yai-yai," and "Oh Sharm el-Sheikh, we have returned to you forever!" Captured Russian trucks, looking like giant Ford pickups, appeared magically on the roads every few minutes; blond Swedish volunteers appeared magically in kibbutz dining rooms. No member of the Israeli government, however schlumpy, could appear in a newsreel (there was no television in Israel yet) without prompting the theater audience to burst into applause. Dayan himself visited West Bank villages and was greeted by "notables," while children on the beaches pranced around him, a hand covering an eye in homage. One international newsweekly put on its cover a bespectacled Hasid, in a phone booth, changing into Superman. The wire services ran the UN speeches of Abba Eban, our Disraeli, showing up Gromyko and his petulant Arab clients. Zionism was proven right by, of all things, Zionism's might.

I got to Jerusalem on June 28, driven in a lurching Citroën deux cheveaux by a family friend, a paratrooper about my own age, who had fought just a couple of weeks before at the Lion's Gate. We explored the ridges around the city, and drove toward the Mandelbaum Gate, the old checkpoint dividing Jewish West Jerusalem from the Arab East, just after noon; we practiced how we might con the guard into letting us proceed to the Old City and the Wailing Wall. But we found no checkpoint and no guard.

We drove on, passing the silenced Arab shops on Salah al-Din Road (named after the Arab warrior who had once chased out the Crusaders, but who now seemed to us a dusty footnote), stopping the car a couple of times to stand silently at piles of rocks, topped by a rifle and a helmet, the makeshift memorials to comrades who had been killed in the assault. Finally, somewhat bewildered, we flipped on the radio, only to discover that the Arab city had been annexed and the whole city declared united an hour before we had gotten there. The government had decided—so I would later learn—to integrate all parts of Jerusalem by expanding Jewish neighborhoods in the Old City and in the eastern part, widening the city limits by more than sixty square kilometers, especially around Mount Scopus, where the old Hadassah Hospital and the Hebrew University had been before 1948. An expanse around the Wailing Wall, we discovered, had already been bulldozed. The radio played the new Zionist anthem, Naomi Shemer's "Jerusalem of Gold." My friend could not speak and I dared not.

NOBODY SEEMED TO GIVE a second thought to the families whose houses had just been razed. Hadn't Jordan used Jewish gravestones from the Mount of Olives to pave roads in the Old City? As for the 70,000 Jerusalem Arabs who might be encroached upon or intimidated, there was land enough for all of us in the "new Middle East." Nineteen countries for them, one for us. King David's city for us, Mayor Teddy Kollek's liberalism for them. There would be one Jerusalem, "never to be divided again."

Only one moment, several weeks later, gave me pause. On a visit with my cousins to the new campus of Tel Aviv University, I noticed a couple of huge posters, with a puzzling map, which seemed exactly like the PLO's sickening Arabic map of Palestine, in which Israel had always been effaced—only this was a Hebrew map of Israel, from which the boundaries of the West Bank and Gaza had been effaced. The posters, my cousins later told me, were from a movement then taking shape, already calling itself the Whole Land of Israel Movement, whose founding statement was signed by, among others, Labor Zionism's poet laureate, Natan Alterman, and the leftist kibbutz leader Yitzhak Tabenkin. (The chief of military education during those years, General Mordechai Baron, told me recently that another one of the group's founders, one of the most popular novelists of the *hityashvut ha-ovedet*, Moshe Shamir, had tried to recruit him, too, seeing how moved he had been accompanying Dayan to the Tomb of Rachel between Bethlehem and Hebron. IDF intelligence strategist Yehoshafat Harkabi was also won over for a while, as was Nobel laureate and author S. Y. Agnon.[2])

My cousins explained that the group opposed returning any part of the conquered West Bank, even for peace, since (as their statement would read) "no government in Israel is entitled to give up this entity, which represents the inherent and inalienable right of our people." The clear implication of their movement was that the West Bank should now be settled by Jews, just like the Valley of Jezreel had been by veteran farming collectives such as Kfar Yehoshua in the 1930s.

But even then, this prospect of annexation and settlement struck me as oddly greedy and provocative, nothing like what my moshav friends' parents had achieved, no matter how many former leaders of the pioneering settlements were joining. The times were completely different, after all. There was no Hitler, no British mandatory government enforcing property law but actually keeping Jewish refugees out, no esteem for proletarian internationalism among the settlers, nothing to compromise Jewish equality in Jerusalem's holy places. There was plenty of land for new agriculture in the Negev and Galilee, elevators for high-rise cities like Tel Aviv and Haifa. Arabs, not Jews, were sitting in miserable camps.

Old Zionists, it is true, had settled some land by force during the chaos of the late 1940s. They had had to "pacify" and make citizens of the Arabs who were left. Settlements seemed of a piece with securing the perimeter of the Jewish state in the 1950s, when the international border was being established beyond the territory allocated by the UN partition plan of 1947. But Jews were desperate then. When Jean Valjean became mayor, he didn't continue stealing bread.

My cousins, too, were skeptical, though they spoke of writers like Natan Alterman—the uncle of my brother-in-law, it happens—with particular reverence. Israel was a Jewish state, they said, but it was "also democratic." The land was ours but, less esoterically, it was also theirs. It didn't matter which people wanted it more or longer. What mattered were boundaries that allowed each people, Jews and Arabs (we didn't use the term *Palestinians* then), to be more or less peacefully self-governing. That, in any case, was the logic of partition, which had established itself as the moral high ground since the 1940s. Only overexcitable Arabs, we were sure, had seemed incapable of grasping partition's virtues. (In 1974, my cousins—the parents of two young boys—were killed by Palestinian terrorists, who bombed their TWA flight out of Athens.)

When I asked others about the Whole Land of Israel Movement, I was reassured to find that few people took it all that seriously. Fewer still (myself included) noticed that this movement was merely proposing for the West Bank as a whole what the government, with almost universal acclaim, had already enacted in Jerusalem.

THIS CURIOUS TRIPLE-THINK about the new occupation—Greater Israel, ours though debatable; Greater Jerusalem, nonnegotiable; Israeli Arabs, theirs but pacifiable—was not much questioned back then by educated Israelis, even people in the orbit of the Labor Party, opposed to West Bank settlement. When, in 1972, I moved to Jerusalem for the first time, to do graduate work at the Hebrew University, my own blinkers had hardly come off. Dayan had essentially frozen diplomatic initiatives, arguing that Israel's new borders had secured a permanent peace; he had left the bridges to Jordan open and argued that commercial exchange would turn the status quo benign. I recall the brilliant political philosopher Shlomo Avineri, with whom I had come to study, praising Dayan's "open bridges" policy as humane, stable—"the best of available options." Meanwhile, talk of returning the territories to Jordan, or engaging Palestinian élites, petered out. About the unity of Jerusalem there was no debate. The first piece I ever published on the subject, which I sent back to a leftist Canadian magazine, lauded the Israeli occupation for freeing Palestinians from their Jordanian "ruling class."

I had, after all, come to Jerusalem as a new Jewish immigrant with *zekhuyot*—my precious bundle of material privileges granted by the Jewish Agency—and a three-year exemption from import tariffs from the state. My young wife and I applied for and were granted a virtually interest-free mortgage to buy a two-bedroom apartment in Jerusalem's French Hill, next to Mount Scopus in Arab East Jerusalem. The new neighborhood was being constructed by subcontractors chartered by the housing ministry, in collaboration with Amidar, a mortgage company subsidized by the Jewish Agency; other *zekhuyot* were provided to

Jews by the Ministry of Immigrant Absorption. All I had had to do was prove myself a Jew by birth, which I had done, to an Israeli consul back in Canada.

I did not think of this apartment complex as a settlement. The land had been part of a demilitarized zone and so was disputed, or so I told friends back in Montreal. French Hill (named after General Allenby's commander, Field Marshall John French) was a promontory on the way to Mount Scopus, which the UN clearly meant for the Jewish state. If Mount Scopus was ours, how could we not keep what was on the way? My neighbors from Latin America were left-wing secular types, refugees from various military dictatorships, supporters of Labor and partition. We opposed West Bank settlements. So we strummed American civil rights hymns. We thought we were righting a balance by moving to French Hill, that our *zekhuyot* were a kind of reward for centuries of benighted Jews being denied their civil rights. I did not think it wrong to be given a neighborhood that was plunked down on confiscated land between two Arab neighborhoods—Wadi Joz (where, proving my magnanimity, I took my car to be fixed) and Shuafat (where King Hussein's unfinished summer palace stood as a monument to war's futility). I did not think it strange that my neighborhood was stringently segregated by the very Zionist laws, dreams, and management I had come to identify with liberation.

Curiously, one of the books I had taken with me to Jerusalem from Montreal, and which I read in my new apartment on French Hill, was Mordechai Richler's *Apprenticeship of Duddy Kravitz,* whose brassy Jewish hero wanted to buy land by a lake in the Laurentian Mountains, owned by good Québécois farmers skeptical of Jews. But imagine—I, for one, could not then—that the land Duddy wanted had been owned in perpetuity by the Québec government; that anyone who wanted a home by a Laurentian lake had to live in a housing complex built by the government, on land confiscated from non-Québécois, and had to present himself as part of a buyers' group subsidized by the St. Jean-Baptiste Society; and that buyers qualified for all of these rights by proving birth to Québécois Catholic parents, or at least proving conversion to Catholicism in a way acceptable to the bishop of Montréal. Imagine Duddy's rant at the end of *that* book.

IT IS TEMPTING to look back on 1967 with a certain wistfulness: young people, heady victories, reckless enemies, unavoidable hubris. Wistfulness goes well with what is probably the most common conception of Israel that educated people in the West—and many in Israel itself—have: that Israel somehow came off the rails in 1967; that this was once a nicely social democratic state and is now being ruined by the blowback from its occupation—by quickly multiplying, pietistic settlers, whom successive governments somewhat naively tolerated; that if only Israel could end terrorist attacks, emancipate itself from the occupation, and replant most settlers back within the Green Line, then the country and its Zionism could get back to being themselves. The original planting of settlements, in this view, was of a piece with an understandable, if misguided, post-1967 concern for security. It is a reversible security strategy, as Sharon's Gaza pullout presumably demonstrated. (When I began writing about these issues, just after the 1973 war, I put things pretty much this way to a critic of one of my articles in the *New York Review of Books:* "Short-sighted as this policy may be," I answered him, "it is rooted in a coherent security strategy which, although somewhat anachronistic, has evolved in response to forty years of raiding, harassment, shelling, and invasion."[3])

But the settlements had manifestly *not* been about security in the ordinary sense of "strategic defense"—security in the face of invasion (like Kibbutz Yad Mordechai's stand against the Egyptian army in 1948). Security strategy was indeed a part of how these settlements were justified by scholars and intelligence officers; security is ontology in Israeli political science. But if there were any illusions about the strategic value of these settlements after 1967, these were shattered by the end of 1973. One reason for the near fatal delay in Israel's counterattack on the Golan in the Yom Kippur War was the unexpected need to evacuate Golan settlers who had come under fire by Syrian invaders. Nobody in Israeli public life disputed this by the winter after that war, which explains why I, a young writer with no military experience, could write cheekily in the pages of the *New York Review* that the Golan settlement policy had been "shortsighted" and "anachronistic." Yet the West Bank settlements grew more quickly, and with wider support, after 1973. Why?

For many of us, intimacy with the ancient land was more than a little intoxicating. My wife, the literary critic Sidra DeKoven Ezrahi, has written about this curiously eroticized impulse—betrayed in Prophets and Jewish lyric poetry since Andalusia—to repossess the distressed, kidnapped, damselland.[4] All of us back then, young and old, religious and secular, were drawn to the Land of Israel's once-prohibited places. After 1967, and even after 1973, we roamed freely to places like Hebron, stopping to watch glassblowers puff out the royal blue vases we would take home to our flats. We sat leisurely in Ramallah cafés, wiping plates of hummus, imagining ourselves in Damascus—as we soon would be, no doubt, when the Arab states finally came to their senses—mistaking the fear and natural hospitality of Palestinian merchants for resignation in the face of Israeli sovereignty. We went on little pilgrimages, in our cars and buses—to Rachel's Tomb on the road to Bethlehem, or the putative Machpelah Cave near Hebron, where the patriarchs and their wives were said to be buried. We then returned home to our block of flats and BBC melodramas at night.

BUT THIS IS ONLY half the story. For the settlements were established so effortlessly after 1967 because the Zionist institutions that built them, and the laws and culture that drove them, had been going full throttle within the Green Line since the 1948 war. Again, I mean the Jewish Agency, Zionist land banks and mortgage companies, the construction companies owned by the labor federation Histadrut, the actions of the Law of Return, the regulations supporting the Orthodox rabbinate's determination of what a Jew is, the abiding conception of Jewish national rights—all of these mechanisms for appropriating and distributing land. Support for the new settlements, which came as much from socialist farmers in Kfar Yehoshua as from Torahhawks, meant steadfastness in the face of threat, which, given the Holocaust, and the losses in the 1948 war, seemed eternal. It was the engulfing threat to Jewish existence that Zionism saw itself answering.

The leaders of the state had seen it all before, you see. One strains to recall this now, but the 1948–49 War of Independence occasioned an Israeli annexation of Palestinians' territory pretty much equal in size to the West Bank. The Western Galilee, the blood-soaked corridor to Jerusalem, areas of the Plain of Sharon, a large area of the Negev east of Gaza—all of these territories had been assigned by the United Nations Partition Plan to a future Palestinian state. Arab countries at first insisted these were occupied territories, too. Except for Nazareth, there was no apparent occupation of large population centers, but that was because in the chaos of the 1948–49 battles, some 750,000 Palestinian Arabs either fled their homes or, as in Lod and Ramle, were driven out.

The targets of blame, and numbers of people suffering this catastrophe—what Palestinians call their Naqba—have been heatedly debated since the archival work of the so-called New Historians in the 1980s. But one decisive fact was never debatable, which was that Arab refugees, understandably leaving a war zone, were not permitted to return. Their "abandoned" lands were then taken over as state property to be used for Jewish settlement. The writer and Mapai leader Moshe Smilansky wrote: "Someday we will have to account for [this] theft and spoliation, not only to our consciences, but also to the law."

So when post-1967 right-wing leaders and settlers say that they've never done anything in the West Bank that was not done in earlier times, they are referring to expropriations like these, presumably, under circumstances like these. This claim is simpleminded and it has back-fired; few believe it justifies the new settlements, while many believe it taints the whole Zionist project. Then again, Arab regimes would no doubt have expropriated Jews had they had the chance—and the Jorda-nians did exactly this, in Jerusalem and around Hebron. But I am raising a psychological point here, not a moral one. The Israeli government that managed the aftermath of the Six-Day War was pretty much the same group that had been in power in the nascent state since the War of Inde-pendence. Ben-Gurion was represented by his protégées, Moshe Dayan and Shimon Peres, and old Mapai leaders Levi Eshkol, Golda Meir, and Pinchas Sapir dominated the cabinet, along with former Palmach com-manders like Yigal Alon. The parallels to 1949 must have seemed un-canny. After 1967, as after 1949, the response to the defeat of Arab states was to deny Israel peace, recognition, and negotiation. The Western world, which had (so my father had said) "sat on its hands" when Israel was besieged, now seemed indifferent to Israeli occupation.

Moreover, if government ministers just followed their reflexes after 1967, these were channeled and strengthened by state bodies that en-couraged settlement. Declassified minutes of cabinet meetings during those heady days—just after the victory but before the annexation of Jerusalem—show ministers speaking about how "very helpful" the JNF would be in settling rings of Jewish neighborhoods around the city. Other Zionist institutions were naturally enlisted. The Jewish Agency raised money in the (largely American) Diaspora. The ILA provided a mechanism for administering new lands.[5]

IT IS WITHIN this context that conquered land was assigned to new settlements. Histadrut public corporations then built and serviced them, while the kibbutz and moshav movements organized farm training and recruiting. Tnuva, the Histadrut marketing cooperative, quickly brought their produce into old distribution channels. State-owned banks provided credit and tax breaks for settlers. All of this had been done before, within the Green Line. And enabling institutions were flush, owing to hundreds of millions of dollars' worth of American Jewish philanthropy after the Six-Day War.

Settlement may now seem part of a grand, premeditated national project—and so it was, especially around Jerusalem. But it was also a spontaneous series of decisions made in quasiofficial Zionist offices to continue putting families formally defined as Jewish in and around where Arabs lived. Boundaries simply disappeared. David Ben-Gurion had speculated in the early 1950s that the leaders of Israeli democracy would have to cut the umbilical cord to revolutionary Zionist institutions. He suggested that major institutions like the Jewish Agency should be abolished. Nevertheless, Zionism's modus operandi remained essentially undisturbed until 1967, and soon there were new kibbutzim on the Golan, and in Gush Etzion. Self-determination through settlement was as natural for Israeli leaders after 1967 as proletarian organizing through industrial unions had been for European Social Democrats after 1945. The key was to establish "facts," so that, again, a provisional border would harden into an international border.

Who knew, so the argument went, how many Jews Israel would eventually have to accommodate, or how many more Palestinians would have to be displaced to make Jews "safe"? Who knew exactly how big Israel would have to be while the Zionist revolution continued? Until it ended, why not continue to assure Jews special privileges— refuge, land, housing, investments—in a word, settlements? And if the old Labor Zionists cut a path to this disaster, subsequent Likud governments paved it. This is not the place to tell that story. Others, like Gershon Gorenberg in his recent book *The Accidental Empire*,[6] have told it in gripping detail. But after 1977, under Menachem Begin, Ariel Sharon, and their allies, the numbers of settlers ballooned. According to Peace Now, which monitors settlement activity, more than 367,000 Israelis now live beyond the 1967 boundary, including 250,000 in areas that are inarguably the West Bank. Something on the order of 157,000 live in areas of East Jerusalem annexed by Israel but considered occupied territory by the UN.

IN THE WAKE of the Hamas victory, reasonable people have written sorrowfully about Palestinians making things worse for themselves, surrendering to rage when pragmatism was called for. The conservative pundit William Rusher, for example, wondered out loud if Palestine would ever have a responsible, moderate, propertied middle class—the builders of civil society, secular in outlook, capable of sustaining economic hope: "What the Hamas victory teaches us is the unappetizing lesson that democratic elections, in nations without a democratic tradition, a substantial middle class, and a viable economy, may result in the triumph of forces even more offensive than the regimes they overthrow."[7] As if Palestine did not have just such a middle class back in 1967, which Jordan repressed. As if, while building settlements, the Israeli government did not displace the Jordanian banking system with its own, and end autonomous Palestinian tourist and construction industries, turning Palestinians into wage laborers on Israeli projects. As if Israel did not preempt Palestinian agricultural marketing companies and insurance companies, and replace Jordanian telecom, postal, electric, and highway infrastructure, bringing in Israeli substitutes. As if Israel does not, to this day, retard the development of the Jerusalem and Ramallah middle classes by denying entry visas to Palestinian American entrepreneurs, doctors, and lawyers.

The folly of such annexationist policies is now more or less obvious to a majority of Israelis, American Jews, and U.S. officials. But the same people who condemn settlements today seem unable to acknowledge the political institutions and mythology that enabled them to get going in the first place. For the settlers' ideals and energy did not just grow out of thin air. Both emerged more or less inexorably from an institutional Zionist logic and a powerful Zionist bureaucracy—right for their time as a revolutionary national movement under the British Mandate, but increasingly wrong for a modern state and civil society. Israeli society has no doubt been transformed by events after 1967—as transformed as the landscape itself. But the quasi–state apparatus that went into the 1967 war was hardly changed by it. The occupation provided a new and enlarged geography for a revolutionary Zionist course that had been set before 1949. This Zionism had been on the street signs, in the songs, in the nuances of political speeches, and so forth, which had turned original settlers into folk heroes. To focus only on the settlers' post-'67 fanaticism is to evade the implications of Israel's most enduring consensus.

I remember reporting on Henry Kissinger's efforts to mediate a disengagement agreement between Israel and Syria in the early summer of 1974, after the unthinkable war had happened in October of 1973. Standing in a crowd in front of the prime minister's office, I was surrounded by a few hundred West Bank settlers; their Gush Emunim, "Bloc of the Faithful" movement was just getting started. Word had leaked out that Kissinger, then inside with Golda Meir's transitional government (she had already resigned in the wake of a commission of inquiry looking into her government's failures on the eve of the October War), was pressuring her to evacuate the captured Syrian town of Kuneitra. But when Kissinger emerged, the settlers, a phalanx of knitted skullcaps, shouted nothing about the security of the Golan. They chanted, "Jew-boy, Jew-boy"—a chant that would become a roar the following spring of 1975, when thousands more took to the streets of Jerusalem to protest Kissinger's efforts to get the new Rabin government to conclude an interim agreement with Egypt's Anwar Sadat over the Western Sinai. The settlers understood that one evacuation might well lead to another. They believed that the renunciation of one inch of promised land was something only a bareheaded, court Jew like Kissinger could have entertained.

Golda Meir gave in to Kissinger on Kuneitra, as Rabin would later give in on the Mitla Pass. Both upbraided the settlers for their impudent behavior. Yet nobody doubted Golda Meir's prejudices (with Ms. Meir, you could not call them judgments), which were not far from Rabin's back then: that Jews had a right to live anywhere in Eretz Yisrael (as I heard her put it, "If in Cleveland, why not in Hebron?"); that the Orthodox rabbis in her coalition, though not her type, were at least the genuine article; that real security would require unilateral actions; that any evacuation from "Judea and Samaria" would require a national referendum. Jerusalem, in contrast, was Israel's "by historic right." Pioneering settlement around Jerusalem and on the Golan Heights was inarguably valiant. The birthrate of Arabs in the land as a whole posed a threat to the Jewish majority, however; Western Jews who had never thought to settle in the Jewish state—assimilated types like Kissinger, or Austrian premier Bruno Kreisky—deserved an Israeli's condescension. (Their unwillingness to immigrate to the national home was the real reason why Israel would have to surrender any conquered territory at all.)

Does this consensus persist? It has faded some, certainly among the iPod-crazed youth of North Tel Aviv. Yet when you think about the declared policies of all governments since 1967, including the current one—exclusive Israeli sovereignty over Greater Jerusalem, a new political border based on annexing large settlement blocs, a commitment to preserving the Jewish nature of the Galilee, etc.—it is hard not to wonder what, if anything, has changed. The emotional and institutional legacy of Zionist settlement still assures Israeli Jews privileges that other people, non-Jews subject to Israeli sovereignty, simply do not get. Again, I am not speaking here of the reasonable discrimination of a state in favor of a dominant national language and culture: a day off for the Jewish Sabbath, or the Star of David on the flag. I mean material discrimination by the state in favor of Jews as individuals and groups of neighbors. I mean me and my *zekhuyot.*

OBVIOUSLY THIS has always been a fraught subject, and is not growing less so. Marxist critics of Israel have long claimed that Israel was to be seen as a colonial-settler state. They intended by this to discredit the entire Zionist project, and suggested that Jews came to Palestine pretty much the way the French *pieds-noirs* came to Algeria.[8] Back in 1974, Yasir Arafat himself concocted a narrative along these lines before the UN General Assembly. He announced, gun in holster, that Jews came to Palestine from Europe "just as settlers colonized and indeed raided most of Africa." You still hear the resonances of that speech in various UN meetings about racism. Some Jewish Israelis, too, have seen in the facts of settlement a case against Israel's founding. *"Yisrael nolda be khet,"* "Israel was born in sin," many of Israel's young radicals will claim, basing their judgments on the work of the New Historians, such as Ilan Pappé. Scenes of Palestinian workers collecting Israeli garbage, or Israeli tanks quashing Palestinian riots in Gaza, have filled our screens for a generation. For many liberal intellectuals, Israeli evacuation under fire, as from Lebanon and Gaza, may seem a portent of how the whole Zionist project will eventually be defeated. We know how *The Battle of Algiers* ends.

Most Israelis, even back-and-forth Israelis like myself, get their backs up when they hear such things. We want at least to defend—as Koestler defended the West during the Cold War—our half truth against the Big Lie. For the charge that Zionism is colonialism is a kind of back-shadowing that not only clouds the truth about how Zionism succeeded but also, ironically, how Palestinians suffered. The latter certainly did not face raids and exploitation at the hands of rootless, metropolitan Jewish settlers seeking cheap labor and resources in the Palestinian hinterland. Zionism did come to Palestine under the auspices of an imperial power at the start of the twentieth century. Everybody did everything in the Middle East under the auspices of an imperial power. But if colonialism means anything, it was the *anti*-colonialism of Zionist settlement that was the foundation of its cultural revolution—also, ironically, the source of the real harm Zionism did to Palestinian peasants and workers. Even Palestinian political economists in the 1930s conceded that historical Zionist settlers self-consciously avoided becoming a colonial ruling class.[9] Zionists lived in closely settled, contiguous collectives, which was the very secret of their success.

I won't go on about this here, either.[10] Suffice it to say that, like Chanan Shiloh's parents, Labor Zionists did their own work, which is what allowed the Hebrew language to be reborn as a language of the everyday. Had Jews been mainly overseers of Arab labor, they would have created much less of an impact on Palestinian political economy; would not have attracted mass Jewish immigration; and would have been eventually forced out of power, or out of the country, as in South Africa or Algeria. The collectives were what engendered the proletarian élan to assimilate immigrants and refugees and devote hard-won economic surpluses to new public, industrial investments. They were what allowed for the development of separate, contiguous Jewish territories and a people's militia to defend them. Zionism's reversal of colonialist habits is the reason why Jews will never just take to their boats. Israeli Jews have roots of their own.

During the War of Independence, there were almost a million European survivors waiting in displaced-persons camps or forced to flee. Six thousand Palestinian Jews died, fully 1 percent of their population. Iraqi and other Middle Eastern Jews were suddenly facing persecution and physical threats. Palestine had become a theater of civil war, with acts of terror on both sides, and populations that increasingly despised each other. The Arab states had rejected partition and had launched an invasion. Not only did Jews from the death camps and the Middle East require homes, but there was reason to believe that a further mass emigration of the Jewish Diaspora, especially from Arab countries, was imminent. Eventually, over 600,000 Jewish refugees came from Arabs countries. To be born in tragedy is not the same as to be born in sin.

And yet the term *Zionist settler state* can be useful to us. It pretty well describes the Jewish colonial settlement, the Yishuv, during the British Mandate. It describes what Israel remained when it pushed out to its cease-fire borders after 1949. It describes a good part of Israel when, later, it pushed into undefined borders after 1967. It is a problem for the way Israelis build their future, not just for the ways they account for their past.

Israel's non-Jewish population is rising quickly: over a million Arabs; 300,000 people admitted under the Law of Return from the former Soviet Union who are cultural if not practicing Christians; another 200,000 foreign workers. Yet the Israeli state continues to cast itself as a kind of work in progress for the world's Jewish people, justifying its borders as provisional by, on the one hand, claiming the elastic, dream borders of ancient Eretz Yisrael, and on the other, recalling the horrific crimes of sixty years ago—crimes driven by anti-Semitic attitudes whose traces are still allegedly found in gentile countries, where safety for Jews is still allegedly provisional.

Other trappings of old Zionist settlement have been changing in Israel. Moshavim are turning into the garden suburbs of high-tech industrial parks; even the most radical kibbutzim are being privatized and broken up into entrepreneurial units. And yet the underlying logic of the Zionist settler state is resilient. It lives on in the shadow government that enables settlement. It lives on in state planning authorities. It lives in the ways Israelis talk to Diaspora Jews. It lives on, mostly, in the ways even the most open-spirited Israelis frame their anxieties. For many older Israelis, the values of old Zionist settlement still imply the national home itself. One can dare give up on it—as the Gaza evacuation proved—but then what values can possibly fill the vacuum?

"ONCE SETTLEMENT GAVE form to the state, but no more," laments my old friend on Kfar Yehoshua, Chanan Shiloh, now a man of seventy-four, still working his dairy farm, his skin leathery, his bloodshot eyes still twinkling. "We take shortcuts, we take the easy way, but also in our social vision, in business, personal relations.

"Once, settlement was the touchstone of civil life," he says, "the answer to the question of what in essence we were doing here." This is mostly changed today. According to Chanan, Israel has become chaotic, bourgeois, for which he blames himself as much as anybody: "You want your children to be among the winners these days, but once, in our settlements, we accepted the principle of equality, with all of the differences among people. We lived in a different atmosphere, doing for one another without asking questions, seeing ourselves as a vanguard for Jews around the world. Today our children are disconnected from the tragedy of the Jewish people."

But does Israel have its own tragedy? "If eventually Jews became a minority in this country, and the choice were a Jewish state or a democratic state, then I would choose to live here in a democratic state, in this county, as a minority. This is my home." (We are sitting on Chanan's lawn, the sprinklers *tap-tapping* behind us.) "I don't know any other, like you do." His distress is palpable: "We aren't going to say, 'Well, we did an injustice, so let's fold up our tent and move away.' But over there in Kfar Zarqa, there were five Arab houses. If there were Arab houses all around here, the Jews never would have come. On the other hand, the moment you take a man out of his home, he doesn't care about history—where Abraham walked or what Mohammed said. It's his home! He will want to come back to his home!"

This may sound like a kind of apology. It is not. It is rather an expression of fear that Jewish settlers—all Israelis, really—must be forever unforgiven and yet are losing the kind of grounded social solidarity that Arabs are increasingly showing. "A person who is not faithful to this land is also not faithful to his friends, and vice versa. I am not at all for Greater Israel; I am ready to forgo some of the land. But I won't forgo the spirit with which we settled the land. I talk about this with all of my friends, including Arabs; you know, I don't just talk to them about calves. And this is not a religious matter. I don't go looking for rabbis; I am for us all becoming our own rabbis. But we are turning into nothing but a part of 'the world out there,' and it is forbidden to us to become like that. We won't be able to stand up to it."

The "it" Chanan still speaks about—empathically, stubbornly, for as long as I've known and admired him—is the challenge of Palestinian grief: "Our parents did not take land the way the West Bank settlers did. But this place, and all the settlements of Jeezreel Valley, were built on land owned by an effendi in Damascus or Beirut. This is no time for fake innocence. We acquired the land of people who were working it from people who really didn't have the right to give it away. Landlords owned it; they were not living on it. And were I not just a kind of down payment [*pikadon*] for the right of the whole Jewish people to be here, I would never have had the right to take it away."

If war restarted, could there be more dispossessions, even of Israeli Arabs? "In a state of war, yes, expulsions may happen again. We can extend all rights to Arabs, try to eliminate all forms of discrimination. But we cannot extend to them the right to return to their lands, which is what they really care about, a right of return we cannot take away from Jews. How, then, can we ever have equality? People talk about land policies after 1967. But it never really occurred to us to return the territories, for peace or anything else, since what we did from 1967 on was continue the settlement that had been our life's responsibility from 1949 on, when we found ourselves new borders after the War of Independence, and we put Jews where Arab towns had been."

When Chanan speaks about these things, he may be paying homage to the Tolstoyan past out of habit. Of his and Esther's four children, none remains in farming. One is a contractor, building "clean rooms" for Teva Pharmaceuticals; one an architect; one a filmmaker; and the youngest, their only son, a software solutions designer for Texas Instruments. This is a kind of global entrepreneurship he accepts, even admires.

And yet Chanan's view of settlement and its discontents is the subconscious in the Israeli collective mind. You do not have to be a farmer to be taken with it, any more than you have to be a cowboy to appreciate the draw of the American frontier. For Chanan, indeed for most Israelis, settlement has been a part of a state-supported culture of survival and renewal. Orthodox Jews speak of *teshuva*, which means "return" in the sense of being born again. For Chanan, settlement still implies the extension and consolidation of a precious Hebrew world, planted on the ancient homeland like a stand of trees, a scar on the map, always in danger of being effaced.

Then again, does not anyone who seeks change in Israel have to explore, as he does, Israel's urbanization and what this means for the country's resiliency? And must they not ask some very hard questions? If Zionism's culture of settlement has created unacceptable problems for Israeli democracy, what can reasonably reform democracy? If an impulse to solidarity has attended communitarian Zionist settlement, will the end of settlement not end the solidarity? If Israel will promote, not settlement, but the globalization that Chanan's children participate in, could Israeli Arabs ever learn to seek integration into *that*?

Let us put this all simply and bravely the way Chanan would. Does Israel's remaining a Jewish state preclude its becoming a fully democratic one? To answer him—to reassure him—must one not change the terms of the conversation?

CHAPTER 3

"A Spade to Dig With"

The paratroopers wandered around the Temple Mount plaza as if in a dream. [Chief] Rabbi Shlomo Goren was among them. I was alone for a moment, lost in thought, when Rabbi Goren approached me. "Uzi," Rabbi Goren said to me, "now is the time to put 100 kilograms of explosives into the Mosque of Omar so that we may rid ourselves of it once and for all." I said to him: "Rabbi, enough!" He said, "Uzi, you will go down in history if you do this." I answered, "My name will already be written in the history books of Jerusalem." But Goren persisted. "You don't grasp what tremendous significance this would have. This is an opportunity that can be taken advantage of now, at this moment. Tomorrow it will be too late." I said, "Rabbi, if you don't stop, I'll take you to jail."[1]

—Major General Uzi Narkiss,
recalling events of 1967,
interview with *Haaretz,* May 1997

After the Rabin assassination, and especially after the Gaza evacuation, political commentators began to speak in cautionary language about the growing alienation of settlers in occupied territory from the majority population on the coastal plain. Some charged that the settlers had created—right under Israel's nose, and with its protection and infrastructural support—a commonwealth of their own, an ur-Jewish state organized with its own district council, living mainly under the influence of its own often-strident rabbis. In January 2006, former IDF chief of staff Dan Halutz described one chilling incident, in which several girls from the Hebron settlements had been detained and were then transported in a military truck: "When we removed them from the truck, we discovered they had damaged and ripped all the seats and inscribed this slogan on the walls: 'Long live the State of Judea, may the State of Israel be ruined.'"[2]

Intimations of this eerie—for urbane Israelis—rhetoric came to public attention most vividly, perhaps, in that remarkable, independent documentary of Channel One's anchor, Haim Yavin, which was aired just before the Gaza evacuation. His report included many searching interviews with settlers and their children. What became disturbingly clear was how, when settlers spoke of moral values, *arakhim musariim*, they meant a willingness to sacrifice for nationalist Orthodoxy and not much more. Immoral, in their view, were Jews who believed in mere Israeliness, or who subscribed to the settlers' Zionism but were unwilling to sacrifice for it. The fiercest resisters of the evacuation—sporting orange T-shirts and knitted yarmulkes—burned Israeli flags and spread oil and tacks on Tel Aviv freeways, defying police efforts to contain their demonstrations. Advisors to Israeli intelligence will tell you that 10 percent of hard-core settlers, perhaps 25,000 people, might well resist evacuation with force of arms.

The inference most Israelis draw from such extremism is that their government will, when the time is right, reverse the power of this Judean state, by asserting Israel's Jewish and democratic character more forcefully, removing settlements for the sake of peace. As with the settlements, however, few Israelis see how their country's stratified state apparatus engendered the Judean state in the first place—engendered introverted Orthodox movements that were reassured by legal exceptionalism, educated in separate schools, and sheltered from the competitions of civil society. Rabbinic power is the other side of the determination to preserve Israel for world Jewry—that is, traditional

Judaism, which world Jews understand much better than Israeliness—
and to privilege citizens and immigrants formally designated as Jews.
Orthodox communities are growing faster than any others; their privilege has a momentum of its own.

The failure of the constitution was the beginning. Four years after
Ben-Gurion withdrew it, in 1953, the Knesset passed the Rabbinical
Courts Jurisdiction Law, which established the Jewish religion as the
state religion, replete with Orthodox rabbinical courts. The law em-
powered rabbis to determine, where applicable, if an immigrant's conversion had been valid, and it reaffirmed the right of Orthodox rabbinic
officials to preside over all marriages, divorces, and burials for Jewish
citizens (though secular kibbutzim at first disregarded their authority).
Official rabbinic bureaucracies determined which restaurants, hotels,
etc., would be declared kosher—a state-sponsored monopoly that has
led to thousands of patronage jobs. By 1955, the state had set up two
school systems for Jews, one secular and the other National Religious,
that is, for children of those identifying with the National Religious
Party who wanted halakhic training as part of the standard curriculum. Ben-Gurion also permitted the sons of the relatively small, non-
Zionist, ultra-Orthodox Haredi (literally, "awestruck") communities
to study in their own schools and yeshivot, and avoid military service.
All of these concessions were absorbed into the notorious Status Quo
Agreement.

THE NATIONAL RELIGIOUS and Haredi communities have very different spiritual roots. The National Religious began in Eastern European
Orthodox parties, whose leaders attended Theodor Herzl's first congress. They saw in Zionist return a rapturous messianism, not unlike
the kind of notions you find today in evangelical movements in the
United States. "All the civilizations will be revived by the renaissance of
our spirit," wrote their first great leader in Palestine, Rabbi Abraham

Isaac Kook. "All quarrels will be resolved, and our revival will cause all life to be luminous with the joy of fresh birth." Early National Religious groups saw the leadership of any new polity leading the people back to divine law. They advocated for basing the state apparatus on halakhic strictures. So the National Religious community never shrank from assuming power in any form, first in the Zionist movement, then in the state. For his part, Kook readily accepted his appointment as chief rabbi by the British high commissioner, who gave his office certain official powers—over marriage, etc. The British wanted to imply that the Jewish community of Palestine was still a religious community, corresponding to the Muslim community, and that secular power fell naturally to the Mandate government. Kook assumed the Zionists would outlast the British and that a religious definition of who is a Jew would outlast any secular one.

Nevertheless, National Religious groups adapted to many of the modernist ideas that the hegemonic socialist Zionists surrounded them with, like a belief in scientific education, technological progress, or social innovations like the kibbutz. The graduates of National Religious schools blended more or less comfortably into the young state; they acquired advanced degrees, practiced the free professions, and attended secular universities, though they also started an Orthodox university of their own, Bar-Ilan. They took management jobs in business or the civil service, and served in the army. Indeed, until the occupation began, the National Religious Party, the NRP, was satisfied to be a junior partner in every Labor government. NRP intellectuals like Joseph Burg had German origins and were proud of their mastery of—if not belief in—the works of German liberal figures like Immanuel Kant and Heinrich Heine.

After the occupation began, however, an Israeli-born and far more radical young guard took over—Haim Druckman, Zevulun Hammer—and the NRP became a fierce advocate for settlements and all

they represented. In May 1967, the NRP's spiritual leader, Rabbi Tzvi
Yehuda Kook, elderly son of Palestine's first chief rabbi, delivered a ser-
mon in honor of Israel's Independence Day; he was seized by a vision of
repopulating the biblical land. "Where is our Hebron?" Kook cried out.
"Can we let it be forgotten? And where are our Shechem and our Jericho? Can we ever forsake them?"[3] Only a few individual rabbis and
scholars, like David Hartman, continued to strive self-critically with
the claims of democratic politics, civil rights, feminism, etc., hoping to
incorporate these into new halakhic norms. For most, the NRP's commitment to democracy was opportunistic. They assumed their own
halakhic life was for the good of the majority, even if this was not the
will of the majority, since it would be the will of the majority—the
Jews' general will—if only all acted in a spirit of communitarian reverence, that is, like the settlers and NRP rabbis themselves.

Meanwhile, historical gentile cruelty—of a piece, presumably, with
Arab enmity and terror—provided the NRP's hatred of boundaries
with a flinty cachet. One member of my family—the child of German
immigrants, the product of the NRP schools, and one of the most decent human beings I know—told me casually over a sumptuous Sabbath dinner that while he opposed new settlements and would roll
some back, he understood the settlers' skeptical opinion of Arab rights
under Jewish sovereignty—an opinion that was as relevant to Arabs
living in Israel as to Arabs living in occupied territory. "Arabs should be
welcomed in the Jewish state," he said, "but they should not have the
right to vote."

The ideology goes back to the origins of orthodox Zionism. Rabbi
Meir Berlin—or Bar-Ilan, after whom Israel's Bar-Ilan University was
named—set out its parameters at one of the earliest Zionist congresses.
"Church and state are kept separate [in Christianity], treated as separate
provinces," Berlin wrote, "but our case is different; Torah and traditions
are not man-made, but are God's own law ... The very sections of

Torah dealing with man's relations to his conscience and his Maker also offer general and specific guidance on the conduct of the state and social life, and also relations with other countries—how to wage war with them and how to live at peace with them . . . Neither have we ever had laws of an exclusively 'secular' nature."[4]

WITH OVER 100,000 students, the state-sponsored Dati Leumi (National Religious) school system has cultural influence everywhere. The Hebrew University Holocaust scholar Amos Goldberg—the father of four children attending these schools—is increasingly troubled. "My sixteen-year-old daughter went to a school program developed to qualify counselors and instructors, about 250 kids. Among a number of mandatory activities, they were instructed to distribute orange ribbons opposing the evacuation of Gaza settlements! Fewer than ten kids refused. Another child, in a putatively more liberal Dati Leumi school, was shipped off to Gush Katif in Gaza, ostensibly not to show support for the resistance to the evacuation, but to express 'identification with the settlers' pain.' So I sent an e-mail to the principal. 'What about the pain of the million Palestinians there, which we don't talk about?' He answered me, 'We are responsible for the Jewish narrative.' A modern man—he learned the postmodern word *narrative.*

"What we lack," Goldberg says of the NRP, which he has all but abandoned, "is a genuine moral language. It is all a dialogue with ourselves, about ourselves—our tribe, our fate, our value, our defense. The other man is the 'stranger' we should 'honor,' like 'we were in Egypt.' But what about the simple question 'What if everybody did this or that?' What about settlers destroying the olive trees of Palestinian farmers? Everybody *else* is a stranger here."

Correspondingly, NRP groups have been using the levers of state power for institutionalizing themselves within Israel's impoverished development towns—money for religious schools, provisional deals with the IDF for protection and national service, infrastructure from the state apparatus, party money allocated by Zionist organizations. *Haaretz's* Yair Sheleg recently reported on two "Torah nucleus" programs, now serving about two thousand families—in effect, local think tanks aiming to serve much larger communities.[5] Natan Natanson, one of the program's leaders, boasts: "We have managed to make people aware that settling in a development town can also be a significant realization of ideological goals." Translation: The main chance is still in the West Bank, but other forms of Orthodox community are coming, especially where poor people feel cut out of Israel's advanced economy.

NRP programs are having an especially strong effect on the army. In 1968, Rabbi Zefania Drori, a graduate of Mercaz HaRav Yeshiva in Jerusalem, founded (in Kiryat Shmona) a Yeshivat Hesder whose students combine Torah study with compulsory military service. In the mid-1970s, similar groups sprang up, from Mevasseret Zion, near Jerusalem, to Ma'alot, in the north; groups affiliated with the Bnei Akiva youth movement established a Yeshivat Hesder in the Negev town of Yeruham. The graduates of the Yeshivot Hesder across Israel proved to be the most passionate resisters of the Gaza evacuation. Tel Aviv University's Yoram Peri, who has been following developments in the IDF's general staff for the past thirty years, has been particularly disturbed by the various ways graduates of the Yeshivot Hesder have penetrated to the upper reaches of the command structure. A great many of the children of the settlers do their service in their settlements, and see guard duty and expansion as entirely consistent.

"A third to half of the general staff are, at any given time, wearing knitted yarmulkes," Peri said; "the commander of the evacuation was such a man and he did his duty honorably. But some did not. Some refused orders. And this was Gaza, not the Land of Israel." Peri was born into a nationalist Orthodox Jerusalem family. But now he cannot find his bearings in the rhetoric he is hearing. "What you hear more and more," Peri says, "is that such institutions as the High Court and secular law in general represent 'foreign values,' 'non-Jewish values.' They do not reflect the 'spirit of Judaism,' the 'faith of Judaism,' the Halakha."

THE ADMIXTURE OF politics and religion is creating something new. "The state of Israel is redefining Judaism," says Menachem Klein, the only prominent architect of the Geneva peace initiative to have come from the Bnei Akiva, and a renowned expert on the politics of Jerusalem at the NRP's Bar-Ilan University, whose administration has blocked his promotion. "To be Jewish now means to be somehow identified with the state." This is a religious novelty that can be dangerously suffocating, he says: "Many Orthodox Jews say casually that they are for a Jewish and democratic state, but they really mean that the source of all legitimacy is Judaism, that Halakha is supreme."

Klein fears fundamentalism is now becoming triumphant in Israel, much the way it has in Islamist republics: "It is very hard for me to accept the idea that there is an absolute distinction between the state, which is something completely secular and apart, and Judaism, which is 100 percent a religious observance, and without implied guidance for political civilization. Judaism is, of course, also culture, historical memory. And it is an identity that is not absolutely religious. Things cannot be black and white when the truth is in tones of gray. But we can *of course* separate religion from the state apparatus. We can emphasize equality of citizenship, even provide for the national rights of the Arab minority. This still leaves the gray.

"This is not the country I grew up in," Klein continues, "with a stable Status Quo Agreement governing relations between a Mapai culture, which was ostensibly secular, but was really a secular religion, and a small Orthodox community. We are now in a society that is more democratic, more liberal, more secular, more Israeli—but yet, ironically, more Israeli Jewish. Two communities are growing stronger, side by side. People adapt. Cultural institutions are often open on the Sabbath these days, but commercial operations are almost completely shut down. This was not the case forty years ago. But it is as if there is a developing cultural consensus now, that halakhic norms are, after all, what 'Jewish' is, and that people cannot avoid grappling with that. I travel a lot and feel like a tourist in many countries. But I feel like a tourist in Israel, too. I feel marginal here to a democratic community not fully liberal and to a Jewish culture that is more overtly halakhic."

HAREDI COMMUNITIES, for their part, have roots in the small ultra-Orthodox societies of Jerusalem and Safed, which lived for hundreds of years on money sent them by Eastern European acolytes, and which kept mainly to themselves while Zionism was taking shape. After the enlightenment, which hit Eastern European Jews in the nineteenth century, Haredi rabbis, both Hasidim and their scholastic opponents, undertook a kind of counterreformation. Formerly, Haredim concentrated in such places as Jerusalem's Mea Shearim and Tel Aviv's Bnei Brak; their communities are now found everywhere in the country. Dressed distinctively in black caftans and rounded hats, even on scorching summer days, they remain pietists connected to Diaspora sects, many of which have since found homes in the United States. Perhaps the best known among these is Habad, whose distant founder, Schneur Zalman of Liadi, is said to have declared in advance of the invasion of Napoleon's armies, "If Napoleon wins, the better for the Jews, if he loses, the better for Judaism."

The Haredi population, Hasidic and anti-Hasidic, now numbers approximately 575,000 people, most of whom are very young. Only about 40 percent are now of voting age. Haifa University demographer Arnon Sofer supposes their total number will be something upward of 20 percent of the Jewish population by 2020. The fertility rate of a Haredi woman is seven and a half children—eight if she is Israeli born. And the political economic foundations of Haredi youth are unique in the Western world. In 1949, the total number of students studying in state-supported yeshivot and ultra-Orthodox schools numbered a few hundred. By 1955, their separate schools enrolled perhaps 17,000 students.[6] The number today is around 200,000. Orthodox students live in virtual isolation from Western democratic and literary culture. Recently, Haredi leaders pushed a new bill to a first reading in the Knesset to exempt their schools from the secular core curriculum.

In the 1950s, when Ben-Gurion established the exemption from military service for yeshiva students, it applied to about four hundred people. In 1977, under pressure from Haredi parties, Menachem Begin withdrew all pressures on young Haredi men to do national service of any kind, and the number of yeshiva students claiming an exemption began to soar. In 1994, 5 percent of military-age Israelis received an exemption on religious grounds. In 2001, this rose to 8 percent. In 2006, it was 11 percent—and it is still rising.[7] Today, some 80,000–90,000 young men are the age of the military draft, not yet married, yet they still do not serve in the army. Virtually no women serve. Men study virtually free of charge in yeshivot, protected religious schools, which are themselves funded largely by the education ministry. Another 45,000–50,000 young, dependent, married men (they are called *avrechim*) are getting support both from their yeshivot and from social insurance and family allowance programs. Currently, only 31 percent of ultra-Orthodox men work, compared with nearly 70 percent of non-Haredi Jewish men. "Imagine," a Tel Aviv friend told me, "the South Korean government financially supporting all the proselytes of Reverend Moon."

Social economist Menachem Friedman, who's followed the money trails in Haredi communities, exposed the pattern: The boys are instructed to study for as long as possible, the girls are instructed to support them; the welfare state takes over where the yeshivot leave off.

Haredi schools are closed, rather cultish affairs, and instructors can be violent in their discipline. Yeshivot teach rigorous observance of Jewish law, interpreted by revered rabbis. The language of instruction may be Yiddish, while Hebrew is reserved for Torah and liturgy. Youth usually marry in their teens, often to partners chosen for them by parents and matchmakers. They study virtually nothing of science and technology in their schools and often seem in positive fear of Western liberal humanities.

Haredi parents fiercely protect the propriety of their large families. I know one father of sixteen children who, after his wife died, broken, shunned his daughter for studying biology and marrying a son of a Bnei Akiva family without his consent. Presumably, Bnei Akiva was not pious enough. No doubt, the other side of this exclusionary life is an enormous homey warmth and the certainty that every moment and particle are impregnated with blessing. But where the eyes of National Religious youth burn through you, the eyes of Haredi youth turn shyly away.

THERE WERE ONCE serious political differences between National Religious and Haredi groups. In the early years of the state, Haredi rabbis thought the NRP's Zionist messianism was an apostasy; the end of days would be hastened, presumably, by keeping commandments, not engaging in politics. For a good many Haredi leaders, a Jewish state is still a kind of aberration. They loathe Zionist literary culture and regard the Hebrew language as a holy tongue, never to be used for secular purposes. Until the 1967 war, no Haredi party served in government. But Haredi politicians came into their own with the ascension in 1977 of Menachem Begin, who wanted them to complete his Likud coalition—what came to be called "the national camp." Leaders like the Haredi-Hassidic Agudat Yisrael's Menachem Porush have since sought to serve in every government. And since the creation of Shas, the ultra-Orthodox political party, in 1984—a merger engineered by the then-Sephardi chief rabbi Ovadia Yosef, and the anti-Hasidic Ashkenazi rabbi Elazar Shach—Haredi parties have also sought to protect the unity of the Land of Israel, which, unlike the state of Israel, they regard as God given. They have also sought to control as far as possible public conversation about the Sabbath on the municipal level and preclude what, by their lights, they regard as defilement. For these purposes, and others, they are happy to make common cause with the NRP.

Perhaps the most egregious recent example of this alliance was their effort to block a gay pride parade in Jerusalem, scheduled for early November 2006 and mapped out to encroach not at all on Haredi neighborhoods. Haredi youth rioted, burning trash and attacking police vehicles. The municipality, in response, forced the parade to become a small rally in the stadium of the Hebrew University: six thousand gay activists and civil rights sympathizers, protected by three thousand police. The writer Sami Michael told the penned-in crowd, "Any society that tries to 'straighten' its citizens is itself warped." *Haaretz*'s Tom Segev later interviewed one NRP member of the Jerusalem City Council, whose views stood for most: "The struggle is over the holiness of the city, against a parade of abomination that desecrates and defiles the holiness of the city," she said. When his interview with her was interrupted by a Haredi member who found that Christian missionaries were distributing proselytizing booklets, both members agreed that the booklets should be burned in a public bonfire. "Book burning?" Segev asked. "Certainly," she replied; "these are books against Judaism. They have to be burned."[8]

Some Israelis will tell you that that rabbinic privileges and rhetoric became seriously oppressive when immigrants from the former Soviet Union arrived in the country. Many of them were non-Jews by Orthodox standards, though they qualified under the Law of Return. But discriminatory laws do not simply harm the people they disadvantage.

They are an education, shaping political culture more widely by shaping the moral imaginations of children born into Israeli society at large. They restrict the choices young people make about how to live their lives, about what is done and not done, or with whom to cast their fate. Laws favoring Orthodoxy have led to an astounding growth in the Orthodox population—and in the spread of Orthodox practices and attitudes. The numbers speak for themselves.

Over the past fifty-five years, Israel's strongly Orthodox Jews—both National Religious and Haredi—have increased from about 10 percent to at least a quarter of the Jewish population, about 1.5 million people. Their number has grown, that is, to five times the number of West Bank settlers, whom they generally champion. One third of all Israeli Jewish schoolchildren will be ultra-Orthodox by 2012.[9] The moral influence of Orthodox groups extends to perhaps another 15 percent of Jewish citizens—in all, to the nearly 40 percent who would choose halakhic law over any competing democratic standard. By the way, precisely the same proportion want the state "to support the emigration of Arab citizens." Thirty-four percent of Israelis say that Arab culture is inferior to Israeli culture. About a third of Israeli Jews would have Yitzhak Rabin's assassin, Yigal Amir, pardoned.

These polls correspond almost exactly to persistent voting patterns. About forty Orthodox and ultrarightist members are regularly elected to the 120-person Knesset and tend to vote as a single bloc. The extremist National Union Party has made common cause with the NRP, whose Bnei Akiva youth groups are a virtual breeding ground for Gush Emunim. More dispersed Orthodox Sephardi voters follow Shas. Ashkenazi-led Haredim divide into two political parties—actually religious societies—Agudat Yisrael and Degel Hatorah. They, too, are identified with Greater Israel these days. In the seventeenth Knesset, the religious parties alone got twenty-seven seats. Another eleven went to the Yisrael Beiteinu (Israel, Our Home) party of Avigdor Lieberman.

No Orthodox Jew, Lieberman argues for a civil marriage law to please his Russian base. But he has a home in a West Bank settlement, and is also for Jewish hegemony in the Land of Israel, often mimicking the way Vladimir Zhirinovsky had argued for Russian destiny; he panders to the Orthodox rabbinate the way any Russian nationalist panders to the Russian Orthodox Church. He wants, and expects, to rule with the religious parties. Like them, he's demanded that Israeli Arabs swear allegiance to Israel as a Jewish and Zionist state, or be deported to a Palestinian one. He calls rather grandly for swapping West Bank settlements for Israeli Arab towns, while Israeli Arab leaders who have met with Hamas should be executed. He likes Cyprus, he told the *Sunday Telegraph,* where Turks and Greeks fought a war and now live apart from each other.[10]

"ORTHODOX POWER may not have been intended by Israel's leaders, but it did not grow haphazardly. The state has, in various ways, supported the new Orthodox in schools of their own, settlements, and neighborhoods of their own, enabling them to keep to a quasihistorical consciousness of their own, even a calendar of their own." I was speaking with *Haaretz* reporter Shahar Ilan, a calm, rumpled, systematic man— you could mistake him for a classics scholar—whose explosive book, *Haredim, Inc.,* blew open the subject of Haredi political economic power for the secular Israeli public. Take the Haredim, he told me, the most obvious wards of the state. When he wrote his book, their basket of economic privileges amounted to something like 17,000 NIS (about $4,000) per month for a family of ten, when tax exemptions were factored in. Families of this size are hardly uncommon.

Support is not quite what it was. Under economic reforms introduced by Sharon's finance minister, Benjamin Netanyahu, family allowance grants were lowered. But the economic dependency of *avrechim* has hardly been broken. "It used to be that family allowance paid five times more for the fifth child than what it paid for the first. The gap is much smaller today, but the pattern is set and the damage is done. No doubt, many of the *avrechim* will now have to join the labor force. But they have been raised to a different standard from other Israelis, and the large, poor families, their treatment of women, and so forth, will persist."

Haredi kindergartens are subsidized by the municipal tax, the *arnona.* Residential middle schools for boys, the *pnimiyot,* are subject to the more or less airless indoctrination of the nineteenth-century one-room schoolhouse, or *heder,* which one might have found in the Pale of Settlement; in these publicly supported schools, there are rarely secular studies and no computer training. The boys learn the mind-bending techniques of scholastic rabbinic debate, but are not exposed to what would pass for critical thinking. When they come of age, Haredi young men often go on to yeshivat and become even more detached from civil society. They do not report their income from such occupations as ritual scribe, the job of scrupulously copying out, on parchment and with a calligraphic hand, Torah scrolls and mezuzot. Meanwhile, the yeshivot pay thousands of salaries to teachers and administrators, reporting such payments deceptively as bursaries for students who are studying.

"If it were clear they were actually coming to work," Ilan says, "they'd have to pay income tax, employers tax, pension, disability, social insurance premiums, and so forth. Students do not even pay the two hundred NIS a month social and medical insurance. So many administrators of the yeshivot pretend to be *avrechim.* If a forty-year-old yeshiva student dies and leaves six or seven children—well, it's a disaster. Their only hope, the last source of Haredi money, is the enormous flow of dollars from U.S. philanthropy, which amounts to a bursary per student of as much as $200 to $1,000 per month."

Needless to say, this kind of thing does not portend meaningful citizenship. "Imagine that a mezuzah must be written in perfect purity, but the fraudulent evasion of income tax in the writing of it does not undermine its purity. Anyway," Ilan continues, "there was a report for an economic institute in Tel Aviv, examining why Israel has experienced a precipitous drop in the rate of participation in the labor force. The research economists were shocked to find that this is the simple effect of factoring in the Haredi community. The women, many of whom are teachers, do pay their share of taxes. But an equal number of women are wig makers—married Orthodox women all wear wigs as a sign of their modesty and piety—and do not report their income. The effective rate of employment among Haredi women is 30–40 percent, about what it is in the rest of Israel. But the women, and the state, are supporting the men!" Incidentally, a small proportion of Haredi women have gotten academic and professional degrees. Since my conversation with Ilan, a council of rabbis has decided to prohibit women from attending any institution offering a terminal academic degree.

Which brings us, finally, to the black market. "There is an underground market for gold; many men engage in gold smuggling, since gold is the most important part of a Haredi dowry. A young man usually gets a watch; a woman, jewelry. Gold is also a kind of political hedge. Unlike the nationalist Orthodox, the Haredi man does not really believe he is home; he believes he is forever wandering, that at any minute he might have to flee. He needs the easiest asset to take with him." Though numbers are impossible to establish, Ilan believes that about 10 percent of Haredi men participate in this underground economy, changing money, laundering money (the Haredi economy is almost entirely in U.S. dollars), periodically selling seasonal ritual objects such as citron (*etrogim*), or boiling cooking implements at Passover time to make them kosher for the holiday. When tax collectors come to Haredi neighborhoods, they have to be accompanied by police. "Otherwise they'd be attacked on the spot," Ilan says. Officials of govern-

ment tax collection agencies almost never prosecute because their in-
vestigators regularly run into violence.

BUT WHATEVER THEIR differences in origin, and however differently
they exploit their economic advantages, NRP, Shas, and Haredi leaders
all count on the Status Quo Agreement to maintain their privileges and
their schools. Again, the Basic Laws do not challenge how, if you are a
Jew, a rabbi must marry you, or how non-Jews still cannot be buried
in a state-supported Jewish cemetery (so, for example, mixed couples
must be parted in death). Non-Jews cannot attend religious public
schools. And state-salaried rabbis still decide whether you are a Jewish
national or not. Most troubling, Ilan says, are the diplomatic implications of this alliance, which have not yet been entirely digested: "Polls
show that about 95 percent of the NRP, settlers, etc., support hard-line
pursuit of Greater Israel; but among the Haredim, responses are more
like 100 percent. They are raised on hatred of the goy. The Arab is the
goy *du jour*." Haredi "Zionism," if that is the word for it, speaks of the
people of Israel, the Land of Israel, and the Torah of Israel—"*Am Yisrael,
Eretz Yisrael, U'Torat Yisrael*"—as a kind of holy trinity.

Jerusalem is ground zero of this emerging Orthodox alliance: The
days of Mayor Teddy Kolleck walking foreign dignitaries and American
Jewish big shots through the antiquities of the Rockefeller Museum
now seem like a kind of lost golden age. More than 45 percent of
schoolchildren in Greater Jerusalem are now Haredi, a number often
linked to the estimated 180,000 mainly secular Jews who have left the
city for the coastal plain over the past ten years. About 30 percent of
schoolchildren are Arab, while about 13 percent are National Religious.
That leaves about 12 percent in secular schools, which Haredi activists
may harass and take over when their neighborhoods outgrow their own.

The current mayor of Jerusalem, Uri Lupolianski, himself Haredi
and the father of twelve children, won election because of the bloc

voting of Haredi citizens. Rates of voting in Haredi neighborhoods are about 20 percent higher than in secular areas, allegedly in part because of votes cast on behalf of people long dead or living in America. Though they are not yet a majority in the city, Haredim are a majority in the city council. Arab neighborhoods get short shrift; the ones I visit lack even street signs. (The dean of radio pundits, Hanan Krystal, quipped that an investigation into election fraud should be initiated if results do not show a 95 percent turnout of Haredi voters for Haredi parties.)

Lupolianski is an affable man, and the nonprofit he founded, Yad Sarah (The Hand of Sarah), has become a model for helping handicapped people worldwide—a kind of lending society for wheelchairs, respirators, etc. And yet, Ilan says, Lupolianski was sent into politics by his rabbinic leader, Rabbi Yosef Shalom Elyashiv, an extreme radical, the spiritual leader of Degel Hatorah, a man renowned for his exegesis of Torah: "It is not a small matter to know that your mayor takes orders from a man like Elyashiv, while the government engages in a massive transfer of funds to officials on rabbinic councils—all in all, tens of thousands of people on the government payroll, acting with state authority to certify food and wine as kosher, counsel couples before marriage, perform weddings, work in ritual baths—disseminating halakhic norms."

For its part, Jerusalem is growing more divided, with Haredi neighborhoods becoming more self-segregated, and Arabs feeling under siege. Fringe Jerusalem neighborhoods planted farther and farther into the West Bank—Maale Adumim, Har Homa, and others—are becoming almost indistinguishable from settlements, which radiate out from Jerusalem on new roads that bypass Arab towns and suburbs. In this climate, applications to the Hebrew University's graduate programs are falling; older students from the more secular coast simply do not want to start their families here. The inner-city streets of Jerusalem, unlike Tel Aviv, are mostly carless, if not abandoned, during Jewish festivals.

The restaurants of the trendy Nakhalat Shiva district will have some after-hours customers, as will the new strip at the Colony Restaurant, adjacent to the old train station; for the most part, the city is tucked in by ten o'clock at night. And the Orthodox wards of the state are poor. Walk along Jaffa Street during the day, from the Machane Yehuda market to Zion Square, and you will see a dinginess as depressing as it was thirty years ago, still surprising in a world capital.

Secular neighborhoods are shrinking, with stores, hotels, and cafés avoiding all commerce on the Sabbath. The German Colony—my own neighborhood along Emeq Refaim Street—was once a haven for secular university intellectuals, diplomats, and journalists. It has now become a mix of secular people and nationalist Orthodox living in somewhat wary coexistence. Orthodox American and French Jews, eager for a foothold, are driving up real-estate prices. On my own short block, there is now a yeshiva on one end and another going up at the other end. There is a sign on the Habad Yeshiva car parked next to my home, bearing the white-bearded face of the (arguably) deceased Lubavitche Rebbe, Menachem Schneerson, looking stern, like a disappointed Santa Claus. The caption beneath it reads: "Messiah the King says, 'Conquer the territories, slaughter the terrorists.'"

THERE IS, just beneath the surface, growing public revulsion in coastal Israel, especially for Haredi power. Several years back, a Haredi group tried to buck up supporters of the Orthodox monopoly over Jewish conversion, plastering the country with posters that said, "*Am ehad, giyur ehad,*" meaning, "One nation, one conversion." Within hours, young people in north Tel Aviv made a mischievous change to the posters, rounding off the letter *resh* in *giyur* to the letter *samach,* so that the message read, "*Am ehad, giyus ehad,*" that is, "One nation, one conscription."

But opposition to Haredi power does not necessarily translate into criticism of Haredi culture. Photos of Nazis pulling beards are etched in the memory. Where everyone is hungry for unity, Haredi Judaism has become a kind of comfort food. Framed portraits of obscure Haredi rabbis hang discreetly behind cash registers in fruit stores and dry cleaners. As one of my students put it, only half-mockingly, "The idea was a Jewish state, wasn't it? So what is more Jewish than a rabbi?" Many secular friends, who otherwise agree with gay rights, opposed the parade in Jerusalem, claiming earnestly that this was, after all, a holy city, and perhaps gays should stick to Tel Aviv. On the day before one recent Yom Kippur, Channel One's national newscast took us to the bizarre scene of Haredi rabbis waving (soon-to-be-sacrificed) chickens over the heads of children, performing the medieval ritual of *kapara* over them. Sins disappear with the slitting of throats. You might have thought this was no more remarkable than an American president lighting the national Christmas tree.

Haredi rabbis capitalize, when they can, on this public sentimentalism. Rabbi Eliezer Menachem Schach, who preceded Elyashiv as leader of Degel Hatorah, has called democracy a cancer. Their "worst nightmare," Shahar Ilan says, is that Israel should become "so much a part of the region that a Jewish woman should marry an Arab." Sephardi chief rabbi Ovadia Yosef once called Arabs "snakes," and has never apologized. Schach dismissed public criticism of the occupation as so much "informing" against the Jewish people. (The language is calculated: The Amidah prayer, at the center of the Orthodox liturgy, denounces "informants," once the bane of Diaspora Jews practicing their faith in secret.) In December 1993, the late Rabbi Shlomo Goren, a former chief rabbi of Israel and chief rabbi of the IDF, published a ruling forbidding Jews to evacuate any settlement in the biblical Land of Israel, declaring that "a soldier who receives an order that runs contrary to Torah law should uphold Halakha and not the secular order."[11] In 1996, Rabbi Eliyahu Bakshi Doron, then the Sephardi chief rabbi, compared Reform Jews to the obscure biblical figure Zimri, who had had sexual relations with a non-Jewish woman. He praised Pinchas, the man who murdered Zimri, and let things stand there.[12]

There is nothing unique about this fundamentalism, of course. Like their counterparts in Islamic countries, Israel's Haredi leaders gain power by trafficking in received truths, claim to reject the materialism of civil society but live off the bourgeois social contract, use information technologies but cannot see that technological advance is the product of open inquiry, depend on women's work but banish the risks of female sexual power, and so forth. They protect male sovereignty, which regularly tips into justifying domestic brutality. They want the comforts of national unity above all, which reinforces the comfort of family love.

"For Haredim," Ilan said, "democracy means majority rule with utter indifference to the rights of minorities, Arabs especially—an unwillingness to accept the rules of the democratic game if this goes against what they perceive as their interests. When I strike up conversations with Haredim in the street, they simply cannot understand why I think that the hypothetical assassination of a Likud prime minister, with whom they know I disagree, would bother me as much as the killing of Rabin—that the rules *themselves* are sacred. For them, all that matters is what is good 'for the Jews'—are you with us or against us? The High Court has made all kinds of decisions protecting the rights of gays, belly dancers, nonkosher restaurants. Rabbinic authorities simply ignore these decisions."

THIS—does it really need to be said?—is not the way things were supposed to turn out in the Jewish National Home. "I have never feared really religious people," Chaim Weizmann, Israel's first president and Zionism's first great statesman, wrote in his 1940s memoir; "it is the new secularized type of Rabbi, resembling somewhat a member of a clerical party in Germany, France, or Belgium, who is the menace, and who will make a heavy bid for power by parading his religious convictions. It is useless to point out to such people that they transgress a fundamental principle which has been laid down by our sages, 'Thou shalt not make of the Torah a crown to glory in, or a spade to dig with.' "[13]

Nor does opposition to a state religion mean opposition to religious imagination. People give prayer, Emerson said, the way trees give apples: The most elementary religious questions are finally inescapable and, lacking answers, sublime. A great many Israeli democrats claim to be deaf to these questions, but then they wonder why their children linger on the banks of the Ganges or, indeed, are drawn to cultish forms of Halakha. Then again, the claim to oppose all religious feeling is in part a reaction to Orthodox Judaism's ubiquity. It is hard to imagine even a word for religion that is not associated with the imposition of Halakha. Quite like Perchik, the freethinking son-in-law in *Fiddler on the Roof,* educated Israelis suppose they must choose between surrendering to dogmatic tradition and standing for the dignity of the individual. Israelis mostly take for granted that being religious—the common word is *dati*—means being an observer of commandments, while being secular—or *hiloni*—means being a scoffer. Actually, there is no word in Hebrew for the English *religious,* which implies personal faith and seeking. *Dati* really means "observant of commandments." The closest to the English is *ruhani,* which really means "spiritual" and can apply to anyone from an inspired artist to a baker of whole-grain bread.

These may seem pedantic distinctions, but their implications are deep and wide. Secular Jews do not much read the Torah, the liturgy, and the Talmud, beyond what is required of them in school or during holidays. They deny, with a kind of aggressive ignorance, that knowing such sources is a benefit to a modern Jew. And yet they revere the Orthodox tradition for nationalist reasons, as the primary source of national survival during Zionism's prehistory. It is rare to find Israelis who will say, what so many American intellectuals offhandedly say, that they are at once secular *and* religious.

Orthodoxy's power to exhaust what is meant by religion is best revealed, perhaps, in the veneration so many proudly secular Israelis feel for the late Hebrew University philosopher Yeshayahu Leibovitz. An Orthodox Jew, Leibovitz spoke loudly against the settlements and for a separation of religion and state, from early in the 1970s until his death in 1994. He argued, moreover, that slavish attachment to the Land of Israel was idolatrous, and that Palestinian self-determination was just; he excoriated both Labor leaders and Orthodox parties for preserving the Status Quo Agreement. His acerbic courage won him many admirers on the left and inspired an Orthodox movement for peace and democracy, led by younger colleagues such as Aviezer Ravitzsky, who became a fellow of the Israel Democracy Institute. But Leibovitz opposed the Status Quo, not because he admired religious pluralism, but rather because he thought that a paid rabbinate would grow fat in government and only bring discredit to halakhic practice—which he expected every *real* Jew to adopt without question. "The Christian God sacrifices His Son for us," he once told me; "the Jewish God expects us to sacrifice our sons to Him."

In this atmosphere, the religious idiosyncrasy we need from democratic intellectuals is hard to find. Anyone who sees Shimon Peres awkwardly adjusting his yarmulke before entering the negotiating room with Shas leaders can only blush for them both (party elders recently delivered the presidency to Peres and were rewarded with larger school budgets). But the alternative is not easy to imagine. Talk about a truly personal faith, and you are branded a kind of eccentric, or worse, an incipient Christian. And what, if not tribalism and apocalyptic thinking, will be taught in Shas schools? The present leader of Shas, Eli Yishai, said of a draft law permitting civil marriage: "Those who have Jewish hearts beating inside them don't promote an initiative as anti-Jewish as civil marriage . . . [The] desire to uproot everything that is Jewish is like a carnivorous germ we have to exterminate."[14]

MOST SADLY, perhaps, their disdain for the tug of religious language takes Israeli democrats out of a fight they cannot really afford to avoid—over the transcendent foundation of democracy itself. The problem is not simply that Israeli democrats surrender the word *religion* to Israel's Orthodox. It is that they don't see how, by doing so, they get caught up in a contradiction that Bertrand Russell once noticed and their children eventually pick up, which makes the argument for democracy seem merely a matter of taste.

Orthodox people—like Haredi groups in Israel—will make grand, traditional claims, which they insist are absolute: the story of creation, the divinity of the revealed word, the promise of the Messiah, and so forth. Israeli democrats respond, dutifully, that all traditional claims should be thought provisional and never absolute. But if traditional claims are provisional, why is not the claim of tolerance merely provisional? Is not the latter merely a Western claim, like claims for the beauty of Bruckner's music? Why not choose Halakha, presumably our tradition, over democracy, the West's? Why not Hasidic music over Bruckner?

The answer, of course, is that tolerance is not a mere tradition, however dogmatically it may now be taught. It is itself an absolute, a tribute to the proposition that humans are ends in themselves, not means to other ends. And that proposition is nothing if not mysterious, grounded in what can only be called faith. Kant was no Tevye, but he was no Perchik, either. Israeli democrats may insist that no book, not even the Torah, is sacred. But what they really mean—or should mean—is that the right to *interpret* books is sacred.[15] Democrats, if they are thoughtful, are nothing if not "awestruck" by the source of this equality. ("Thou shalt see it," Melville wrote in *Moby-Dick,* "shining in the arm that wields a pick or drives a spike; that democratic dignity which, on all hands, radiates without end from God; Himself! The great God absolute! The center and circumference of all democracy! His omnipresence, our divine equality!")

Orthodox Jews, or at least those with a progressive streak, will rush to say that this notion of absolute dignity can itself be found in the Torah. Men and women were created in God's image, after all. But Orthodox Israeli Jews do not generally take this as the starting point of moral autonomy and improvisation. They take it to be yet further proof of the Torah's perfection, including its ability to anticipate everything good. Like Leibovitz, they are merely claiming the moral prestige of a democratic principle to justify obeying everything else that is divinely commanded, the whole burden of Halakha. The sages, it may be said, freely interpreted Jewish laws. But are those laws worth debating endlessly, to the exclusion of other principles of action? And do only rabbis have the right to pronounce which laws to obey or what ceremonies to practice? Ask such questions in a yeshiva, and you'll be smacked upside the head.

What all of this comes down to is the debasement of religion as well as democracy. In his *Varieties of Religious Experience,* William James writes that the most constructive faith begins in a kind of rational unhappiness, which can never be put right. ("Unhappiness," he says, "is apt to characterize the period of order-making and struggle. If the individual be of tender conscience and religiously quickened, the unhappiness will take the form of moral remorse and compunction, of feeling inwardly vile and wrong, and of standing in false relation to the author of one's being and appointer of one's spiritual fate.") James called this formative experience the "sickness of the soul." Truly religious people, he thought, cannot stop doubting that matter *matters.* They will not achieve sanity, humility, etc., if they are sure it does.

Yet like the author of Ecclesiastes, such people always come up against overtly religious, that is, untroubled people, for whom a just order is pre-ordained by totemic force. Those people are inclined to a disquieting, naive piety, providing them "passports beyond the bounds of conventional morality." James called them, with graceful irony, "healthy-minded." The point is, surrendering the privilege of defining religion to Orthodoxy guarantees the triumph of healthy-mindedness. Just after the catastrophic tsumani in Southeast Asia, the chief Sephardi rabbi, Shlomo Amar, declaimed: "God is angry, and we must pray more and ask for mercy; the nations of the world are obligated to observe the seven Noahide laws, such as prohibitions against murder and illicit relations."

Such theology is a public tragedy, but it is felt most subtly in private spaces, touching each of us differently. For my part, I can't stop noticing the dubious fate of the traditional blessing after the meal, the Birkat Ha-mazon. It has a famous coda taken from Proverbs, which Isaiah Berlin once called the "harshest lie in world." This goes: "I was a youth, and I have become aged, and I have never seen a righteous man deserted, and his children begging for bread."[16] (Na'ar hayiti, gan zakanti, v-lo raiti tzadik ne'ezav, v-zaro mevakesh lahem.) Even as a young child, I thought those words fatuous. But the melody that accompanied them—so it was sung by my father, aunts, uncles—was in a minor key and among the most mournful, lovely melodies I had yet heard. I could not articulate subtle feelings at the time, but the blessing's words accompanied by that music seemed deliciously ironic to me. The two together suggested justice accompanied by a fascinating, bitter skepticism—a juxtaposition that, I dare say, made my soul a little sick. This was, I thought, an introduction to the edgy splendor of the Jewish people's election. "When I say Judaism," the writer Aharon Appelfeld told me, "I mean a basic disquiet, that you are never completely rooted, in this or any place, that you are never serene."[17] My father put it more bluntly in an old Yiddish adage: "Der mensch tracht un Gott lacht"—"Men strive, God laughs."

But when I moved to Jerusalem in 1972, I noticed that something had gone awry with the prayer. Its haunting melody had been superseded by a new one—which had come, so I was told, from the Bnei Akiva youth movement—a catchy tune in four-four time and in a major key, reminiscent of the University of Michigan's fight song. With that rhythm, and in that register, the final words of the blessing could only be taken as a kind of intelligent design. I have often been offended by this melody, but could not be bothered to say so. Who wants to spoil the *gemutlich* feeling at somebody's holiday Sabbath table? ("Surely all this," as *Moby-Dick's* Ishmael says of his own little smoothing hypocrisies, "is not without meaning.")

THERE IS ONE last question that needs answering. Can the expansion of Israel's Orthodox citizenry be explained by the fecklessness of Israeli secularism alone? Was Orthodoxy not—given a Jewish polity speaking the holy tongue—unavoidable? "We don't like to think about this," my wife, Sidra, says, "but people like the young Gershon Scholem put things radically. What religious nuances do Hebrew words naturally carry? Scholem feared that Zionism's political fevers would awake more primordial fevers; that the Hebrew language contained long dormant but easily activated agents of messianism and apocalyptic thinking. How can we stay close to this sacred center, yet keep our distance?" Scholem put these fears into a famous 1926 letter from Jerusalem to Franz Rosenzweig back in Berlin:

One speaks here of many things that could make us fail, more than ever today about the Arabs...[M]ore uncanny than the Arab people another threat confronts us. It is absolutely impossible to empty out words filled to bursting...If we transmit to our children the language which has been transmitted to us, if we— the generation of transmission—resuscitate the language of the ancient books so that it reveals itself anew to them, must then not the religious violence of this language break out against those who speak it?[18]

What Scholem most feared was the atavistic power of Hebrew itself. Can Israel's politicians, conducting affairs of state in Hebrew's biblical words and phrases, avoid implying the authority of religious practice and hierarchy? Can democracy even be grasped in Hebrew? Scholem was not alone. The young Koestler, who (in his capacity as a journalist) also tooled around Palestine in 1926, wrote that Hebrew could never convey the private emotions of the free, bourgeois experience. Later he would put it this way, in his 1949 chronicle, *Promise and Fulfillment*: "The instrument on which the Hebrew novelist has to express his twentieth-century emotions has no half-tones or modulations of key or timbre . . . Hebrew is admirably suited for producing prophetic thunder; but you cannot play a scherzo on a ram's horn." Koestler's friend George Orwell had by then written in a well-known essay, "Politics and the English Language," that when an Englishman used the word *liberty* he immediately implied freedom in the sense of personal rights. Did the word *herut* from the Passover Haggadah mean *that*? Did it not mean, rather, collective freedom from oppression, which is why Begin appropriated it as the name for his first ultranationalist political party? Koestler implied that people who spoke of individual conscience in Hebrew were swimming against a subtle current. Do they not still? (Scholem's letter goes on: "People play with words in writings and newspapers, lying to themselves or to God that this means nothing, and often, out of the ghostly shame of our language, the power of the sacred speaks out."[19])

YET THE FATE of Hebrew has been more complex than anyone could have fully anticipated in the 1920s. "There is Tel Aviv Hebrew," the poet and Hebrew University scholar of South Asian languages David Shulman told me; "it is the most juicy, delicious Hebrew imaginable, all about going out and getting laid, all very personal and loaded with slang from Arabic and English. I learn it from my kids and students. Some prissy old writers hate it; but I love its wonderful cutting directness, its *hatakh*. The individual can almost certainly live in it." Are external influences decisive? "It is also true that Hebrew lends itself to the life of a tribal ghetto. 'The nation will dwell alone.' Phrases like this are everywhere. Just listen to the rhetoric of the army, which is full of classical allusions to the sacred nature of individual sacrifice for the people. Yet it was the achievement of Agnon and others to have ironized all that, though many seem to have overlooked Agnon and other modern Jewish writers."[20]

Shulman was referring to Israel's Nobel Laureate, S. Y. Agnon, the undisputed (if not the unchallenged) father of modern Hebrew prose. It was Agnon, Shulman implies, who demonstrated how to both validate and undermine—how to *manage*—the sacred character of Hebrew. And he did so not by rejecting, but rather by ironizing Jewish scripture and liturgy, by playing self-consciously with its texts the way Milton did with the King James Bible.

Sidra elaborates the point: "Agnon and the other giants of the modern literary revival were masters of a kind of ironic distance. Their juxtapositions of the sacred and the profane, of Diaspora and Zion, reflected this binary consciousness. Their great heir was Yehuda Amichai. We all love the way he rewrites the prayer intoned at Jewish gravesides, El Maleh Rahamim: 'God full of mercy / Were God not so full of mercy / Then there would be mercy in the world / And not just in Him.' Such delicious irony. But Amichai," Sidra continues, "goes beyond these divisive binaries to a more inclusive vision. He is our poet of the sacred quotidian, not unlike Emily Dickinson in America. The Zionist project collected, reunited, and reintegrated people, territory, and texts. Amichai assembled these into a poetics of compassion. 'Not like a cypress,' Amichai writes in the poem that is often read as his *Ars Poetica,* 'Not all at once, not all of me / But like the grass, in thousands of cautious green exits / To be hiding like many children / While one of them seeks.' "[21]

What scope do ordinary citizens have to find ironic distance, rhetorical compassion, the way their poets do? A great deal, it turns out. The week before the disengagement, I heard a pundit on the radio who was trying to assure listeners of the Gaza evacuation's inexorability: "The evacuation will come," he said, "and even if it should tarry, it will come" *(Ha-pinui yavo, v-af al pi she-yitmahameha, bo yavo).* The unspoken reference in this phrase, which any schoolchild might have picked up, was to the ancient declaration of faith in the ultimate coming of the "tarrying" Messiah, chanted yearly, lugubriously, on the Ninth of Av (the fast day commemorating the destruction of the Temple). The pundit's ironic twist was compounded by his use of the language of Jewish messianism to discredit Jewish messianists.

And yet it is never quite clear in contemporary Israel just who is the butt of the joke. For the ironic phrase here drew attention to the pundit's talent (privilege, ability) to play with classical messianic formulations, and yet also to the authenticity of the messianic longing itself. If he had said, less colorfully, "The evacuation will come as surely as the sun will set," he would have encouraged quite another frame of mind. At critical times, in other words, even ironized Hebrew creates a mental atmosphere in which one can never be sure whether rabbinic authority is being superseded or sanctioned (and if sanctioned, merely asked to live up to its transcendent promise).

Another radio commentator, speaking on the same program, wanted to call attention to the mad, loving loyalty of the settlers to the land. So he said that Israel was being threatened by *"ahavat hinam"*— "baseless love"—the ironic opposite of "baseless hatred" (*sinat hinam*), to which, so the Talmud teaches, the destruction of the sacred Temple can be attributed. The commentator wanted to make the settlers seem extreme. But he actually sanitized the phrase while yanking us back into thoughts of how talmudic wisdom was enough to account for the ancient, apocalyptic destruction of Jerusalem—and might still be relevant today.

"Languages no doubt have characteristics," Israel Prize–winning critic Menachem Brinker summed things up for me, "but I doubt that they have essences. I don't feel in my own use of the language that there is anything which would keep me from laying the ground for a democracy. The Hebrew language as we know it today, at least 15 percent of it, is words coming from international languages, broadened to the needs of the community.

"When an Israeli eats his salad in the morning, the names of his vegetables have come from different places over a 2,600-year period: Radishes and onions are from the Bible; cucumber is from the Mishna; the tomato is an innovation from Kibbutz Degania, the first kibbutz of the Second Aliyah at the turn of the century; then there is the word for lettuce, which comes from Arabic. On the other hand, innovations don't all work. People," Brinker continued, "wanted to call the telephone *sah-rahok*. It didn't take. The Arabs still have their own words for socialism and democracy. Not the Hebrews. We are 'Europeans.' How then to believe that the language will decide the nature of the society that this people is capable of?"

What, then, about Scholem's fear? "He was sure that as long as Jews spoke Hebrew, there would never be a full-fledged Jewish secularism—they would never get rid of the load of religious connotations," Brinker said. "And Scholem had a point, which was much more penetrating than certain Zionist thinkers, who thought that Hebrew would have its victory when, say, the Jewish state would have thieves and whores who spoke it. Anyhow, other, more important Jewish experiences are getting in the way, like Diaspora attitudes. There is something about this two-thousand-year-old culture of the Diaspora, which sees state sovereignty as merely instrumental, as something used by gentiles against the Jewish people's interest, which is interfering with laying the ground for democracy. The Diaspora mentality is coming back to haunt us here. The settlers think of the state as a kind of enemy of some purer Judaism. And who will tell us what to do, with a nuclear weapon in one hand, and the story of the Holocaust in the other?"

Brinker's words were hardly cheerful, yet there was an implied optimism in the hybridization he spoke of, especially in the Tel Aviv Hebrew he and Shulman both love—a language growing and changing at an astonishing rate. That Hebrew is more and more impregnated with what might be called global English—allusions to the politics, popular culture, science, and business life of North America, particularly. Global English is hardly a sacred language, but its ubiquity does seem a kind of saving grace. Its democratic nuances are built into everyday Hebrew much like jazz and rock have been built into Israel's music. This English alleviates Hebrew, the way it has alleviated Japanese and German. It is, I think, a kind playful accompaniment to classical Hebrew that works for democracy the opposite way sad melody works with the climactic passages of Birkat Ha-mazon.

Sidra, for her part, argues that poets such as Amichai and T. Carmi, both now dead, alas, absorbed Anglo-American influences from Whitman to Auden, along with global English. Such poets have already proved how playful encounters with classical Judaism is the peculiar gift of Israeli democracy. "Amichai knew the danger of forgetting that any human descriptions of the divine are necessarily metaphorical, a kind of grown-up child's play. What are our settlers if not people who've forgotten that their exotic, compelling descriptions of the land are just the poetic inventions of medieval Jews? You literalize Psalms and you kill others and destroy yourself. There is a language for loving Jerusalem, but there must also be a language for loving *in* Jerusalem. In any case, Amichai knew secular does not mean faithless. He wrote that wrapping yourself in a towel after the beach can be a sacred act much like wrapping yourself in a *tallis* [prayer shawl]; that a part of what makes the towel sacred is the memory of your father's *tallis* in the synagogue. And would the *tallis* be sacred if not for the towel?"

LOVING JERUSALEM or loving *in* Jerusalem. There is a Hebrew for both, but only the latter Hebrew is self-ironizing, playfully anglicized—erotic, brassy, metaphorical, mischievous. This is the Hebrew every with-it Israeli knows and every democratic Israeli unknowingly counts on.

At the same time, you cannot live in Hebrew and expect no repercussions from its archaic power. You cannot live in a state with an official Judaism, in addition to this Hebrew, and expect no erosion of citizenship. You can, as most Israelis do, speak the language, ignore the archaism, and tolerate the Judaism. But then you should not expect your children to understand what democracy is.

PART TWO

The Decline—and Rise—of the Hebrew Republic

If the weight of its Zionist past confounds Israel's democracy, what would an unencumbered state—a Hebrew republic—look like? Its contours are implied between the lines so far; but the necessary changes are worth summarizing before we go on. The sequence is not as important as the package, all of which could be in place in about one generation.

First, a democratic Israel would have boundaries. It need not remove a single soldier from occupied territory just yet, not until demilitarized zones, the precedent of treaties honored, and NATO forces guarantee Israel's security; but it would immediately freeze all settlements, remove outlying ones, and agree in advance to a border based on the internationally recognized Green Line. It would welcome a Palestinian capital in East Jerusalem in return for an internationally recognized Israeli capital in West Jerusalem. Where Jewish settlers could not be moved, Israel would execute land exchanges. It would require special protections here and there, such as in Palestinian airspace close to Ben-Gurion Airport, but it would in any case adopt the principle that sovereignty derives from the just consent of the governed. Israel would declare its ultimate intention to end the occupation and negotiate a peace treaty with the Palestinian Authority (PA) under international auspices. Negotiation itself would be taken as proof that both sides would eventually recognize the other and work for peace. In places where a clear division of territory would, like the Old City of Jerusalem, be impossible, Israel would be open to the presence of international forces, including multinational Arab forces from Jordan and Egypt. (These principles are consistent with the Geneva Initiative, whose solutions command widespread support; I'll return to peacemaking in this book's conclusion.)

Second, a democratic Israel would pass a bill of rights and a formal constitution, guaranteeing all of its citizens an impartial state apparatus such as the one promised in Israel's 1948 Declaration of Independence. It would recognize Israeli as the only nationality it has the jurisdiction to confer. It would set out clear standards for immigration and naturalization. Accordingly, it would retire the Law of Return, and replace it with an immigration bill extending landed-immigrant status on, among other categories, refugees from anti-Semitism. All landed immigrants would qualify for citizenship, if they learn Hebrew, after a minimum of five years of residency.

Third, Israel would guarantee equality of property rights. It would, within ten years, privatize all lands in open, impartial auctions—except for national parks, rights of way for public transportation, etc., which benefit all of its citizens equally. It would set up a civil rights commission. It would immediately end the participation in its state planning boards of the Jewish Agency and Jewish National Fund, and rescind the quasiofficial status of all Zionist institutions, inviting them to become, if they desire, registered nonprofit institutions, operating in Israel the way any others do. Israel would retain its national symbols and anthem, but also add to them, so that all citizens might more easily identify with the state. It would require national service from all of its citizens.

Finally, Israel would separate religion and state. Consistent with its democratic bill of rights, it would end state support for any rabbinical institutions or offices. It would offer civil marriage, divorce, and burial. It would establish a true public school system. It would not necessarily run all schools, and may even opt for a voucher system. But it would

refuse state subventions (or parent vouchers) to any schools that refused to teach a standard curriculum in science and the humanities approved by the Ministry of Education—and in the Hebrew language.
The privileged place for Hebrew would be a critical characteristic of this
reformed state. Hebrew would be Israel's one official language. At the
same time, all children, from the first grade on, would learn English
and Arabic. High schools would be integrated on a regional basis.

There is more to be said about this Hebrew republic's relations with
the world—how it would naturally establish federal arrangements
with Palestine and Jordan, and aim for some kind of association with
the European Union. But what already seems so remarkable about this
list is how unremarkable the changes are. All they do, so to speak, is
bring Israel's democracy up to code. If we were debating, for example,
the reform of Turkey, so that it might qualify for the European Union,
such changes would cause little fuss. Why do they seem so audacious
when applied to Israel?

A Jewish state—it cannot be emphasized enough—does not have an
identity like that of a Jewish person. A state is also not a family, or a
club, or a congregation. It is a commonwealth, a social contract, in
which individuals who are subject to equal rules of citizenship work out
their lives—if they wish, in voluntary association with people, families,
clubs, and congregations. Nor is the call for a Hebrew republic a desire
to replace the Jewish people with a people called Hebrews or to impose
Jewish identity on Israel's Arabs. On the contrary, I am just Zionist
enough to believe that the Hebrew language is the best possible
medium in which Jewish individuals, congregations, and so forth, can
try out whatever practical definitions of who is a Jew they please. Hebrew is also spacious enough for Arabs to absorb its nuances and yet remain Arabs, at least in the hybridized way minorities everywhere adapt
to a majority's language and the culture it subtends. Diaspora Jews are
nothing if not proof of how this can work. You do not have to be a

Catholic descended from Frankish clans to be a Frenchman or to enjoy the rights and cultural blessings of France. But if you *were* a Catholic descended from the Franks and wanted to explore Frenchness, where else but in the French republic would you rather live? Similarly, Hebrew is the best possible context for communities to forge Jewish identities, secular and also religious. What a Hebrew republic does preclude is the monopoly that Orthodox rabbinic hierarchies have arrogated to themselves to define who is a Jew and Jewish values. A democratic state can tell you what to speak, not what to think. In a Hebrew republic, rabbis would have to compete for minds and hearts with, say, poets.

Moreover, if all of these changes were to come, not in a generation, but in a single day, most Israelis would actually not notice that their lives had changed very much. Formally, it is true, this would not be the state Israelis have grown accustomed to without quite knowing why. But it would hardly be unfamiliar. The result would be a state that feels very much like Tel Aviv, or Haifa, or the towns in the Valley of Jezreel and the Galilee. It would integrate its minorities and immigrants in growing urban areas: Already 95 percent of Israelis live in cities, nearly a third in the four biggest cities. Hebrew is already Israel's primary language.

In 1942, at the Biltmore Conference in New York, when Ben-Gurion's Zionist executive first called for a state, it actually called for a "Jewish Commonwealth integrated in the structure of the new democratic world." A Hebrew republic would be something quite like that. But it is hard to speak about these matters precisely, so Israelis tend to scare one another with disconcerting anecdotes: about trips to sprawling Arab towns in the Galilee, or encounters with Russian immigrants walking through Tel Aviv with crucifixes around their necks.

ALL OF WHICH raises the next crucial question for this book. If the Jewish-and-democratic state needs repair, just who will advance a fix along the lines of a Hebrew republic? Israel, after all, would have to reform diplomatic and constitutional arrangements that have endured since before 1967. These changes would have to be acceptable to a reasonably broad electoral majority; they cannot just cascade from decisions of the High Court. Reform would have to be promoted, one link at a time, by a more or less cohesive group of leading politicians.

It is time, in other words, to consider the politics of the situation. Which political élites are likely to have real influence? Who believes what? Israelis, obviously, do not lack political groups making sharp arguments that cut across party lines. What pressures can be expected to grow on them?

If we go by the headlines, there are three broad groups to watch. The settlers and their rightist supporters are one, using the freedoms of the democratic process—demonstrations, government coalitions, squatting, or the panic of the demos—to preserve the status quo. Again, something more than a third of Israeli Jews would subscribe to their view. Their numbers are growing—naturally, as it were—in view of the Haredi birthrates and out of a spreading fear of Arab birthrates. Second, there is a solid centrist majority, 55 to 60 percent of Jews, challenging the settlers. These people claim that the occupation (including the settlers who want its perpetuation and the terrorists who force its perpetuation) has presented Israeli democracy with a demographic threat. Maintain the occupation, so the argument goes, lose the Jewish majority between the Jordan River and the Mediterranean Sea, and Israel must become either an apartheid state or a binational state—and in this sense, must be either Jewish or democratic, but not both. ("The danger," Ehud Olmert told me in February 2007, inadvertently stepping on Jimmy Carter's mine, "is that we move from an Algerian situation to a South African one.") The center is dogged by a third group, buoyed by Arab voters, who believes that no Jewish state could be democratic, because a state founded on a desire to privilege the Jewish people is inherently discriminatory. Some kind of binationalism, they say, is preferable, if not inevitable.

From a distance, the noisiest and most interesting fight is the lopsided one between centrists and electorally insignificant advocates for some kind of binational state. Both sides are educated and progressive, and both would claim to be democrats in the Western sense. Both refuse to see Jewishness as a blood type. Yet the former calls the latter naïve, post-Zionist, or patsies of anti-Semites—and prominent American Jews have reflexively gone along. The latter group, much smaller among Jews, but much larger in the world at large, calls the former racist and committed to the vestiges of colonialism. It draws to itself Europe's (and the developing world's) growing number of *intellectuels engagés*, whose desire to distance themselves from Zionism has, if anything, only gained strength by the revolt of Islamic minorities in bourgeois European cities.

But the headlines are missing something important. Those preoccupied with demographic trends, including leaders of Israel's peace camp, have not only an intuitive grasp of what it takes to preserve Jewish culture, but an understanding of democratic rights that is shallow and mechanical. They are painting by numbers. Should the settlers and their advocates regain power—which is hardly impossible in the short run, and almost inevitable if peace breaks out—all this talk about preserving a Jewish majority could lay the ground, not for withdrawing from the West Bank, but for ethnic cleansing of Israeli Arabs. For their part, advocates for a secular binational state miss how radically, and for the better, historic Zionism has already changed Jewish culture.

Nor is this the only way to define the groups determining Israel's political fate. The most important and least specified force comes into relief when we look at the center in a different light, not as political leaders, but as economic players. I am referring to a new generation of élite professionals whose talk about demographics is actually a place-holder for a potentially open-minded vision—people who are willing hostages to the market pressures and liberal values inherent in globalization.

If they intend to maintain their country's economic vitality and retain their own power, this élite will have to nudge Israel in the direction of global integration, no matter what their traditional prejudices about Zionism's cause may be. The only Israel that could integrate in this way—so they are discovering—is a country that looks much like the Hebrew republic I've just described. If Israel were to take shape in this way, would Israeli Arab élites agree to join it? And if they did, would Israel's Jews accept them?

CHAPTER 4

The Center's Liberal Demography

Deterministic processes are threatening to destroy Israel. We won't succeed with democracy and pretty words. If we do not exert all our efforts in the Negev and Galilee, with an emergency regime, in another three to five years a dictator will do it . . . In a few years there will be an Arab axis from Biranit in the north, through the Galilee, Acre, Shfaram, Jerusalem and to the Negev. Jews will drink coffee in Tel Aviv and that will be the end of the state.

—PROFESSOR ARNON SOFER,
Haifa University,
interview with *Haaretz,* February 25, 2003

When Ariel Sharon formed the Kadima party in advance of the March 2006 election, much hopeful talk focused on the emergence of Israel's political center—in electoral terms, the partnership between Kadima, Labor, and some smaller liberal parties, but as a larger political force, a coalition of what has been called Israel's silent majority: globalist, pragmatic, stabilizing, even hip. If Israel could move to peace, what if not the center would take it there? Hasn't the Likud, the majority party since 1977, remained a prisoner of rightist forces ideologically committed to Greater Israel?

Much of this hope dissipated immediately after the 2006 Lebanon War, when Israelis reviewed the performance of top government leaders.

But the trends producing Kadima and the center will not soon disappear, even if Olmert's government and party do. Indeed, the fate of Israel's democracy is bound up with the center, whose ideas are seriously limited, but still evolving. In a way, the word *center* only obscures why.

IF ALL ONE MEANS by center is a vague desire to contain Palestinian terrorism yet distance oneself from settlers' excesses—to do the former without alienating Washington, and the latter without splitting the Jewish people—then a stable majority has been centrist since 1967. But this is a free-floating desire, not the basis of a political identity.

Israelis anguish over five issues, actually. First, there is the question of whether to rely primarily on military power when dealing with the troubled Middle East. Second, there is the collateral but more ideologically charged question of whether to withdraw from occupied territory, historical Eretz Yisrael, in order to advance to a "two-state solution" with Palestinians. Third, there is the question we have examined thus far, whether a democracy can accord exclusive privileges to those legally defined as Jews—a question linked to the first two, but not limited by them. Next there is the question, tucked into the last one, of whether to privilege Orthodox religious practice. Finally, there is the question of economic privilege, even class: Who wins and who loses in a global market economy?

One cannot easily find a center in the permutations these questions produce, which is why as many as twenty political parties typically compete in Israeli elections. But when pundits now speak about a center, they mean leaders who, though they'll want to have things both ways on many of these issues, have tipped over in certain directions: immediate toughness over eventual diplomacy; "painful concessions" in the territories over "Zionist" devotion to the Land of Israel; some civil reform, yet Jewish privilege over scrupulous attention to Arab rights; the religious Status Quo over secular discomfort; and global markets over working-class discomfort. Some of these choices are shortsighted, no doubt, but the ambivalence is promising. Centrists will often advance contradictory positions: shows of social compassion for the poor, wedded to reassurances to venture capitalists; civil marriage, yet jobs for rabbis.

To add to the complexity, Israel's elections bring out five more or less permanent tribes to debate these issues: groups of electors defined by primordial ethnic or religious loyalties. Each comprises about 20 percent of the electorate, or something around a million and a half people. The tribes have had immigrant experiences at very different times, and so tend to think of Israel in different ways. They sometimes meld into one another and more often chafe against one another. For some time now, Israeli coalition politics has been a game of temporarily patching them together.[1]

THE FIRST TRIBE—call it Tribe One—is dominated by veteran Ashkenazim (of European origin), most of them Sabras. They were born in the country, are now well educated and cosmopolitan, secular, and (if anything) observant of Judaism in the emancipated sense—live and let live—and living very well indeed, in fashionable neighborhoods like North Tel Aviv, Jerusalem's Bak'a, or Haifa's Carmel. These are the Israelis that Americans usually run into, members of the educational and professional élite, often drawn by opportunities abroad: a visiting appointment at the University of Pennsylvania, a stint at A. T. Kearney. Their old-timers tell harrowing, personal tales of ideological nonconformism and political prescience, of immigrant courage and pioneering struggle during the Mandate. Successful entrepreneurs will still justify their businesses in the rhetoric of the old pioneering communitarianism. Tribe One are Israel's WASPs. Clearly, they are crucial to an understanding what the Israeli center is and can yet be.

Tribe Two, in contrast, is the residual core of the rather larger North African immigration of Mizrahi Jews, who came to Israel in the 1950s and '60s en masse. They were as shocked as the Arabs by Tribe One's ideological and sexual avant-garde. Most had been petit bourgeois, small merchants and tradesmen back in Casablanca, Tunis, Tripoli. Their most educated or affluent leaders often went to Paris or Montréal. Back in the Maghreb, men ruled and plotted family survival. Women were generally illiterate. The collapse of colonialism and the birth of Israel left Mizrahi Jews exposed to unexpected retaliations in their countries of origin; businesses and friends were left behind in heartbreaking haste. Once in Israel, however, the Mizrahim found themselves in an underclass, much less well educated than the Eastern European Labor Zionists who ran the place. They were pressured to work for, and become like, the socialist bosses who presided over the kibbutzim, union-owned factories, and government agencies. Their old culture heroes were the French bourgeoisie.

On average, Tribe Two still actually earns a third less than Tribe One. Pride in Tribe Two is pride in the family, not in tales of some old commune or movement. But it is a pride that tips easily into social anger, for they see the state as a kind of great family that ought to take care of its own. Many have now made it in retail businesses, or car repair shops, or real estate. Their children have become lawyers, police officers, and contractors. Yet most of Tribe Two remains hungry for status, and tens of thousands still struggle with unemployment in inner cities and neglected development towns. Unlike Tribe One, they follow Halakha naturally, if not quite piously. They still feel they have a score to settle with "the Arabs," the Muslims, who drove them out, mainly after the Sinai War. They still cannot believe how they could have been so marginalized by the Labor aristocracy. As with the Boston Irish, their social resentment gets passed on from generation to generation and gets channeled into cultural politics: overzealous devotion at soccer matches, or overt nepotism in the smaller city councils, where Tribe Two politicians tend to dominate.

Tribe Three, the newest tribe, has its origins in about 900,000 immigrants from the former Soviet Union, most of whom came in the 1990s. They include people from the Ukraine, the Baltic states, and so forth, but are generally known as "the Russians." Hypereducated, hypersecular (about 25 percent were never "real" Jews back home in Moscow or Kiev), the Russians were beneficiaries of both a rigorous Soviet education and a vital anti-Soviet refusenik underground. They are repelled by the Orthodox and are gluttons for high culture: symphonic music, experimental theater, mathematical sciences. In the 1990s, when Israeli high tech was taking off, about a third of the research programmers, materials scientists, and others were from Tribe Three. But they are also hypernationalist, certain of their purchase on Europe's grim history, scornful of Muslim fanaticism and backwardness (their Vietnam was Afghanistan, after all), and dismayed by the squishy liberal intellectuals of Tribe One, who allegedly pander to the Muslim world. They came to Israel to join the West and to save it from itself. They are searching for an Israeli Putin.

Haaretz's Lily Galili, who has followed this community for years, told me that a majority of the Russians are feeling chronically embattled, "a combination of seeing impending catastrophe and a certainty that toughness will bring progress." They are quick, she says, to see the Nazis in Palestinians, and yet they are certain about Israel's ability "to exercise a kind of omnipotence" on a world stage: "This is very Russian, the idea that liberalism is holy and yet something for Jewish suckers, which is why they have such common language with American neoconservatives. Natan Sharansky is in many ways their hero—the chess player, the intellectual, the world prophet. He appealed to international liberal conscience while he was in prison, but after coming to Israel, he seems

to have found that he could both lecture to the world about democracy and lecture Israelis that the Jewish claim to Jerusalem was a 'higher
value' than liberalism—that the Arabs had better learn to accept it—
that Israel, being a better democracy than its neighbors, should be im-
mune from Western criticism."

These first three tribes intermarry at a high rate, and their edges are
getting blurry. Some vote their class interests, some their security
fears—none of the three is monolithic. The melding of Ashkenazim
and Sephardim is especially great in the twentysomething generation.
More educated Mizrahim and more cosmopolitan Russians tend to
vote Labor and embrace liberal ideas. Nevertheless, identity politics play
out among these tribes in unpredictable ways, depending on who leads
or what buttons get pushed—for example, whether security concerns
or economic issues dominate the headlines. (On the whole, economic
issues pull people leftward, that is, toward concessions to the Palestinians, while security issues pull rightward.)

Historically a majority in each tribe has tended to hold to certain directions—Tribe One to Labor; Two to Likud; Three to rightist splinter
parties, claiming Russian loyalties—but it was in tribes Two and Three
where virtually all of Israel's swing voters have lived. In the fraught
election of 2001, which brought Sharon to power, the affluent, mainly
Ashkenazi suburb of Kfar Shmaryahu voted 78 percent for Labor, while
81 percent of the comparatively poor Mizrahi town of Beit Shemesh
voted Likud. In 1999, some 65 percent of the Russians voted for Barak;
in 2001, about 70 percent voted for Sharon.

Finally, there are tribes Four and Five, familiar to us by now, also more
monolithic and predictable. Four is made up of Israel's ultranationalist,
theocratic groups, bronzed West Bank settlers wedded politically, if not
temperamentally, to pale Haredi yeshiva students. Tribe Four are devo-
tees of the Land of Israel. Yet they tend to be economically socialist—
"national socialist," one settler told me with a kind of creepy pride—for

many of the Orthodox live off the state, either in state schools or embattled settlements. They seem to suffer from what Koestler once called
"claustrophilia." Tribe Four disdains Israeliness as an effort to decouple
the national life of the state from the Jewish world of Torah and commandments. It refuses the distinction between the covenantal people
and the Israeli nation. Its bane is Tribe Five, Israeli Arabs, living in towns
segregated by both archaic land policies and the discrimination of Zionist institutions. Poor but up-and-coming, willing if not eager to enter Israeli democracy, Israeli Arabs are enraged by the existing version of the
Jewish state. Five is counting on, if anything, Israeliness.

ORDINARILY, THEN, Tribe Three hates Four, condescends to Two, and
doubts One; Two hates One, resents Three and (for different reasons)
Four; One is afraid of Two, patronizes Three, and hates Four; Four hates
One, proselytizes Two, and is afraid of Three. All four are afraid of Five.

And to say that the center holds, at least in terms of electoral politics,
is merely to say that the descendents of the original Zionist settlers—
the original labor aristocracy, the first Israeli establishment—have been
joined by educated Sephardim and liberal Russians and are thus able to
focus the country as a whole on economic hopes, demographic anxieties, and a vague pluralism. Most Sephardim and Russians will naturally support more right-wing views: They have been much of the
wood behind the Likud's arrowhead. But the key for the center, in 2006
and from here on in, is to get a decisive number of swing voters among
the tribes to join the camp of globalism and pragmatism. The center
cannot expect many Orthodox votes. Arabs have at times supported
the Labor Party in impressive numbers and will play an increasingly important role in centrist calculations; but most will not support a center
still indifferent to their legal and material concerns.

Which brings me back to Kadima. The party does not have a coherent social vision or stable political following. Sharon intended it to be

a mixed bag, including Labor's Shimon Peres, who fathered the Oslo Agreements, and Likud's Tzahi Hanegbi, who opposed them. But Kadima's election did mean that certain stalwarts of Israel's natural (more educated, more affluent, more cosmopolitan) élite triangulated their way to control of the government. Many had felt that they'd been living in a kind of internal exile under Likud's "national camp." There is no guarantee that Kadima will retain control of the Knesset, though the government's mandate runs out only in 2010. With Hamas a force in the Palestinian territories, and Hezbollah still creating a ministate in Southern Lebanon, a rightist coalition led by Benjamin Netanyahu could well make a comeback; if, say, a terrorist shoots down a jumbo jet landing at Ben-Gurion Airport, a rightist victory would be certain.

Yet—and here is the main point—the center's leaders and brains-trust cannot really be eliminated from the exercise of power, whatever party is in government. The people who came together to form Kadima, and then organized the centrist coalition, are the very people who run much of the state bureaucracy, IDF intelligence, veteran consumer corporations, high-tech start-ups, banks, press and media, universities, and nonprofits. In effect, they represent the recapturing of the public agenda by Tribe One, an agenda lost to Menachem Begin in the 1970s—that is, to his pandering to tribes Two and Four. Netanyahu may win an election by playing to those same tribes. But he cannot govern without the center's people; indeed, he and what is left of Likud are pretty much centrist themselves. The most ideologically romantic of Begin's old Land of Israel leadership, including his own son, left Likud a long time ago. Netanyahu and the people around him want—and expect—to keep Israel in the world.

Incidentally, this panoply of centrist leaders, from Buzi Herzog in Labor, to Tzipi Livni in Kadima, and Bibi Netanyahu in Likud, comes from families that have known one another for years, which is why they call each other by their pet names. They run, and are enriched by, an intimate city-state. Former prime minister Ehud Barak, who lost and then regained Labor's leadership, made something like eight million dollars from international consulting—that is, selling access—in the six years he was out of office. In many ways, the election of Shimon Peres as state president confirmed all in this subtle solidarity. In recent years, the people of the center have gathered every winter to exchange views on the country's "strategic resilience," together with American policy analysts, European diplomats, and mainly neoconservative Jewish intellectuals, at the prestigious Herzliya Conference, convened at Herzliya's Interdisciplinary Center, the fabulously successful private college where the well heeled send their children (and where I myself have pleasurably taught). These people are often longtime friends or friendly adversaries, increasingly cosmopolitan and sophisticated, patrons of the arts, loyal to their smallish world of buddies and gossip, eager to share talk of their exploits in combat units, or triumphal tales of high-technology IPOs. The increasingly liberal *Haaretz* (which recently spawned the hot business magazine *Marker*) is their newspaper of record.

Centrists, then, may disagree about the pace of change, or whom to trust, or how to deter enemies. They may be more or less consciously liberal, or emphasize demographic trends without seeing the racist implications. Yet their globalist consciousness is, if anything, spreading. "The center's democratic front," says *Yediot Ahronot*'s business editor, "sends a clear, reassuring signal to people investing in Israel, foreign and local."[2] Even the Russian exponent of ethnic cleansing, Avigdor Lieberman, has unexpectedly begun to advocate Israel's inclusion in NATO and the European Union.

But then, globalism presses from the outside in, as well as from the inside out. Kadima's hodgepodge coalition works, at least for now, since most Israeli voters assume that any conceivable peace process, with its attendant social changes, will be driven by some larger constellation of American diplomacy and European investment—not by an Israel that dwells alone. Key centrist leaders like Foreign Minister Livni and Defense Minister Barak pretty much go along with this. It seems enough for Israel's government, they think, to gesture that it will undertake confidence-building steps, like the Gaza disengagement, and then enter negotiations with whatever moderate Palestinians the U.S. and G8 pressure can deliver.

"THERE IS A VERY identifiable part of the state of Israel today," Ehud Olmert told me in a quiet breakfast, joined by his wife, Aliza, at the prime minister's residence in February 2007. "You may call North Tel Aviv a symbolic, representative category, but you find them in the center of the country a lot, and you find them in Jerusalem. They are already thriving on globalization. They are equal if not identical to young executives in high-tech companies in New York, on Wall Street, in the city of London, in Paris, or any other place. They are wealthy, they are successful, they are similar—they actually speak the same language. When they are in Israel, among their friends, they speak Hebrew. But when they are abroad, they speak the same English as Wall Street investment bankers or Silicon Valley high-tech executives."

To be sure, he admitted, not many people in the country live this way. ("Is it all of Israel, is it part of Israel—what part of Israel is it?") But this was just the surface of things: "It's important enough to have an enormous impact on the economy of Israel," Olmert continued. "The economy of Israel is an unbelievable story. This past year we've had a growth of over 5 percent, which is higher than the growth of any European country last year ... and the highest ever amount of foreign investment in history—which manifests a certain degree of trust, not only in the strength of the Israeli economy, but in the stability, consistency, continuity of the Israeli political system. Because nobody invests billions of dollars in this country if they don't believe the country is stable . . . We sold last year more than we bought—in fact, our growth during the last quarter of last year was 8 percent, on a annual basis, which is really unbelievable."

The world of the Israeli center—Olmert, too—has been tarred by scandals of various kinds, alleging insider deals. Given its relatively small size, the Israeli economy is particularly susceptible to being dominated by a few superrich families—the Dankners, the Offers, the Arisons. But on the whole, Israel's indigenous professional classes are not especially corrupt or unusually rich. They are simply a success on the European model. "So on the one hand," Olmert continued, "Israel is a fantastic story, a fantastic success, a very innovative place, and very much a part of globalization. [But] how many does it touch? Obviously a minority. Enough to have an impact on the entire country in terms of its economic success, but not enough yet to change the nature of the lives in this country . . . [These successful entrepreneurs] have private planes and go back and forth for the weekends to Paris, to eat in good restaurants, and for them distances are irrelevant, because they are citizens of the world . . . But if they care to think about the possible political ramifications of this life, then they may be in another place."

Olmert believes, in other words, that the élite with whom he is so closely identified has not—or not yet—drawn political conclusions from their globalized lives. The transformation only began, really, in the late 1990s. He did not mean to allude to this when he spoke of people in the élite considering "another place," but it is often said that as many as a third of the children of the élite (including two of Olmert's four children) are living abroad. And the undigested changes suggest still more changes: "If you are part of the EU and there are no barriers," he said, "and people can move in and out without any restrictions, then what is the significance of the Law of Return, how can you keep that nature of the state of Israel, which many still feel is essential for self-preservation? Most would say that we are not yet strong enough to be part of globalization in the sense of being immersed within the European Union."

Most would also say, alas, that Olmert was himself not strong enough to lead anywhere new when I spoke with him—certainly not to propose any of the drastic changes democratic globalization entails. But the center as a whole almost certainly does have the strength to renew itself, given the collapse of the old party system. With the press forever hyping new leaders, as Olmert was hyped for a while, it is easy to imagine new leaders for Kadima, or new parties forming spontaneously, as circumstances change. Yet the profiles of the people who will godfather them are already fairly predictable. They will be younger versions of Yaacov Peri, the former head of the ultrasecret Shabak, who became head of the cell phone giant Cellcom, or Iscar's Stef Wertheimer, who came out of the old Palmach strike force. Israel's global business daily, *Globes,* runs a yearly conference of its own on Israel's business prospects. The people who show up at it are almost indistinguishable from the participants in the Herzliya Conference.

These people move easily into circles of American Jewish philanthropists, who, like them—and often in partnership with them—invest in knowledge companies; endow educational institutions; provide distribution channels for Israeli companies in America; and sponsor museums, art collections, and other ventures. They also have natural allies in American journalists specializing in Israeli affairs, who reflect their political pragmatism. Jeffrey Goldberg expressed their common view succinctly in his bellwether 2004 *New Yorker* article attacking the West Bank settlers: "Israel is faced with two options: keep the settlements, and risk either apartheid or binationalism; or separate cleanly from the

Palestinians, by withdrawing settlements and raising a wall between the two sides."

GOLDBERG'S SYLLOGISM expresses the center's rallying idée fixe: the demographic warning that Jews would lose their majority if they do not separate cleanly from occupied territory. This leads to binationalism, which is code, they say, for dismantling Israel. One hears this argument from Kadima and Labor supporters, from respected social scientists and writers, from former heads of army intelligence—even from Oslo strategists like Yossi Beilin, who put together the Geneva Initiative with Palestinian officials in 2003. Poll after poll shows that about two-thirds of the country now believe in some version of the demographic threat. Demographer Arnon Sofer, the center's number-crunching Cassandra, has long campaigned for a two-state solution, but has simultaneously proposed a national Zionist unity government that would move the Israeli Arab city of Umm el-Fahm to a Palestinian state ("our insane and suicidal neighbor") and move Negev bedouin off state lands.[3]

What's so bad about this demographic argument? The center's fear, after all, seems to be that the loss of a Jewish majority would mean the loss, not of a Jewish state, but of a democratic one. They have turned against settlement. Even politicians who once made their careers coddling Jewish settlers are fretting publicly about the South African precedent. "I shudder to think," Olmert said back before the Gaza evacuation, "that the same Jews who led the struggle against apartheid in South Africa will be at the forefront of the struggle against us."[4] He repeated this theme after the Second Lebanon War, on November 27, 2007, when he announced a peace initiative at Ben-Gurion's grave at Sde Boker:

When we were faced with the choice between the entire land of Israel without a Jewish State, or a Jewish State without the entire

land of Israel—we chose a Jewish State without the entire land of
Israel . . . David Ben-Gurion, already a retired statesman, ruled
that in exchange for true peace, Israel must relinquish a vast majority of the territories occupied in the Six Day War. Much has
happened since then, facts were established on the ground, agreements were signed, the international and regional arena changed
beyond recognition. The bloody conflict with the Palestinians has
not ended. Ben-Gurion's basic diagnosis remained valid and continues to guide—with the necessary amendments—the position
of Israeli governments in our peace policy today.

Indeed, their globalist impulses notwithstanding, centrists assert—
and not unreasonably—that there needs to be a critical mass of Jews to
sustain Jewish national life. So if Jews have resisted being "thrown into
the sea," should they now choose to be swamped? Would not Israel
then have only reproduced the ambient pressures for Jews to assimilate
that they had found in the Diaspora—pressures that inspired Zionism
in the first place?

BUT THIS IS not the whole story. For centrists are also increasingly strident about Jewish national unity; and they can hardly see their nationalism apart from the legal and institutional anachronisms valorized by
the state. This keeps centrists from seeing how toxic and mechanistic
the demographic argument can be. It also keeps them from seeing beyond vague claims for binationalism, which they loathe, to federalism,
which they need.

Nothing made all of this more disturbingly clear than the reaction
of the center to a rather hypothetical article about binationalism,
written during the al-Aqsa Intifada. As suicide bombers were attacking Israeli cities, the modern European historian Tony Judt, a distin-
guished professor at New York University—who once spent time on a

kibbutz—made the case for a binational state of Israelis and Palestinians in the *New York Review of Books*. The two-state solution was not only not imminent, he argued, but not morally intelligent. He did not really spell out what a binational state would look like (it "would not be easy, though not quite as impossible as it sounds: the process has already begun de facto"). He did not seem to fear mixing together in a single democracy a rich, educated, Hebrew-speaking population and a poor, less well-educated, Arabic-speaking one—populations that still hate each other. But neither did he mince words. "The very idea of a 'Jewish state,'" he wrote, "a state in which Jews and the Jewish religion have exclusive privileges from which non-Jewish citizens are forever excluded—is rooted in another time and place. Israel, in short, is an anachronism."[5]

The article caused an immediate sensation among educated Israelis (it was still referred to with dismay in my Montréal friend's letter, three years after it was published). In part, this was a defensive response to Judt's stinging and not exactly misplaced criticism of Israel's legal structure. But the real problem was Judt's extrapolation from that structure to a misty future, in which Jewish national life, engendered by the Hebrew language, would seem inconceivable—a move that has echoes in Zionist history. Before the founding of the state, when socialist internationalism was still in vogue, certain leftist Zionist parties—most notably, Hashomer Hatzair—argued for a binational state with the Palestinian proletariat. They assumed most Jews would be socialists living in pioneering kibbutzim, and that their novel national culture would be protected by a kind of cloistering. You find that forlorn hope in the early writings of Noam Chomsky.[6] Various intellectuals in prestate Palestine, such as Martin Buber and Judah Magnes, the founders of the Brit Shalom movement, argued for a quite different form of binationalism—in effect, a liberal state with two distinct populations, which would continue to coexist under the aegis of the British Mandate. Yet you still find serious Western intellectuals (not only Judt, but the late Edward Said, Judith Butler, Jacqueline Rose, and others) who have thought it useful to revive the vision, or some version of it. Binationalists who argue in this vein seem to regard the problem as one of creating a melting pot, Jews and Arabs living in a common society, each community presumably speaking a nicely accented English.

It is not surprising, therefore, that Israel's centrist élite assumes that people who speak of binationalism are simply trying to reset the clock to 1948 and reintroduce ideas that call into question the very logic of launching Israel in the first place. Judt is a great historian. But there is, ironically, little sense of history in his attack on Zionism. He mentions not at all, for example, the urgent need for the Zionists to have settled a million Holocaust refugees in 1948, something the Arab part of a binational state would never have agreed to. Nor does Judt have any obvious affinity for Hebrew culture. He is an eloquent defender of the European Union, but he does not seem to take for granted defenses of national life in Israel that are common among all European member nations.

Why, after all, could not Israel end exclusive privileges for Jews as individuals, and for the Jewish religion as an established state religion, and yet privilege Jewish national culture—by maintaining an official language, or focusing on Jewish history in the national school system, or investing in public institutions like the Israel Museum or the Hebrew University? A democratic government cannot dictate the shape of cultural forms, but it can establish certain outer limits by teaching a cherished national language and mandating one focus (among others) for studying the past. The Montréal I came from was the product of the Quiet Revolution. Was it not obvious that Québécois—a French majority, but living on a largely English-speaking continent—were justified in taking urgent action, consistent with accepted standards of human rights but irritating to English Montréalers, to preserve their national culture?—things like compulsory French education, compulsory French signs, a holiday on St. Jean-Baptiste Day when the rest of Canada celebrated the tie to the English Crown. Would not Israelis today be obviously justified in taking action to preserve *their* national culture?

ANYWAY, ISRAEL'S centrists dwell on demographic trends, a Jewish majority, and so forth, in part because they fear a Judt-like vision—a blurry, sudden enfranchising of Palestinians in a unitary state called (but not for long) Israel. Wasn't this how Yasir Arafat spoke of Jews and Palestinians before Oslo, when his PLO, engaging in terror, called for a secular democratic state? Meanwhile—and sadly—centrists ignore federalist voices, Arab and Jewish, who take Jewish national life for granted.

Indeed, strident claims for binationalism seem so important in this context mainly because they are so distracting. What the center needs to learn is that secular and federal reforms do not mean this vague binationalism—not, certainly, in the sense of spelling the ruin of Jewish national life. Federal arrangements can actually enhance the staying power of the Jewish nation where Israelis and Palestinians and Israel's Arab minority are so thoroughly interpenetrated.

Perhaps the most vigilant exponent of a workable new federalism is the crusty Israeli historian (and a former deputy mayor of Jerusalem) Meron Benvenisti. He's argued that the occupation has "scrambled the eggs," which cannot now be entirely separated again. He does not call into question the original making of Israel (as Azmi Bishara has), but has, at times, argued that Israel-Palestine has evolved into a complex, single entity whose only democratic solution is some kind of binational state. "Institutionalized ethnic separatism," he writes, "is a direct result of a mistaken policy; it is not the Arabs who have created the separatism but rather the Jews. Their oppression of the Arabs and their discrimination against them are, in every area, based on clearly ethnic criteria, and the crystallization of an alienated Arab minority is an inevitable result."

What is the solution? Benvenisti means for us to work toward some eventual federal state with Palestine (and possibly Jordan), in which inseparable jurisdictions would be shared, but national cultural distinctions maintained: "The correct comparison," Benvenisti writes, "is with the dozens of countries where national minorities are granted recognition of their collective, political and cultural rights, as defined in the laws of the European Union, or in the southern Tyrol, Spain, Canada, Australia and many other places."[7] Benvenisti, in short, is laying a foundation for regional justice that will minimize the drift toward religious fanaticism—ending, that is, the ways the Israeli state apparatus incites its own Arab minority against itself. If, as many have argued, the latest war with Lebanon suggests that it is already too late for such an approach, then it is certainly too late for the hard-line approach that helped precipitate the war and brought no victory or definition of victory. The fire is burning; the choice, Benvenisti implies, is whether or not to pour gasoline on it.

Imagine that a border between Israel and Palestine were at last to be negotiated. Could Israel and Palestine ever exercise the jurisdictions of sovereign states without the other's permanent cooperation—or that of Jordan? I have myself written on this question. Think of policing Jerusalem, which will have to fill with tourists to jump-start development. Think of developing the Jordan Valley, or water carriers, or managing traffic between the West Bank and Gaza. Think of developing a currency when, as now, 95 percent of Palestinian exports go to Israel; or of telecommunications infrastructure; or the need to monitor the migration of desperately poor migrant workers from the Nile Delta. How could one imagine Israel not associated with Palestine at least as tightly as Québec is with Ontario?[8]

IT IS NOT immediately clear why federalist views of this kind, especially when qualified by allusions to international precedents and calls for international guarantees, would prompt allergic responses from the Israeli center. But they do, or at least the mention of the word *binationalism* does, like the mention of United Nations officials or European peace-keepers—people you can't quite hate, people you obviously need from time to time, but don't have to like. Most Israelis find the demographic argument hardheaded. They find binationalist arguments, even federalist ones, hardhearted. Indeed, the Israeli center's skeptical attitude toward federalism reveals the trap set by their own focus on demography. While many centrist leaders are tantalized by a globalized Israel, they nevertheless live in a mental atmosphere created by state Zionism.

Consider, again, Jeffrey Goldberg's formulation in this context. Note especially how Arabs who are Israeli citizens, including three generations who have been born and educated in the country, are casually folded into demographic projections. This is not just sloppiness; Goldberg knows Israel as well as anyone. Rather, his formulation is an authentic expression of Israeli constitutional tradition and political economy, which engenders a fuzzy Jewish defensiveness. "If there is a demographic problem, and there is, it is with the Israeli Arabs who will remain Israeli citizens," former finance minister Benjamin Netanyahu (now the Likud leader) told the Herzliya Conference in December 2003. "To stop democracy from wiping out the Jewish nature of the country we must insure the Jewish majority; incorporating the Arab Israelis fully into Israeli society should be done hand in hand with protecting the Jewish nature of that society."

Wiping out the Jewish nature of the country. The real problem, you see, is that all Arabs, including Israeli citizens, are immediately grasped in terms of the same organic solidarity that proponents of official Zionism assume for Jews—all Jews, no matter what their origin, religious imaginations, or national commitments. The presumption works in all directions, and is most visible, perhaps, when aimed at American Jews, whose distinct experiences Israelis don't really know what to do with.

Back in the winter of 1988, at the beginning of the First Intifada, I brought the writer Philip Roth to lunch at the Knesset with then backbencher Ehud Olmert, whose political sophistication I had come to trust. Almost before we sat down, Olmert began to complain how the Palestinian revolt was the result of American Jews "not coming" to Israel. Presumably, two million American Jews flooding the territories would have made the claims of Palestinians moot. When Roth suggested that American Jews might have ambitions of their own, Olmert dismissed these as "inauthentic." The lunch did not last very long. Around the same time, Shlomo Avineri, the Hebrew University's most eminent political theorist and a pillar of the Labor Party for a generation, wrote a famous open letter to American Jews regarding the Pollard Affair, criticizing them harshly for not acknowledging their "ambivalence, alienation, homelessness." He then got to the point: "Zionism grew out of the cruel realization that for all of their achievements and successes, when the chips are down Jews in the Diaspora become vulnerable and defenseless, are seen as aliens—and will always see themselves as such."[9]

Such views have, if anything, grown more shameless in the intervening years. In 2003, I was present at a speech to the Herzliya Conference by then Jewish Agency chairman (now ambassador to Washington) Sallai Meridor, which was delivered in a session some time after Netanyahu spoke of the demographic problem posed by Israel's Arabs. Meridor said that the "loss" of six million Jews through intermarriage in the U.S. since World War II was comparable to the loss of six million Jews in the Holocaust. Nobody in the hall raised an objection.

ISRAELI CENTRISTS like Meridor have mostly been born into secular Zionist homes. They will tell you cheerfully how they never go to synagogue, for example. Yet they see how readily present-day Diaspora Jews—whose economic power they respect and cultivate—identify with Israel through Judaism. So they promote what Menachem Klein calls the peculiarly Jewish Israeliness he did not know in his youth. Meridor put it this way to *Haaretz*'s Yair Sheleg: "If the state stands on two legs—the Jewish and the democratic—what has happened in recent years, through the Basic Laws, is that the democratic leg is very long, and the Jewish leg could find itself dangling in the air."[10] Uzi Arad, the eloquent, Princeton-educated former director of research in the Mossad, co-authored with Uzi Dayan and Hebrew social scientist Yehezkel Dror a new "Zionist Manifesto" for Israel, which was presented to the Zionist Congress in Jerusalem in November 2003.[11] It aimed to give constitutional status to Israel as a "Zionist-Jewish state," a state of the "whole [read *world*] Jewish people."

How should this feeling be realized? More recently, Arad wrote in the *New Republic* what Sofer had proposed to him, that if a Palestinian state could be negotiated, Israel's largest Arab towns in the "little triangle," from Umm el-Fahm in the north to Kfar Kassem in the south, should be annexed by it—something most Israeli Arabs bitterly oppose. There should be a land swap, he insisted, that would exchange "for example, the Gush Etzion and Ariel blocs and towns in the Jerusalem district for the towns and surroundings of Umm El Fahm, Arara, Bartaa, Qalansuwa, Taybe, Tira, and Kfar Kassem." (Tira is, by the way, the hometown of Israeli author Sayed Kashua.) "The various land swap plans," Arad writes, "proposing a tradeoff of territories aim to increase ethnic homogeneity . . . [so that] the Jewish majority would remain at 81 percent until 2050. In other words, the land swap has great potential to preserve Israel as both a Jewish and a democratic state well into the latter half of this century."[12]

Arad's manifesto called for a state that would teach "the feeling of a right to the Promised Land, which is a central principle of Judaism." It also called for "the preservation of democracy for all of its citizens." It did not say if *this* was a central principle of Judaism.

THIS IS WHERE the demographic argument gets you. You expand your border to include most West Bank Jewish settlements. You subject a quarter of a million Arab residents of Jerusalem (and their ancient mosques) to the sovereignty of a Jewish state. You hive off a half million Arab Israelis and put them in the Palestinian state. You maintain existing political economic barriers for the remaining Arab Israelis—barriers of institutional practice and law, barriers of land and common ideology. And this is the demographic vision under conditions of peace. You also accept formal rabbinic definitions of Jewishness—vaguely tribal, spiritual, international. And you use terms like *ethnic homogeneity,* which, presumably, intelligence professionals like Arad can define for Arabs and Jews. Then you say these ethnic parts must be separated, because even if Israel's Arab citizens will make the most of what liberties Israel gives them, they could not possibly want to be absorbed into Israel, which is also what makes them a physical threat.

Then come the people swaps, the snap disenfranchisement of hundreds of thousands of Israeli citizens, justified by "professional" estimates, projecting assumptions about Jewish identity forty or fifty years into the future ("the Jewish majority would remain at 81 percent until 2050"). As if Arad could imagine what the Israeli scene will be in 2050 any better than Allen Dulles, the head of the CIA under Eisenhower in 1956, could have imagined America in 2006. Meanwhile, you dismiss as vestiges of a failed liberalism the stringent constitutional protections and cultural hybridizations now common in America and the European Union. And you suppose yourself a democrat because you're speaking of—and for—a Jewish majority.

Clearly, the idea of democracy is being perverted here, presented only as some vague notion of national majority rule. And this is in nobody's interest. Even if terrorism from the territories could be crushed, even if the West Bank and Gaza could be taken completely out of the equation, even if the little triangle from Umm al-Fahm to Kfar Kassem could be dispatched to a Palestinian state, something the residents of these towns utterly reject, Israel would still be left with hundreds of thousands of Arab citizens (if Arad is right, 19 percent of the population in 2050). A burgeoning number of these people will be young and ambitious. If a great proportion of them will not be absorbed as equals into Israel's civil society, then the country will face—not fifty years from now, but in the foreseeable future—virtually the same dynamic that post-1967 Israel began to face in the occupied territories in the 1970s. This will be a condition of war, not peace.

And here we get to the heart of the matter. For the demographic argument, even as an argument for two states, is not really premised on conditions of peace. Its first premise is that every Israeli Arab, like every Palestinian, has a little Mufti inside struggling to come out (the way every Jew, presumably, has a little Menachem Begin). The Israeli center, in consequence, increasingly traffics in a new master narrative, which sees the state's founding in an exchange of populations, beginning with the Shoah, and moving to attacks on all fronts by Arab states in 1948. In this flattened history, 750,000 Palestinian Arabs either fled or (for more daring tellers) were driven from their homes, while the Arab states dispossessed and expelled Mizrahi Jewish refugees to Israel. Israelis were not perfect, they say, but the pattern is unmistakable.

The historian Benny Morris, who has written unsparingly about

1948, probably speaks for most in the center when he applies the lessons of that time:

> The Israeli Arabs are a time bomb. Their slide into complete Pales-
> tinization has made them an emissary of the enemy that is among
> us. They are a potential fifth column. In both demographic and
> security terms they are liable to undermine the state. So that if Is-
> rael again finds itself in a situation of existential threat, as in 1948,
> it may be forced to act as it did then.[13]

Morris became famous in the late 1980s, tracing the fate of Arab refugees during the first Israeli-Arab war, showing what was flight and what was expulsion. His outburst suggests an ominous direction in Israel's political center. For there is an obvious way to safeguard a Jew-ish majority that is hardly named in polite conversation, though the polls, and the way most Israelis now grasp their history, should be giv-ing us pause.

I mean *"ha-transfer"*—reducing by forced expulsion or economic pressure the numbers of Arabs living in the country. There is simply no way to get the "clean" separation Jeffrey Goldberg writes about without extensive ethnic cleansing. Israelis know this in their bones, even if they do not feel comfortable talking about it. When Meir Kahane voiced such views in the 1980s, his party was banned from the Knesset. Today, exponents of *transfer* serve in the government. The center would no doubt prefer the status quo to any ethnic cleansing, yet they know that the status quo—numbers, occupation, and all—is unsustainable: An April 2002 poll of Tel Aviv University's Jaffee Center for Strategic Stud-ies revealed that 46 percent of Israelis entertain the idea of expelling Palestinians, including Israeli citizens. Thirty-one percent, roughly the number of people who favor a state of Jewish law, favor the expulsion of Israeli Arabs.[14] The settlers, for their part, do not have to convince a majority of Israelis that their settlement program is right. They only have to prove something proponents of the demographic argument concede in advance: that the Jewish people are something organic, which Israelis dare not divide.

THE ETHNIC CLEANSING Morris talks about assumes another big and cataclysmic war, like 1948, not the low-level conflict Israel is actually living with. But even in the current context, there are many ways to encourage the emigration of Palestinians, both from occupied territory and from the state. Consider the security wall, which began as a Labor Party idea, and which Olmert and the defense establishment have entirely embraced and largely built.

Now it is not unreasonable for Israel to put up a barrier to keep out rogue terrorists, any more than putting up metal detectors at the airport. Even PA leaders have conceded that, much as they'd regret it, they'd have no objection to a wall on the Green Line. But the route of this wall is something else. It does not so much wall Palestinians out as wall them in, creating numerous enclaves running north-south, separated from Jerusalem, their cultural metropolis, and from one another. These enclaves are surrounded not only by fences but also by numerous established Jewish settlements, linked together by exclusive settler highways and bypass roads. All along their eastern border, the enclaves are hemmed in by the heights overlooking the Jordan Valley, where Olmert expects the IDF to stay. In all, about 16 percent of the West Bank has been confiscated just to build the wall. Follow Olmert's route, and only about 43 percent of West Bank land will be left for a Palestinian state.

The real danger of the wall is the separation of hinterland towns from Jerusalem's commercial core, a rupture that denies any prospect of economic viability for either. No Palestinian entrepreneur can hope to build an advanced business under these conditions. Kalkilya, a West Bank Arab town of about 40,000 residents near the Israeli border northeast of Tel Aviv, is surrounded by a triangular barrier. By 2004, about one-third of Kalkilya's 1,800 businesses and shops had closed, and about eight thousand people had left. As their prospects become desperate, will not more Palestinian youth turn to terror? Jerusalem, the most disputed city, is also the most explosive. The Palestinians do not see a viable Palestinian state without Jerusalem acting as its administrative and religious hub. While Olmert is being depicted—by the settler zealots he once championed as Jerusalem's mayor—as caving in to Palestinians, the route of his fence is already responsible for the migration of thousands.

In Jerusalem itself, the Arab minority population has grown relative to the Jewish majority over the past decade. The fence will reverse the trend toward equality. As many as 60,000 of greater Jerusalem's 250,000 Arab residents are already caught directly between Israeli Defense Forces checkpoints and other fences; at least 50,000 suddenly do not qualify for Israeli health insurance or travel documents, being stateless, and those who do qualify receive virtually no government services; it is common for them to fight their way through choked queues in front of government offices. The notorious Kalandia Checkpoint between Jerusalem and Ramallah can turn a fifteen-minute trip into a humiliating two- to three-hour ordeal. The Old City, which can reasonably house about 18,000, is sleeping about 40,000. People fear they will not be allowed back into Jerusalem if they visit their homes in neighboring towns.

About two miles from my home is the neighborhood of Jabel Mukhaber. The fence cuts it off from one of its own neighborhoods, Sheik Sa'ad, whose 2,500 residents are themselves cut off from the rest of Palestine by steep cliffs. One leader of Jabel Mukhaber told me that a third of those people—their own family members—have left, while the remaining villagers are living off the gifts of family abroad. Another Palestinian I know, who runs the butchery in the supermarket near my home, spent the savings of twenty years on a spacious home that he built in Beit Hanina, which turned out to be located just on the other side of the wall's route. To keep his right to live in Jerusalem, he abandoned his house ("to the birds," he told me with resignation) and took a small, two-bedroom flat for his wife and three children in the nearby neighborhood of Abu Tur. His eyes welled up speaking of the shock to his children. Six months later, his brother's house in Abu Tur, built on land that has been in his family for generations, was demolished by Israeli police.

Considering the Jewish people's past, it would be tactless to call these enclaves ghettoes. So let's just call them walled-in, endlessly patrolled, increasingly impoverished places for people with diminishing political rights and unlimited encouragement to leave. Yasir Barakat, one of the most established merchants in the Old City, tells me he knows "nobody whose educated children are not planning to leave Jerusalem if they can." One of his children lives now in Dubai. With the government placing ever harsher restrictions on Palestinians seeking tourist visas, it is no simple matter for children to visit parents left behind. On the other hand, Sam Bahour, a Ramallah entrepreneur holding (like myself) an American passport, fears leaving for overseas. "They won't let me back in," he told me.

TALK ABOUT THIS cruelty to friends in the center and you will be told that Israel offered the Palestinians "95 percent at Camp David" and that "they came back with terror." I must have heard this claim a hundred times. It is a dubious claim, as political analyst and former president Clinton's Middle East advisor Robert Malley explained.[15] But to argue against it misses the point. For the assumptions behind it are unconsciously apocalyptic. For most in the center, politics seems little more than preparation for the worst possible contingencies. It is as if you have to prove, first and foremost, that you can think the way one is paid to think in the intelligence services. Your dimmer friends always start conversations by solemnly predicting war "this summer," year after year. And some years there are wars. Justice and survival are lines that never quite come together, one cousin told me, confident in his philosophical geometry.

There is a peculiar affectation at work here. Moshe Dayan once said that when he saw the sun going down, he simply saw it going down—unlike Ben-Gurion, the too-brainy, too-broad-minded Diaspora Jew, who saw the earth spinning on its axis. For Dayan, this was a perverse source of satisfaction. Israelis see the world *as it is*. It is not a place for prissy intellectuals. An enemy is an enemy, power is (military) power, and liberalism requires a general willingness to be nice, which goyim are not, at least when Jews are involved. This is what Avineri, who once brilliantly exposed the democratic bluff in Marx's thought, was getting at when he wrote that Diaspora Jews would learn that "when the chips are down," they are nothing but vulnerable, and their democratic values would be of no use. If democratic liberalism was not a failure, why would Zionism ever have been necessary?

As if democratic rights were some extravagance Western societies, fattened on capitalism, give themselves only after national self-determination has been achieved; as if constitutions were instrumental just to the nation's business, a kind of operating system installed to modernize backward immigrants or allow for freedom of the press or élite succession—the most advanced system, perhaps the most moral, but its full version too expensive for a discontented, embattled startup like Israel. Surely it must have occurred to Avineri (if not to other centrists who join him in condescending to American liberalism) that tough constitutional principles grew out of an even crueler realization than did Zionism: namely, that civilized people are always one generation away from barbarism; that without strict constitutional protections, the chips can fall everywhere, and for everyone.

What if instead of settling the Palestinians' land after 1967, Israeli officials had simply said they wanted for Palestinians what American officials said they wanted for the hated Germany in 1948: that it should have an integrated population and economy, the rule of law, conditions for the investment of advanced corporations, schools and universities that teach liberal values—and that an occupation army, reinforced by a Western coalition, would stay in place until it was safe to withdraw and not one day beyond this? Would Israelis and Palestinians not be facing a very different reality today?

FOR NOW, perhaps not forever, the center is evading such questions. There are demographic trends, enemies at the gates, business is good. But time is not working for the center, and not only because of Orthodoxy's momentum. The situation prompts an urge for national unity, which can be a little embarrassing for élites who are conspicuously rich, cosmopolitan, and eccentric.

During the last war with Lebanon, hundreds of thousands of families opened their homes to people living in the north and seeking respite from the missiles. One friend called this an "ecstasy of solidarity." But people in the north meanwhile condemned Tel Aviv for keeping its bars and restaurants open. Over 150 Israelis were killed by missiles or in combat. Young Israeli soldiers, for their part, killed and injured many times this number of Palestinians and Lebanese, and live with memories they'd rather forget. Yet politicians, officials, even writers usually identified with the peace camp, were quick to pronounce this a just war, if not a successful one. People are seeking the relief of solidarity, what with the embarrassments and divisions of occupation. They instinctively condemn tensions between Orthodox and secular Jews, social privilege, corruption, etc., as undermining the common front.

It was the same during the Al-Aqsa Intifada. Over 830 Israelis were killed in suicide bombing and over 4,600 were injured or maimed. A short walk from my home in the German Colony is Café Hillel, which was bombed in September 2003. Across the street, Emeq Refaim (the Valley of the Ghosts), is another café, Caffit, where two suicide bombers were foiled on two separate occasions. At the summit of the main street's rise, near Terra Sancta in the Rehavia quarter, another café, Moment, was bombed in 2002. Walk another half mile into the city center and you come to a pizzeria that was bombed twice. The Ben Yehuda Street mall was bombed. When I draw an imaginary radius around the outermost of these neighborhood landmarks, I can remember five bus bombings in the area, each kicking off a new round of sirens, days of mourning. My wife's cafeteria at the Hebrew University was bombed. These are not times when you extend compassion to the other side.

You do not feel a mortal danger, given the law of probabilities, but you do feel a moral danger. How, day in, day out, can you do or say the right thing? So you try hard not to avert your eyes from those of the guard standing in front of the restaurant you are entering—usually a student or an Ethiopian immigrant working for minimum wage, ostensibly there to check for weapons, but really there, as everybody knows, to take the brunt of the blast. You consider moving to the back wall and then think better of it, reluctant to be hypothetically sacrificing the diners who are sitting near the entrance. (Next time, you just automatically move to the back wall.) You sit with friends and give thanks that your kids are beyond the age when they must ride the buses to school, and then realize, ashamed, that your friends' children and grandchildren *are* riding buses. You sit with family and decide to avoid certain subjects. You pass a young man, obviously an Arab, sitting with a full schoolbag next to a construction site, and check his armpits to see if he is perspiring more than he should be for the weather. You pass by an Arab man in his forties, dressed neatly in faded clothes, rummaging for bottles in your trash, and impulsively check his midriff before thinking to press a twenty-shekel note into his hand—and then feel doubly ashamed when, as periodically happens, he refuses it.

Pretty much everybody in Jerusalem is exhausted from juggling such thoughts. Unlike political matters, these things are rarely talked about, but now and then their weight becomes touchingly obvious. A *hudna* (cease-fire) with Hamas was announced in the summer of 2003, and the suicide bombings abruptly stopped; the Malcha Mall in South Jerusalem was so unexpectedly packed with parents and children that you had to wait in long lines to get on an escalator. You believed you could feel what every child was feeling.

Even during the Gaza pullout, which was ostensibly a small triumph for antisettler forces, national disunity, or *pilug,* became the real story, as the country spontaneously broke into a kind of color war, portending divisions that almost every reporter and pundit warned about. Supporters of the settlers tied orange ribbons to their side-view mirrors, porches, baby carriages. Supporters of withdrawal tied blue ones in response. Jerusalem was a virtual sea of orange ribbons. The settlers' obvious fervor played best of all in the headlines and sound bites that in Israel, as in most Western countries, clamored for attention from broadcast media, in which the more complex opinions all seem to cancel one another out.

The week before the evacuation, on a drive north, I passed a couple of billboards in the main square of the town of Hadera. On one side of the square was an orange sign, with the face of a young man who had Zhivago-like eyes; beneath him was the caption "Brother, don't force me from my home." On the other side, a royal blue sign, not from any political group, but from Bank Leumi, exhorting its depositors to borrow against their home equity ("up to 60,000 shekels") to take the family to Europe. I thought of that famous line of Yeats: "The best lack all conviction, while the worst are full of passionate intensity."

AND SO WILL the center hold? Can it liberalize and globalize when Jewish solidarity is framed in ways kept evergreen by Arab solidarity? Some of the most considerate centrist voices insist on doubt. "The whole Jew was Kafka," the writer Aharon Appelfeld told me, "and you know, this attitude of his, this restlessness and disquiet, contributed to the Holocaust in a way, because Jews thought a restless frame of mind would qualify them to be Europeans—they thought that Europe was the distillation of humanity, music, science, everything. After the Holocaust, the liberal certainties, including certainty in this uncertainty, evaporated again, and Jews who had endured the Holocaust both divorced and internalized the divine. They thought: 'God won't make justice, so I will. God permits atrocities. I shall, to the extent that I can, prevent them.' Trust in the God of Israel, in the old intimacy? Impossible. You cannot simply say, 'the God of our fathers.'

"And yet"—Appelfeld was coming to his point—"you have Jewish sources which allow you to play out this tension or in which, it turns out, some tension was already played out. I go to London, I take two books. A novel of Kafka's and a book of the Torah, or Aggadic Legends, or the mystical Zohar. A Jewish book that grapples with the commonwealth, or relations between a person with a person, or a person with God—this kind of book is precious to me." The question he left me to play out was whether Arabs had such sources.

"I knew the nations living in the town of my birth, our maid, my father's clients, the people in the shops. There was a life. There was a symbiotic life. And I'm not even speaking about the gymnasia or university where Jews and non-Jews were taught. I absorbed it and understood it, even as a child. I have written lovingly about non-Jews, even though I have been treated very badly by non-Jews, but I absorbed this symbiosis; it became a part of me. I spoke their language. But here," Appelfeld continued sadly, "my encounter with Arabs was very small—mainly through my students and certain scholars—especially scholars—and their reaction to me was almost immediately hostile. You are a colonialist, an invader. And we almost never live with each other, house to house, or study with each other in the high school. So I still wonder: There are things I cannot understand. You speak of writers like [Sayed] Kashua. I haven't a drop of hostility toward him. But I'm sure he thinks himself a part of a majority of 250 million, and we are the intruders."

Nevertheless, is not this thing Jews have constructed here powerful enough to bring others into it? Appelfeld was skeptical. "Look, the four people who blew themselves up in London were born in England." What about the many more born in England who did not blow themselves up? "There are surveys," he said, "and the longer people from Pakistan remained in England, the more they wanted to be Pakistani, and many went back to find a madrassa. I have been teaching for thirty years, and I have had Arab students in every class. They say, 'You have come from Europe and will have to go back.' Good students, good heads, even students who were especially open to me, I dare say. They say: 'You are from Europe, big army, nuclear weapons, you terrify us; you don't belong to this place; we don't want you here; *we can't do anything about this*—but we don't want you here; you don't belong to this place.' This is not symbiosis."

But wasn't Israel, for its part, becoming a place full of the very nationalist certainties he disdained? Look, after all, at the orange ribbons. "The political questions of Israel that preoccupy you so much do not preoccupy me. What troubles me is how do we preserve, culturally, in our souls, what is essentially Jewish, from the Torah to Kafka. I listen to the news, too, but what I am listening for is the answer to the question of whether this Jewish phenomenon will disappear from the world. I found it in Malamud, Bellow, and in Philip [Roth]—also in Scholem and others here. This is my family. Joyce's Bloom."

Appelfeld then jumped a quantum: "Look, I have to see that this Jewish essence is in a way the essence of modernity. Here was a free creation. In Czernowitz, the people next door had their homes, their lands, their religion. You say these were people who weren't free, who couldn't express themselves—even their anti-Semitism was an expression of their lack of free imagination. Jewish freedom—it is *characteristic*." Did one have to be born Jewish to qualify for this essential disquiet? Did we both not know very many non-Jews who fit this idiosyncratic definition? "Look, this feeling of restlessness has a history. I don't open windows without thinking that perhaps someone might jump in. Somebody once noticed that I always walk near the wall, not in the center of the room. It is hard for me, this idea: 'They've suffered, you've suffered, it's all the same.' Obviously anyone who's gone through a pogrom or a holocaust, if he is Armenian, say, will have this feeling. This is wired into the collective now. I'm not proud of it—'Bravo, you've endured a pogrom.' Not at all. But what can be done? It is a part of our specific character, including a certain generosity. Look, we pay 50 percent taxes here. It comes from the idea that you are a guest on this earth, just a little while. The sages said that 'A minute can save you from death.' The meaning? Give. *Give*. Give—it's healing. Give—it makes you *more*. Give—you save the world from death."

ONCE I HEARD a Unitarian minister preach that Unitarians were the only religion on earth that was not intolerant of other religions. Appelfeld, and many other supremely decent Israelis of the center, leave you feeling off balance in this way, uncertain whether you are hearing arguments for a transcendent form of liberalism or a recalcitrant form of tribalism—or both at once. When you think about it, however,

Appelfeld's governing assumption is not really that Jews are uniquely
fit for civil society. It is rather that Arabs have yet to prove that they can
live in civil society at all. At bottom, there is the same fear that makes
for solidarity in the Malcha Mall.

One would think centrist jurists, unlike writers, would be easier to
pin down. Not so. I sat down with X, somebody often mentioned for
a judicial appointment, and who (therefore, perhaps) preferred not be
identified. X had made a brilliant career as a civil rights scholar and activist but had of late surprised friends by exploring common ground
with rabbis advocating continuing privileges for Halakha in the Israeli
state ("My less delicate friends think I have crossed the line," X says).
How could X's two approaches—liberalism and halakhic privilege—be
reconciled? What about the implication for Arabs?

"I am not migrating," X said, "I am struggling with the implications
of political liberalism. Human rights, democracy, liberalism—all of
these things include a commitment to freedom of religion and freedom
of association, the freedom of people to belong to groups. What I am
going through is the realization that in a society where the right to Jewish self-determination is challenged, and where liberal democracy is
sometimes seen as limiting freedom of religion, then liberal frame-
works of thought need to do more than they have done in order to give
a full answer to life in a complex society."

I tried to parse what could possibly be meant by liberal democracy
"limiting freedom of religion." In what sense could religious freedom
be thought to be under threat by, of all things, liberalism? X seemed a
little taken aback, apparently surprised that I did not think *religious* and
liberal were in obvious contradiction. "Well, I agree we have personal
freedom of religion, except in two cases, which should be changed for
both Arabs and Jews: namely, the monopoly of Orthodox religious authorities over marriage and divorce. But this is moving in the right di-

rection." (X provided no evidence for this claim, but I let it go.) "Anyway," X continued, "the debate in Israel is not now about 'narrow' freedom of religion . . . It is over the public sphere, religion as culture. The prism through which I look at a Jewish and democratic state is the deep and uncomfortable connection between Jewish as non-Arab, Jewish as non-Christian; that is, Jewish as *origin*."

The penny was dropping. To say that liberalism threatened religious freedom was a kind of code. Liberalism meant the centrist custodians of secular Israel—not perfect, but "moving in the right direction." Religion meant Jewish, which implied national affiliation, a biological fact, a specific religious practice, an historical consciousness. To say the Jewish people needed religious freedom actually meant that Jews needed political power. Radical Israeli liberals—people who refused to see the importance of "groups"—were a threat to that.

"I am against Israeli nationality," X said; "I am for Israeli citizenship. I am for Jewish collective identity, which allows a variety of Jewish forms of life, and includes the Orthodox."

Fair enough, I said. But why does collective identity need to be defined by the state apparatus? Why should not personal or community identity be voluntary? X broke into laughter: "That's fascinating!" X exclaimed, though the laughter was not sympathetic. "That's Zionism, after all." Was it? I persisted. The Québécois defined their nation as having an origin in a distinct religious community. Yet the Québec government does not seek to impose a religious tradition on its citizens. "But it does impose a language!" X declared. Yes, I readily conceded, Israel might impose Hebrew, but the language does not exclude anyone, or make observance of halakhic practice the basis of a social contract.

"*What* privileges for Halakhic life?" X interrupted. Well, the National Religious school system, I answered. But X interrupted again, not calm anymore—"Okay, you now want to discuss disestablishment; this is something completely different." I was stunned. Just how was the question of disestablishment different from the question of the separation of religion and state? "Because," X replied, "in most of the countries of Europe you have a different approach than in America. Some states support private religious schools." Schools that do not teach a standard secular curriculum? "It is just a question of their gaining material benefits for their concerns. I might fight to deny money to these schools politically, but I do not believe they should be excluded, any more than in sports, or football, or whatever."

SOMETHING IMPORTANT was not being said. No serious liberal could believe that state support for a widening network of Orthodox schools was comparable to state support for a football league. X relented: "I agree that no religion should be able to enlist the power of the state to further its goals. You cannot take from religious people their belief in the supremacy of their religion and their God. But we can lay out a deal, which is that they cannot act on this, or enlist the state to act on it."

But they *are* enlisting the state, I said. Finally, the unspoken thing was spoken.

"This is a public struggle. What schools teach must come under public scrutiny. We have to consider how to create a civic identity that transcends group identity. We have to be secure enough to trust that our liberal vision will win. But in countries like Israel, with large fundamentalist communities—not only Jewish—and in this region, where fundamental Islam is very dangerous, you can afford to be democratic only when you can be sure that you can, indeed, govern. We need Jewish particularism in order to fend off Jewish fundamentalism."

X's argument was finally becoming clear. Empowering the rabbinate was a form of realpolitik. You surrender to Orthodox interests in order to govern at all. The Arabs had their schools as a symbol or a means to their survival as a group in Jewish Israel. The Orthodox had *their* schools to survive as a group in secular Israel—and, implicitly, to underpin the survival of a Jewish nation. The solution was collective rights. And what was the problem? It was the survival of groups, and in this case, the Jewish group, challenged by terrorism, and by some of the things Israeli Arabs would teach their children were it not for public scrutiny.

"The center is really a minority," X continued, "and it has to hold its own against the national Orthodox, the ultra-Orthodox, and the Arabs, who all refuse to assimilate. And you have an armed conflict about the legitimacy of the whole state. If a Jew is secular and does not have a Jewishness that is valid, robust, and strong, then of what value is a Jewish state? You must permit a Jewishness that is not fundamentalist, but maintains physical security and cultural security. You must permit a fabric of life, a language that permits Israeli Jews, unlike, say, American Jews, to be a nation and not a religion." Then should we not, I countered, anticipate, indeed, welcome, Arabs and other minorities freely assimilating into this fabric of life?

"The problem with the Arabs is that as long as the conflict goes on, they do not have the freedom to assimilate," X insisted, echoing Appelfeld; "they would never become Jews. Not at all. Some would assimilate into Hebrew and Western values, while some others would become more fundamentalist in response. Anyway, such an assimilation is the hope of this country." But do we not then have to remove the barriers to this assimilation? What about privatizing land? What about replacing the Law of Return, which valorizes a racial-religious definition of Jew? Why not naturalization to Israeli nationality?

I had stepped on a mine. "Israeli Arabs who say they merely want Israel to be a democratic state—you must understand, most Israeli liberals see such people as a great threat," X replied heatedly. "This is the opening for a binational state, which I strongly reject. Israel is not going to be a neutral state, because Israel is the only state where the individual and cultural rights of Jews are protected. This state will not be binational, it will have Hebrew as its language. The Arab school system cannot, cannot, cannot teach that Israel is not legitimate. They want this to be a bilingual country. It will not be!"

Had we reached an impasse? Israel could certainly privilege Hebrew, I suggested, and insist that all citizens learn it as the primary language of education. This was hardly binationalism. But X was adamant. Language education was, after all, only a part of the problem. There would be no end to demands that would make Israel binational on the sly. Arabs wanted Arabic on all Tel Aviv street signs. An Arab who was injured at the ice rink in Metulla sued because a warning was not posted in Arabic: "They want to live in this country without learning Hebrew. We don't want languages of equal status."

It seemed obvious to me that X, who otherwise expected secular Israelis to live confidently in the world, completely underestimated the power and attraction of Hebrew for others. Put Arabic on a street sign, and national life is undermined. Compete and you lose.

WHAT IS MOST common to Israel's center are these elisions, airs, and doubts, which are a restatement of my friend Chanan's more humble anxieties—that Palestinians cannot forgive, that Jews are getting soft, that two states may be necessary but will only postpone some final day of reckoning. And nowhere are these attitudes more deceptively understated than, of all places, in Israel's community of legal scholarship, which is otherwise devoted to press freedoms, electoral processes, and so much of what Israel has become justifiably proud of as democratic process.

"I am always amazed," former Interdisciplinary Center law school dean Yoram Shachar told me, "how my students fail to see the connection between law and underlying political commitments or political fights. I start my classes on legal systems asserting that most of Aharon

Barak's legal decisions were not liberal. Shock waves go through the hall. Reflective thinking *must* be liberal. It's the thing that lefties do. Right-wingers feel. Left-wingers think."

I protested: What about Barak's fight to extend the reach of the Basic Law on Human Dignity and Liberty? Shachar seemed amused. "There is kosher and, as Americans say, kosher-style. Barak was liberal-style. Compare police power and military power in Britain and America, where the rights of individual citizens are so much on people's minds. Barak put the communitarian first. He does not have to defer to professional military people on security matters, he often *leads* here. Think of arrest-and-detention pending proceedings, where the accused is not released on bail. The average time for these cases, mostly Arab detainees, is eight months to a year. Trials can be delayed for two, even three years. Barak takes the worst stand on this, even to the right of various ministers of justice."

What about the changed route of the fence? "He could have made that decision months before," Shachar insisted, "but he waited for the World Court, and then grabbed the limelight—upholding the government's legal right to move the border, the occupation, but then moving the line a few meters. And has he raised major opposition to the rabbinical structure? Barak has called the Law of Human Dignity a constitutional revolution. Has there been even a minor revolution? How has the domain of civil rights grown at all? Decisions about personal status, material rights, the educational system?

"We live in a political vacuum," Shachar said. "The Orthodox, reactionary, strictly Jewish types are so organized, so positioned to tip things into a kind of Jewish state that real liberals would choke in— well, a small number of Orthodox have power over hundreds of thousands, and it is hard to see how to emerge from this. American Jews"—here he winked at me—"are of no help. I find it enormously difficult to find national affinity with American Jews. What is Jewish to them is foreign to me. There is gefilte fish in common, I suppose, like pizza, a way of making something out of junk. But really, the good Dershowitz is no closer to me than Tony Soprano."

Shachar may yet rue the day Barak retired. Barak has long warned that the Knesset was increasing its power, in particular to minimize the court's jurisdiction to interpret the Basic Law of Human Dignity. Justice minister Daniel Friedmann, who has threatened to subordinate the interpretive prerogatives of the High Court to the Knesset, has often accused Barak's High Court of "activism." The epithet is, of course, drawn from American judicial debates. What Friedmann precisely lacks is an American constitution that an implied constructionist like himself might fall back on.

Still, Israelis like Friedmann do not just live in a political vacuum—certainly not as they accommodate to the pressures of world markets and Western political institutions, over which rabbis and bureaucrats have no control. There has always been a struggle for the soul of educated Israelis, with the conflict pulling toward atavism, and the outside world toward democratic forms. Once there was no question which pull was greater, or at least more immediate. But are not the new facts of globalization changing the balance?

CHAPTER 5

The Business of Integration

The growth sector—the amazingly growing sector in Israel—is the
high-tech sector. And that is the most impervious to political or military developments... Their investments in plants and equipment are
not substantial. Their real assets are carried around in people's heads.
Peace would be a useful, additional condition, but it is not the primordial, necessary condition, which is, anywhere, economic freedom.

—PRIME MINISTER BENJAMIN NETANYAHU,
interview with the author for *Fortune,* 1998

A writer I admire once described Voltaire as a man who gave the impression of playing chess while everybody else played checkers. Most
people in Israel's power élite give the same impression, thinking out the
contingencies, counting on sequenced actions playing out just so—projecting how human nature responds to power and enticement. If Palestinian terror could be mitigated, either through force or by building a
wall, could not negotiations resume and the momentum of settlement
be broken? If—so the center's logic continues—the demographic threat
could be reduced, and if less affluent tribes could be economically appeased for a while, could not the country refocus on making globalization work? If Israel grew stronger in global markets, could it not make
itself indispensable to regional players and, *en passant,* outlast Israeli Arab
and foreign doubts about the Jewish state being democratic? If Rudy
Giuliani is elected, won't that buy time? Moshe Dayan once chided

reporters that he would not answer a question "with more than two 'if's in it." But what was Dayan's engineering of Anwar Sadat's visit to Jerusalem in 1977 if not *his* belated effort to move from checkers to chess?

There are strategic disagreements in the center, of course, but they seem to boil down to opposable historical archetypes. A few days after Operation Defensive Shield began, in April 2002, I attended a faculty meeting at the Interdisciplinary Center in Herzliya. As we sat around, chatting sullenly about the spreading war, worrying most of all about the students who'd been called up by the reserves, the college president, Uriel Reichman, walked in and announced (with an obvious show of satisfaction) the arrest of Marwan Barghouti, leader of the Tanzim, the Palestinian armed underground close to Fatah. Actually, we already knew this; the news had flashed on our cell phones a few minutes before. We knew that Barghouti had been implicated in revolting acts of terror; the press had been full of allusions to the Tanzim as a throwback to Nazi brownshirts. But we also knew that he was a charismatic figure and had publicly renounced terror in a *New York Times* op-ed. He spoke excellent Hebrew, from a previous stint in Israeli prisons, and had called for recognizing Israel. Anyway, Ehud Sprinzak, an expert on terrorism (who, sadly, died several months later), walked into the meeting. "What's going on?" he asked. "They got Barghouti," Reichman said. Sprinzak shot back: "You will negotiate with him."

This exchange has stuck in my mind, for it represents pretty well the historical grooves you slide into most often in the salons of the Israeli center. Some think they're in danger of Munich, so they want to nip new Hitlers in the bud. Some think they're in danger of South Africa, so they're hoping for the Palestinian Mandela. Anyone who's heard Santayana's aphorism is condemned to repeat it. It is much harder for Israelis to accept what is truly novel—in this case, the promising implications of global integration, the evidence for which is everywhere except in history.

One would think that the politics of globalization would feel natural to Jews. Globalization is an old promise fulfilled. And Israeli centrists of all stripes will readily admit that Israel is a hostage to commercial globalization. They count on a world-spanning information platform to make their fortunes, and have seen the European Union rising around them, with a charter of human rights. Yet few let themselves imagine how Israel's current crisis might be transformed by the country's integration into this larger political system, which is evolving and unprecedented. Educated Israelis dutifully scoff at the idea of joining the European Union, yet many privately acquire European passports (a Polish grandparent is enough); and they implicitly take the Western world's integration for granted, certainly when they get to the airport or switch on their laptops. How long before they realize that their presence in this world is not merely virtual?

EUROPE'S MODEL, more and more, seems the Israeli center's forbidden fruit. Israelis all link naturally to the United States and American Jews; American English, Hollywood, Congressional politics, and the NBA are in the blood. Nevertheless, most in the Israeli center suppose that if Israel were to partner with some larger entity, it would be the European Union. Even the prospect of free trade or federal arrangements with Palestine (and other neighboring states) do not get in the way of this idea. Israel already enjoys free trade with Europe, and a preponderance of its high-technology exports goes there. Educated Israelis, including North African Jews and Russians, speak a wide spectrum of European languages. Israeli students study (and in many ways feel themselves the products of) European history, ideologies, and philosophical movements. Israelis compete against European basketball teams, emulate European styles, play European symphonies, collect European literary prizes. Much of European history is terrifying for Israelis to look back at, of course, but it is terrifying for Europeans, too. Official commitments to memorialize and overcome the past give younger generations of intellectuals and entrepreneurs, in Israel and in Europe, something of a common language.

And yet the very things that make joining the union seductive make it vaguely disturbing. Israeli Jews are anxious about getting lost, if not losing their distinction, in European multiculturalism. Their most explicit fear is being forced to give up residual Zionist obligations, like the Law of Return. They think of Europe as a space of Jewish assimilation. But why, to press the point, would building from commercial integration to political integration endanger the Jewish character of Israel? Some will point immediately to the prospect of Europeans, seeing the large number of Israeli Arabs, demanding that Israel be binational and not Jewish. But don't large minorities present different kinds of manageable challenges to European member states themselves—Basques in Spain, Turks in Germany, and so forth? Of course they do. And Israel could benefit from their models. What minorities there do not face are legal arrangements that, in effect, prevent them from undertaking voluntary acts of integration. Moreover, any citizen of the EU could choose to work, or start a business, in any other member country—a privilege that might well appeal to many Israeli Arabs.

The EU could also teach Israelis how to handle naturalization. It is true that some member states, like Greece—so legal scholar Amnon Rubinstein points out—have naturalization statutes that also give preference to returning Greek nationals. The criteria can be as vague as Israel's Law of Return.[1] Rubinstein expects us to conclude from this that Israel does not fall short of European standards. But all countries in the EU, including Greece, provide secular guidelines to earn citizenship. And however you came to be Greek, you are also a European with rights. Tens of thousands of Russian Jews have, for example, become Germans since the fall of the Iron Curtain. "Europe is not only an economic bloc with profitable trading opportunities," writes EU Commissioner Benita Ferrero-Waldner, "but also a group of nations sharing common ideas and values. Israel can be associated with this group, but at some point it will have to make the strategic decision of whether this is what it really wants."[2] Carl Hahn, the former chairman of Volkswagen and an architect of the union, was more blunt. He told me that Israel would "certainly strengthen" the EU, but Israel must first have peace with its neighbors "and civil rights that conform to European law."

Can Israeli centrists remain forever ambivalent about such invitations? Not likely. Europe's knowledge economy, at which Israelis excel, blurs its political boundaries. Israeli entrepreneurs, who also feel kinship with Jewish minorities abroad, cannot but welcome the logic. If Israel were actually a member of the union, moreover, the strident constitutional demands made by Israel's Arabs would almost certainly be moderated. The Adalah draft constitution, for example, insists on rigid binational protections for state symbols, which Europeans just wince at—for example, the proposal that Israel's flag be determined by a Knesset committee, half of whose members are Arab. Europeans, in contrast, have simply become accustomed to flying the European flag next to every conceivable national flag, from Germany's to Sardinia's. If the Israeli flag flew next to that of the union, and Israeli Arabs knew that in addition to flying what they wanted in their towns, they had the right to work and live anywhere in Israel, Palestine, or Europe for that matter, would they be worrying about the composition of committees to modify the Star of David?

Finally, association with Europe would mean gaining strength in numbers, through collective security arrangements—something Israel has never enjoyed. Israel cannot hope to live at war forever with the entire Islamic world, or achieve secure borders by relying on unilateral military power and strategic arrangements. Olmert has floated the idea that Israel might eventually join NATO. It is obvious that coordinated European action on Palestine, including NATO boots on the ground, is the only way to a sustainable regional peace. One of the most prescient strategic demands the Israeli government made before the last Lebanon war was that European forces must occupy Southern Lebanon—something that would have been unheard of a generation ago. But European forces—not just in Lebanon, but also in Palestine and East Jerusalem—would only reinforce the larger truth: that Israelis and their neighbors cannot build their states unless they succeed at economic globalization together. This vision of economic integration—of economic hope—is the only real rival in the region to rage and fanaticism, which has taken on a religious cast and an increasingly apocalyptic rhetoric.

AND YET, for all of Europe's gravitational pull, you do not find many in the Israeli center speaking about their future in this way today. Talk is still about separating from Palestinians, not joining Europeans. Let's separate, so the argument goes, and if we can't cut a deal, then to hell with them, because any line we would draw would not be based on trust anyway, so we can always do what we did in Gaza, pull out settlers, leave our informants network, and hunker down behind a wall. Anyway, the most perverse thing about this despair is that it suggests political and economic self-sufficiency just when globalization is making nonsense of it. Israelis urgently need, and are accustomed to having, global markets, investments, and technology. Yet Israel is integrated into a world that, according to a recent BBC poll, considers it a major threat to global peace. Israeli élites are thus more economically vulnerable than ever to local political violence, especially violence that would be the natural extension of demographic reasoning—and foreign censure and boycott. Continue the polarization between Israeli Jews and Arabs, and ethnic cleansing becomes inevitable. But if the Israeli government dares initiate ethnic cleansing, in response to whatever provocation, would not the economy unravel through isolation? That is a question with just one "if" in it.

The point is dawning on educated Israelis, most quickly on Israel's business community. It has been a kind of rite of passage for Olmert himself and other centrist politicians. Back when he was minister of trade and industry in 2003, for example, Olmert was unexpectedly confronted by an EU demand that goods from occupied territory be labeled as such, as distinct from goods coming from Israel proper. The EU spokesman was clear: The union did "not recognize settlements over the Green Line as being part of Israel." Israel then exported more than $7 billion in goods and services to Europe (this number is much higher today). Olmert feared that for the sake of $120 million in goods from the settlements, all Israeli exports would be subject to European tariffs. Reluctantly, he agreed to change the labels.

Settlers condemned Olmert for knuckling under. They charged Europeans with wanting to have a yellow Star of David fixed to Israeli products. Olmert lashed back: "Whoever is playing politics with this is endangering all of Israel's exports to Europe . . . What we have done is in keeping with the desire to protect the Israeli economy."[3] Dan Propper, a food processing magnate and past president of the Manufacturers' Association of Israel, backed him up. ("It was clear this was going to spread to all of Europe," Propper said.) Revealingly, after this incident Olmert began to speculate openly about the logic of the Gaza evacuation (and to work discreetly to form Kadima). "The economy is the pivot upon which a revolution may turn," a high-tech manager told me; "Israel either goes forward as a Hebrew version of that global thing or falls back and becomes a little Jewish Pakistan." ("Diplomatic isolation will lead to economic isolation," Olmert admitted.)

Integrationist logic is the same for Israel and Palestine, by the way. One needs a certain political imagination to see two states, two parliaments, two language communities, and so forth. But one needs no imagination at all to see the impossibility of two economies, that is, two disconnected states. Think again of building tourist infrastructure, or just coping with labor migration from the Nile. Think of electrical power, or water, or telecommunications, or the currency, or management of investment zones, or air and sea transport—the list goes on. On this front, however, attitudes are slower to evolve. Few centrists will just say that Israel's economic future is tied to Palestine, or even to peace with Palestine. For Kadima, Labor, and the constituencies they organize have an opposition to contend with: several hundred thousand settlers in the West Bank and around Jerusalem, ultra-Orthodox parties, Russian immigrant hawks, combat officers nervous about losing "deterrent power," Diaspora Jews for whom the year is perpetually 1938 and they are perpetually Churchill. Government leaders are understandably reluctant to take them on for the sake of a peace process that could at any time be subverted by either the Palestinians' weakness or their unity.

ALL OF THIS raises a critical question. If external economic pressures will not give the center courage, will they give it something worse to fear than the settlers' opposition and momentum? The polls may be telltale. In 1998, some 48 percent of Israelis believed that the peace process would have no effect on unemployment, or would actually increase it, as opposed to 43 percent who believed that peace will create new jobs.[4] Today, over two-thirds of the country see a strong connection between the peace process and economic growth. What is more, Israeli leaders are growing increasingly aware that to manage its immanent social tensions, Israel must generate unprecedented growth, 6 or 7 percent a year over ten years, according to Bank of Israel governor Stanley Fischer. "We can grow without progressing toward peace," he told Haaretz in January 2007, but with peace, growth would be much higher: "We are talking about the difference between 4 percent growth a year and growth of 5 to 6 percent a year. And the difference between 4 percent growth and 6 percent growth is not 2 percent—it's 50 percent."[5]

Consider the economic dangers and opportunities implied by Fischer's projections, both of which are stark. Israel only recently emerged from a political economy dominated by the Histadrut labor federation and a command economy. A generation ago, in 1984, five years after the peace with Egypt, failing, state-subsidized manufacturing industries (textiles, chemicals, etc.) and a largely corrupt network of state-owned and union-owned public corporations still accounted for around 50 percent of the GDP. The rate of inflation climbed to an Argentinean 400 percent when a Likud government desperately bought votes by increasing welfare-state subsidies to staple consumer goods like milk and eggs. The huge defense establishment soaked up more than a fifth of the government budget.[6]

The country has come a great distance since 1984. But until the reforms of the first Sharon government, presided over by then finance minister Netanyahu, the public sector still accounted for more employment than the private sector did. (In the United States, where the public sector is admittedly smaller than in Europe, the figure is somewhere between 10 and 15 percent, and the total number of people working in the public sector is roughly equal to the number working in big business alone.) Since 1984, Israel's GDP has quintupled, to nearly $150 billion; and per capita income is now on average about $21,000 per annum, a comfortably Western standard.

But the numbers are deceiving. Israel under Ben-Gurion's old Mapai party was famous for having the least inequality of Western mixed economies. Israel today has among the highest rates of inequality, something like the inequalities between Silicon Valley entrepreneurs and the Hispanics who cut their lawns. As of this writing, about one-third of Israelis earn about $800 per month or less.[7] The top decile earns about $8,200 a month. One-third of children live under the poverty line. Between 1990 and 2002, the top decile of the population saw their income grow by about 6 percent, to $106,000 per annum, or 30 percent of the total national income. The next decile saw no growth in earnings whatsoever, and the remaining 80 percent of workers actually witnessed a decrease in their income. The bottom decile earns about 2 percent of total national income.

At the 2006 Herzliya Conference, Uriel Reichman (who was then Kadima's education minister–designate) laid out the problem with unusual bluntness and poignancy. In the Western world, Israel was among the countries most afflicted by educational inequalities between rich and poor, Sephardim and Ashkenazim, Arabs and Jews. "[And] Israeli children are generally among the lowest of OECD countries, in all areas of knowledge, and all ages; and there is a lowering of language skills." While the rate of completion of matriculation exams is falling, and stands now at about 50 percent overall, Reichman reported, "in Gavatayim 73 percent complete the matriculation, and in Tel Aviv 61 percent, while in the Arab town of Tira, it is 23 percent, and in Jerusalem 33 percent." Translation: 75 percent graduate from relatively affluent neighborhoods, about 40 percent from Mizrahi development towns, under 30 percent from Haredi neighborhoods, and under 20 percent from Arab towns. In affluent neighborhoods, close to 20 percent are entering college. In Arab towns and Jerusalem, well under 8 percent.

Arie Ben-Shachar, an economist specializing in employment data (and who served as the youth secretary of the Israeli Communist Party in the 1960s), was never invited to the Herzliya Conference and would no doubt have been amused to hear the intellectual conscience of Israel's centrist élite speaking of class divisions leading to a "social explosion." Yet there was little in Reichman's warning that Ben-Shachar would have disagreed with. "None of the educational data," Ben-Shachar said, "reflects 'discouraged' workers who aren't even seeking work, which was as high as 3 percent in 2004, on top of the formal unemployment rate. Then there are workers who are partially employed, less than thirty-five hours a week, who are more than a quarter of people employed. Two-thirds or more are women. But a third are people who cannot survive on what they are earning. The real unemployment rate in Israel is at least 18 percent—*18 percent!*"

Did this include Haredi men, who do not seek work when supported by their yeshiva? Ben-Shachar was waiting for the question. "For economists, the question you are begging is the general level of participation in the Israeli labor force. It is very low in Israel—around 55 percent, as compared with OECD countries, which are 8 to 12 percent higher or, say, about 67 percent in Japan. The higher the level of education, the higher the level of participation. This is clearest among women. But the level of participation among men has been declining here in, of all times, the 1990s, when the economy has been growing impressively. Something unheard of in the West. This is obviously attributable to the Haredi influence but also to the limited availability of acceptable jobs. People won't work for pennies, not Jews, not Israeli Arabs. They'll find relatives or other ways to survive."

Ben-Shachar was despondent: "All of this is the prelude to a culture war, not just an economic one. Education and income go hand in hand. Perhaps the Likud has had an interest in this—they have been able to sell undereducated people their bill of goods. Anyway, without significant economic expansion, this is a ticking bomb."

IT WOULD NOT be a simple matter to prevent an explosion under the best of circumstances, what with the class tensions, the ubiquitous sense of possible violence from occupied territory, the economic divisions taking on an ethnic-immigrant character. Organized crime, a social marker, is on a precipitous rise. Former High Court justice (and, before that, attorney general) Yitzhak Zamir is appalled by the spread of bureaucratic corruption: "We have to shout and say, 'Listen, we are sick.' Corruption really is a kind of chronic disease, which can be terminal."[8]

One former Israeli police chief, Assaf Heretz, claimed recently that almost $3 billion in dirty money has been invested in Israel over the past few years.[9] Crime figures for 2003 show that there were 484,688 criminal files and unprosecuted cases, 20,000 more than in the previous year. But these data do not tell the whole story. Youth unemployment in Arab towns is at 30 percent. "Many despair," a *Haaretz* editorial confesses, "and give up on filing complaints that are dealt with sluggishly and often produce no results. The prevailing public sentiment is that the police are helpless."[10]

The Israeli government, which has spent 50 billion NIS, or $15 billion, on settlements since 1967,[11] is hardly in a position to intervene with substantial new spending on school reform, vocational training, or crime fighting. As I write, Israeli teachers and university professors are on strike, protesting how their real incomes have fallen by more than 30 percent since the late 1990s. The so-called security wall costs approximately a million dollars per kilometer. The 2006 fiscal year left the government with an unexpected surplus of over 5 billion NIS. But the state suffers from a huge national debt. It is trying to make up for infrastructural neglect on the coastal plain: new roads, high-speed rail between Tel Aviv and Jerusalem, subways in Greater Tel Aviv. These projects create quality jobs, but also significantly increase the number of foreign laborers. They do not really reverse the long-term trend toward inequality.

Granted, the government budget has been kept under control since the grim days of 1984; inflation has been reasonably low for the past twenty years, thanks mainly to the diligence of Bank of Israel governors. Successive finance ministers, whose staffs have become increasingly professional, have maintained fiscal discipline and enabled critical Western borrowing—bonds subsidized, in effect, by American loan guarantees. Among the very positive reforms Netanyahu introduced during his last tenure as finance minister was an end to the monopoly Israeli banks had on the management of pension funds, which made Israeli capital markets more competitive and fluid than ever before. Low inflation has permitted the development of high-tech entrepreneurial ventures. Direct foreign investment in Israeli companies and financial institutions in 2006 rose to an unprecedented $6 billion. Growth, which was flat during the Al-Aqsa Intifada, rose to over 5 percent, the best among Western developed nations.

But the cost of fiscal discipline is a budget-allocation process in perpetual crisis, including arbitrary cuts to all kinds of social welfare spending: schools, universities, hospitals, aid to mothers, support for the handicapped and the elderly, support for the arts, support for public media.[12] The number of cases of children who have been abused or neglected by their families since 1995 has risen by 130 percent, to about 39,000, while the number of children who have ended up in emergency wards as a result of such abuse has risen by 166 percent.[13] Nor has austerity put the Israeli budget in the clear. The government deficit in 2004 was 12 percent of revenue and, more critically, almost 4 percent of GDP. If Israel were a member of the European Union, it would be in serious breach of the EU's Stability and Growth Pact provisions, which insist on a deficit of no more than 3 percent of GDP. (The U.S. federal government is currently running a deficit of about 3.5 percent, but all of its state budgets are balanced.)

Since 2004, Israel's accumulated national debt has hovered near 80 percent of GDP, a number very difficult to bring down without stringent fiscal measures. Maastricht agreements set a limit of 60 percent for EU members. (Irish national debt to GDP was, for example, about 31 percent and moving downward.) Debt service in Israel was about 20–25 percent of the budget, but that was when global interest rates and oil prices were at lows not likely to be seen again for some time, perhaps not ever. And yet the Israeli defense budget remains at approximately 20 percent of the entire budget, while social service entitlements of all kinds command 40–45 percent of government revenues. Without

American guarantees in 2002, Israeli bonds would have been close to junk.

THESE STRESSES exacerbate inequalities with, and opportunities in, Palestine. The Israeli annual per capita income of about $21,000 is about twenty times what Palestinians beyond the wall average. No Palestinian economist or entrepreneur I have talked to imagines the Palestinian economy making any headway without Israeli businesses taking the lead. Palestine will grow initially, if at all, from high-rise and road construction, which require fairly high levels of technology, integrated information systems, and networks of global suppliers. West Bank towns are really suburbs of Jerusalem: Palestinian businesses will remain both customers and stepchildren of Israeli food-processing companies, banks, farms, and telecommunications providers. Then there is tourism: The new Palestinian state will count heavily on visits to the holy mosques and Jerusalem, especially by pilgrims from the Arab world. Israelis are the bridge to global hotel companies, booking networks, car-rental agencies, restaurant supply companies, and more. Over 90 percent of Palestinian exports go to Israeli markets.

The pattern of dependency is even clearer in high-technology businesses. Yahya al-Salqan, the CEO of Jaffa.net, Ramallah's leading software solutions house, told me even before the Hamas victory in Gaza that he could not imagine Palestine thriving "without having some kind of federation with Israel and Jordan, where businesses would find no differences," no "barriers to entry." A former Sun Microsystems engineer, al-Salqan has built information technology platforms for the PA's banking and educational systems, and also a novel data warehouse and billing-system solution for Jawal, the Palestinian cell phone company. He teaches computer science in Al-Quds University in Abu Dis, an eastern neighborhood of Jerusalem.

"I have no doubts about the technical competence of our graduates—and we graduate perhaps seven hundred software engineers on the West Bank every year. This could be a five-hundred-employee company. Our people are so motivated, so intent on keeping their jobs, that they become productive in six months, whereas this used to take as much as two years in the Silicon Valley. I just got 140 CVs for one opening. Heartbreaking. But they need better communication skills, in English, and better business orientation. They need to learn enterprise culture. This is what they lack. Academic training is not what allows you to go up that learning curve. In school you learn the concepts of a data-base design and architecture, not the things about Oracle and Microsoft applications they learn here. For that you need world-class, challenging projects."

Does this mean exposure to Israeli companies? "If you think about a software company starting from scratch, then you are absolutely correct! I could take what I did for Jawal to other, larger-scale companies and governments. The solutions would scale beautifully—if I could ever get to Gaza, and from there to the Gulf, for example. But for companies starting out, needing knowledge capital, experience, a level of business engagement, then absolutely, they'd need Israeli partners."

I AM DWELLING on al-Salqan's logic because his grasp of Palestine's dependency on Israel is, when you think about it, an obvious parallel to Israel's dependency on the rest of the developed world. The same way the knowledge economy pushes him toward economic integration with Israel and Jordan, it is pushing the great majority of Israel's élite toward integration with, especially, proximate European businesses. Though the scale is different, Israeli high-tech businesses desperately need from global markets what Jaffa.net needs from Israel—insider knowledge of major product development efforts, or of corporate supply chains, or customizations for companies that have learned to trust proven suppliers. High-tech solutions require know-about, not just know-how.

To sustain their growth, Israeli firms have needed not only market intelligence, but the prelude to market intelligence: an open, even welcome conversation with companies in Europe and Asia. To get their start, Israeli companies need to receive direct infusions of insider knowledge from global companies and consulting firms. The government needs many more such businesses to succeed if the country is to defuse its social bomb. This realization—that money is not enough—is turning a great many Israeli entrepreneurs into peace advocates, but the old, discouraged Israeli peace camp has not really caught on to their potential support. Not long ago, I attended an omnibus meeting of peace groups in Ramallah, which purported to represent the whole spectrum of activists: Israeli democrats, Palestinian liberals and nationalist moderates, foreign Catholics, Quakers, evangelicals, feminists. How many, I asked the hundred or so people in the room, were associated either as students or teachers with universities or colleges? About sixty hands went up. How many, I then asked, were from business schools? One hand went up, in addition to my own. But two Palestinian entrepreneurs dropped their business cards into my pocket.

THE CENTER has a formidable dissenter here, Benjamin Netanyahu himself. Like Netanyahu, most centrist leaders have proclivities toward apocalyptic stubbornness, and suppose that Israel's economy can muddle through, even with tensions and periodic violence. But business leaders and writers are generally a reliable constituency for peace negotiations today, and are certainly willing to make concessions to globalization. Netanyahu, for his part, is unimpressed by their moderation. He insists there is virtually no connection between the peace process and the state of the nation's economy. He has argued over the years, not without sophistication, that peace is beside the point, at least insofar as the global economy is concerned—that a knowledge economy actually enables Israel to make minimal strategic or territorial concessions. And though

Netanyahu is of the center, his position frees him to lead the Likud back into a coalition with Land of Israel ideologues, settlers, and Orthodox parties. He's been gaining ground, not only politically, but intellectually as well.

What's his argument? High-tech growth, he says, is most impervious to military developments on the ground because it requires little in the way of manufacturing infrastructure—investments in plants and equipment—that might come under threat. Real value is in people's heads, and investors, particularly venture capitalists, know it. So what Israelis really need is economic freedom, which the Israeli government must provide: tax cuts, lowered government spending, "regardless of the political and security situation, regardless of our relationship with the Palestinians." At the same time—so he told me directly—"the drive for Israeli high tech has come from the perpetual motion machine called the Israel Defense Forces." The stresses on the IDF have, if anything, engendered innovation. Israel has to keep up its science and the supply of conceptual workers: "Peace would be a useful, additional condition, but it is not the primordial, necessary condition." He might have added that war industries have billion-dollar markets, too.

There is something nicely daring about Netanyahu's argument. Enduring Israel's perpetual conflicts, in this view, fits with a trendy, even futuristic model for succeeding in a global knowledge economy. Intangible assets, ferreted out by venture capital, will make Israelis rich irrespective of violence in the streets. All you need, presumably, is brainpower, the IDF, and investors—which Israelis have had. In 1993, just one venture fund operated in Israel. Today there are sixty, which have invested over $10 billion during this period.

And there is a good deal of truth to his general approach. His prestige as an economic prophet has only grown since he successfully oversaw market reforms during Sharon's tenure. Meanwhile, the resilience of Israel's economy after the last war with Lebanon has given him an added credibility. Even Olmert, his old rival, graciously defended Netanyahu's point to me, conceding that Israel's economy has seemed peculiarly able to slough off the war.

But Netanyahu's argument is an immensely dangerous illusion. Most centrists know it, or will come to know it. Its real value is that it provides an ideal foil to explore how Israel's knowledge economy really works. Let's start with what his argument gets right, and then see what's misguided and ominous about it.

TO HIS CREDIT, Netanyahu overturns the common-sense proposition, often stated by people around the Histadrut labor unions, that unemployment cannot really be alleviated by knowledge businesses, since these create relatively few jobs per company—certainly as compared with large-scale assembly operations, labor-intensive manufacturing, or low-end service jobs (such as call centers and so forth). Netanyahu is certainly right that Israel's leading sectors will have to be those that depend on conceptual workers, on creating value in a knowledge economy, not on cheap labor in manufacturing or services. But he is also right that lots of smaller knowledge businesses can eventually employ as many people as a few large manufacturing ones—or stimulate the need for thousands of service jobs.

Besides, Israel could never compete globally on labor or elementary services. Israel will compete, if at all, on innovation: design, integrative services, infrastructural advances, and content. As Natan Linder, the young founder of Samsung's Israeli technology center, put it to me recently, "Israel's real demographic problem is in India and China. What is their top 10 percent—two hundred million people? Assume real geniuses are just 1 percent of the total population—that is twenty million people. They have four times more geniuses than we have people. So how does Israel survive in this scenario? We have to live on our academic excellence and our capacity to innovate, as we are doing now. We may be sunk anyway, but this is our main chance, our *only* chance. If we don't have a system that promotes this innovation, what do we have?"

By the way, Israel has at present 135 scientists and engineers per 10,000 workers—more than any developed nation. Over 20 percent of the Israeli citizens now have university degrees (ranking third after the U.S. and the Netherlands). Over 35 percent of Israelis between the ages of twenty-five and sixty-four hold a university degree, 12 percent hold advanced degrees, and 77 percent of the population has graduated from high school. Israeli immigrants maintain special cultural ties with Russia, Eastern Europe, and more recently, India.

And Netanyahu is right that the government has been shrewd to liberalize capital markets and entrepreneurial freedom. The deteriorating state of public education aside, successive Likud and Labor governments since the 1980s have done well to engender a high-tech business culture. They have stabilized the shekel. They built out the transportation infrastructure, including a new airport, privatized the major telecommunications company, privatized the national airline, privatized the major state-owned bank, allowed for the development of genuine competition in cellular telephony, opened the public media to many new channels.

The government has created a transparent stock exchange, in which many capital funds are now invested; in 2005, Tel Aviv 100 equities grew in value by over 26 percent. The government funded a formidable system of entrepreneurial incubators, which the governors of various American states have learned from. (In 2005, twenty-three were up and running, seeding over 200 active projects; 735 graduated the incubators, with private investment funding over 50 percent of their launch capital.) Over the years, the Office of the Chief Scientist has provided seed money for dozens of start-ups. And the Ministry of Trade and Industry has set up a system of investment zones for new facilities, in some cases offering tax abatements of up to 38 percent, and various cash incentives for companies prepared to locate in the periphery—a policy that has helped Intel, for example, to make investments amounting to over $5 billion in a chip fabrication plant complex in Kiryat Gat.

"OUR SECRET," Netanyahu told me, "has often been thought to be the Russian immigration; the real trigger of the Israeli technological explosion is an effective army, which we've needed—will always need—to survive. The telecommunications sector comes directly from defense research, encryption businesses, for example. We have had over three thousand high-tech start-ups in this country. Many of these have been put together by graduates of special units in the army.

"And the corollary advantage is a certain culture—heavily, heavily weighted toward fast results," Netanyahu said. "You look at a telecom company like ECI; their advantage, they tell me, is that their decision making is roughly one-half to one-third the time of their competition in bringing a product to market. Their people come from the army— 'Get it done'. . . Our new companies are $50–$100 million in sales, even half a billion dollars—they are small. They could be ten times bigger, but they don't have the people, especially marketing people. We haven't had a market economy and have lacked marketers—the scale to penetrate foreign markets. But that will change as we head toward a more open economy. In the long run, we are going to have to prepare all of our children for this kind of work, solve the social gap, with ideas like our computer-for-every-child program."

Would this change in the Israeli economy imply a larger cultural shift? Netanyahu could not deny it. "The role models have changed. When we were young, there were the khaki shorts and the sandals— and a collectivist ethos. People admired the army general, the agricultural pioneer. Six-year-olds didn't compete with lemonade stands. Now it's not a crime, by God, for a Jew to make money—by skillful enterprise. The high-tech entrepreneur is seen on another scale; there is no question that we are moving to an individualistic ethos. It is troubling to some: the fear of a centrifugal force that will tear the country apart. That is not my fear. We can appreciate the value of the individual in a way that will not interfere with national goals."

Some have assumed that the IDF has stimulated a huge Israeli arms industry and, true enough, military sales were $5 billion in 2004 and have been growing every year since. But this is not the point, and Netanyahu knows it. These days, the base technologies incubated in the IDF—network management, logistics, optics, electronics, cellular communications, materials, etc.—have any number of civilian commercial applications. A cousin of mine, when he was in the air force, helped to develop an algorithm for aircraft to regroup into attack formation after one plane veered off to avoid a missile; this algorithm became the heart of a company that doubled the capacity of old telephone lines to manage data traffic.

Which is why Israel's start-up culture became so eclectic. In electronics and information industries, Israelis had about 260 active businesses by 2004. There are over three hundred today. Over ninety Israeli advanced technology companies are listed on the NASDAQ, over two hundred on all American stock exchanges. (Only Canada has more.) Nearly 40 percent of the start-ups Netanyahu heralded have been in telecom, over 20 percent in software solutions and Internet components, and another 20 percent in life sciences. Israeli exports are well over $40 billion today, including Dead Sea chemicals and cut diamonds. In total, Israel has seen five thousand start-ups since 1990.

The total of high-tech exports is about two-thirds of all exports, in office and computing equipment and software, electronic components, aircraft and avionics, electronic communications, electronic control and supervision, pharmaceuticals, machine-tool cutting blades. Electronics and information industries alone employ about sixty thousand, about 60 percent of whom are engineers: They are global leaders in

Internet telephony and video, generic pharmaceuticals, telecom billing and load management, desktop graphics, cryptography, optics, retrieval and categorization, flash memory, network security and management, bioinformatics, and many other areas of special expertise.

Global investors have been paying attention. In May 2006, Warren Buffett's Berkshire Hathaway bought an 80 percent stake in ISCAR, the high-tech metal-cutting blade company, for $4 billion, providing the founding Wertheimer family with an unprecedented fund to expand Tefen, the industrial park and company incubators they developed around company headquarters.[14] The limiting factor, CEO Eitan Wertheimer once told me, is not the number of people companies employ, but the levels of education produced in civil society. That same year, Erel Margalit's Jerusalem Venture Partners opened an animation studio in Jerusalem's old railway station, attracting some of Hollywood's most experienced filmmakers to the project. "We could move beyond high technology and security, to a combination of arts, spirituality, design, philosophy—to learning in the full sense Jerusalem represents," he told me.

At the same time, higher value-added businesses, bringing Silicon Valley–type salaries to engineers and managers in Tel Aviv, Haifa, and Jerusalem, will spur the development of decent jobs in, if not properly a service economy, then a "servant" economy: restaurants, landscaping, renovation, house cleaning, car repair. Early on, Netanyahu was justly proud of the fabulous number of entrepreneurial ventures Israel had engendered since 1990.

SO WHAT'S WRONG with this picture? First, Netanyahu is wrong, even cavalier, to underplay critical, immediate peace dividends from lower-technology employment. Despite the Bank of Israel statistics, real Israeli unemployment is high, and the wages paid to the working poor are low. The Palestinian economist Hisham Awartani told me in Ramallah that he sees a serious peace dividend for both lower-skilled Israelis and Palestinians. He argues that in construction, food processing, tourism, etc., there are hundreds of thousands of semiskilled jobs to be had, which Israel needs as badly as Palestine does; these could create a great deal of politically beneficial codependence. Think especially of tourism in and around Jerusalem. Prague gets over eight million tourists a year, compared with Israel's (at most) two million. Israel's superb new airport is seriously underutilized.

But high technology is not what Netanyahu thinks, either. Gil Schwed, the CEO of Check Point Software, once put the matter to me this way: "In the short run, nobody is going to cancel a distribution agreement with Check Point because of a terrorist attack; our customers and stockholders assume a peace process is evolving. But in the long run, if the peace momentum goes away, we will lose our edge in attracting customers and top-flight management to Israel—in the next two years, the economy will go downhill and the impact will be measurable." Schwed did not anticipate a full-scale intifada, yet his words were prophetic. They reflect how companies like Check Point work.

Check Point today is the world's premier network security company, with over $500 million in sales. It was, by 1998, the market maker for security firewalls in corporate intranets, owning perhaps 50 percent of the burgeoning market. The first thing you notice about its headquarters is that the company would be as much at home in the Silicon Valley as in Tel Aviv: halls inhabited by casually dressed people with purposeful eyes, walls covered with testimonies to the company's latest releases from *PC Magazine* and *Network World.* Then again, Check Point *is* at home in Silicon Valley, maintaining a U.S. headquarters—and from its start in 1994, a strategic alliance with Sun Microsystems. That alliance is now over, but Sun's bundling of Check Point's security products with its own network management systems accounted for about 17 percent of Check Point's initial revenues.

This is not an atypical story. The technology is in Israel, but the markets, and the marketing organizations, are elsewhere. Market leadership is established with foreign alliances. Israeli managers do not dwell alone; Israel cannot hope to have serious, ongoing violence and expect foreign managers, customers, suppliers, and strategic partners to come back and forth, the way normal business needs them to. From 1994 to 1999, the five years of Oslo and the Internet boom, the Israeli GDP grew from $57.4 billion to $102 billion, a remarkable 74 percent. Ireland, in contrast, grew by 58 percent. But from 1999 to 2004, Israel grew only 18 percent. From 2002 to 2004, growth was negative. Netanyahu insisted that this drop was more or less the result of the bursting of the high-tech bubble, which happened about the same time. But Ireland grew by 74 percent after the bubble burst while, again, Israel grew by only 18 percent. Israeli stocks soared immediately after the evacuation of Gaza. Bubble shmubble.

Perhaps the most precise way to explain Netanyahu's mistake is by focusing on one of Israel's most successful high-tech industries, which is often dismissed as a low-tech industry, namely, plastics. Keter Plastics, for example, is one of Israel's most successful exporters, nineteenth on the list between Motorola and ECI Telecom. In 2004, Israeli plastics as a whole exported about the same as the Israeli pharmaceutical industry did, about $1.5 billion. Keter alone had a sales turnover of $700 million, exported about $420 million in various products, and put up twenty-three factories worldwide, employing 3,500 people. The company CEO, Sami Sagol, predicted Keter would be a $3–$4 billion company by the end of the decade, competing successfully against a division of much larger companies such as Rubbermaid, which Keter offered $200 million to acquire. A childhood friend of mine, Sheldon Schreter, was an investor in another Israeli plastics company called ZAG, which made tool chests and other hardware; it, too, competed successfully against Rubbermaid and was finally acquired by Stanley Tools.

How can a lawn chair be considered a high-tech product, and why are Israelis so good at this kind of thing? Does the military provide certain competitive advantages Netanyahu fails to see? Here we get to the heart of how Israel's advanced businesses are really sustained. A plastic chair, you see, is made by a huge injection molding machine and corresponding robotics that can cost millions of dollars to get up and running. Any plastics company has to keep it running 24/7 for as much as two months a year just to pay the interest on the capital equipment.

But to keep the machines up and running, you need monitoring software and equipment to make sure PVC temperatures are just right, visioning software and equipment to make sure the chairs are coming off the line just so, scheduling software to make sure that the inventory of raw material is right. You need other scheduling software to make sure trucks will show up on time to cart chairs to the port, pick-and-place robotics software and equipment to make sure the chairs are prepared for shipping correctly, point-of-sale software and information to make sure you know how many of what color to make.

So plastics companies like Keter and ZAG need a highly integrated system of very expensive capital equipment wrapped in multiple envelopes of software. And they need small teams of problem-solving employees, accustomed to improvisation, comfortable when keeping such highly integrated systems up and running twenty-four hours a day. Getting all of this integration right is just table stakes in the plastics business, where companies all over the world can acquire and eventually learn to use the software and equipment. Real profit comes from design innovations—for instance, a lumbar support for the lower back—and getting the innovations into production (dyes, robots, etc.) faster than the competition. But this means getting ever more subtle customer needs reflected in designs and product offerings. It means managed information networks in place so that teams can know, not only how to do things more efficiently, but also about what customers want, or how many customers there are, or what the competition is doing. "Our secret weapon," Schreter told me, "was a guy who could put new designs together and get them into production better than they could. That was the whole difference between swimming or going under."

WHAT SCHRETER was really saying is that a chair or toolbox is not a static product. It is an evolving solution to a customer problem—the same kind of thing Check Point information-technology consultants sell. Again, technical know-how is critical to getting the offering into the customer's hands, but marketing know-about is critical to sustaining the business and engendering its growth. Profitability comes from being good at operational integration, but also from managing complex design processes, which means that employees know what customers need, and also how to work with one another under stresses of all kinds. Anything that can be made merely by some set of routines will be made profitably only where both labor is cheap and logistics and telecommunications are advanced, as in China. (This, by the way, is why Keter is slowly moving away from making lawn furniture and migrating to markets where knowledge of customer needs is ever more complex, for example, custom piping for large-scale construction and irrigation projects.)

Can Israelis innovate where competition in solutions is global? The answer is yes, though a qualified yes. Israel has many things going for it: Technical competence in various sciences allows for innovative ideas in medicine, telecom, the Internet, and all kinds of process technologies. And here is, as Netanyahu says, where defense technologies shine. But even more important, Israeli youth who spend several years in the IDF attend, in effect, a finishing school for the kind of team-based problem solving that sustains, for example, Keter's integrated operations. Keeping a massive injection-molding machine and its requisite software

raeli genius. Israeli capital is already voting with its wings. In 2006, Israelis invested more capital abroad (some $7 billion more) than global investors sent to Israel. Perhaps $100 billion total is invested abroad, and something like half of that is estimated to be the private fortunes of Israelis—not the capital needed to expand Israeli businesses.

MOST EDUCATED ISRAELIS have now figured all of this out, if only intuitively. Sure, economic freedom matters; an educated workforce matters; the IDF matters, though more to teach team skills than to create base technologies, which also derive from universities and advanced companies. But if Israel does not become a place where educated young Israelis want to live, the opportunities proffered by venture capitalists will not make Israel seem more attractive to them. Another war—or the revival of the intifada, which also would lead to a worldwide shunning of Israelis—will be another kind of horror. Direct investment by global corporations will taper off. Already, reports from Gaza suggest the development of missiles with a range capable of reaching Intel's five-billion-dollar complex in Kiryat Gat.

"In an industry like ours, a culture like ours," Check Point CEO Schwed told me, "people who think they are going to suffer here for long will go live someplace else." According to recent polls, nearly half of Israel's young people "do not feel connected" to the state, and a quarter of them "do not see their future" in the country. A 2006 study by IDC's Institute for Policy and Strategy (the Herzliya Conference group) found that 44 percent of young Israelis "would seriously think of leaving Israel if it would result in an improved standard of living abroad." Attitudes about emigration among youth from Russian immigrant families are even more discouraging. According to one study, from 2000 to 2004 the number of scientists leaving Israel increased by 6 percent annually. For its size, Israel is the largest exporter of brainpower to America in the world.[15]

So Netanyahu's model of an economy, driven by venture funds, is not a prescription for sustained growth, but for the acceleration of a disastrous brain drain. Over half a million Israelis already live in the United States. The working hypothesis among my friends is that a third of the children of educated Israelis are working abroad. Of the forty-five top-flight students I mentored at IDC's entrepreneurship program, fifteen are now working in the U.S. and England.

"The vital signs seem okay," Dov Frohman, now retired from Intel, told me recently, alluding to the macroeconomic data Netanyahu trots out at every opportunity, "but we are really in the dumps, socially, morally, culturally, everything." Frohman is not a natural pessimist. He is an extraordinarily gifted strategist who's seen it all. His parents were killed in the death camps, yet managed to save him by spiriting him to a courageous family in the Dutch countryside (with whom he is still in touch); after the war he came to Israel as an orphan immigrant. His jeans are a tribute to Berkeley in the sixties; his patience, to his stint as a teacher in Ghana; his white beard, to Tolstoy. His serenity, these days, comes from Eastern wisdom literature. Frohman was one of Intel's original employees. He was responsible for the invention of the EPROM, then for bringing Intel to Israel, and then for making the most advanced microprocessors. He flies a plane and rides a motorcycle for "fun"—his favorite, most deadly serious word.

"This is a drugged democracy, which is worse than a dictatorship, because in a dictatorship you try to rebel—and in this place you don't do anything. We need some kind of catalyst to get people to the streets. We need to start talking about social issues—and without generals doing the talking." But we cannot go back to Mapai's world, I countered; do we not have to continue with a process of globalization, which will help the lower strata only after it has precipitated growth? "By the time globalization would be in a position to help the lower classes, we'll have another intifada," Frohman said, his smile turning ironic. "Anyway, if I have a concern, it is really the younger generation, who will have to drive the process, and for the time being are without light in their eyes. People keep talking about security, and I wonder who will be left to give security to. Young people are saying, 'Why do I want to be here, if we are going to a global environment anyway?' Of course, you think you'll be better off and then you have adjustment problems, or your kids do. But this will continue in any case, and we are very vulnerable, because this is one of the worst countries to live in right now."

Worst countries? "You feel you are under life threat all the time. People move from Jerusalem to Tel Aviv, but Jerusalem is just a mirror of the country. I tell them, if you leave this city you might as well leave the country. Tel Aviv means you just put your head in the sand and say everything is okay. Most of the pleasures are fake. We do it in order to boost our spirits. Look at the Maccabiah Games, which brings Jewish athletes from around the world. When I was a kid, this was a big event; now all I know about it is that I couldn't play tennis because the courts were being used by the kids who came to compete. There is no real vitality. The Jewish Agency brings Jewish kids on the Birthright program. They go around in buses and wave flags and wear hats. But we shouldn't need this kind of fake, feel-good stuff by now. We should have our jazz festivals and other festivals bringing people here who are chasing their real passions. I don't believe in a step-function improvement, where nothing is happening and then all of a sudden everybody wakes up. Sharon was a very capable manipulator of public opinion, a good druggist."

THIS DID NOT sound like fun. Was there not something inspiring about globalization that a center coalition could rally the country to? "I think about who has tried to address the problems of global poverty and the sources of terrorism at the root, and I think of Tony Blair, who makes speeches that are then forgotten—and then the bombs go off in

London. It is very hard to focus on those things when you have the issue of terrorism distracting everybody, and with politicians like Bush and Sharon, and with Sharon claiming that we are here most experienced in fighting it. In Britain, they now want to start monitoring Internet transmissions. You keep talking about vision and here things are falling apart at the seams. You hope for America to intervene. But you don't see that Americans are tired of this direction. The talk is still about using force. The ground is very treacherous for someone who wants to create hope."

Netanyahu has a different view of this, I reminded Frohman. Can we not depend on the world coming to us for our technology? "This is bullshit. *Bullshit.* Investors will not come to us in a big way unless there is political stability. Personal and economic stability, or the hope of stability—a process. In the global economy, you don't only need Jewish investors, you need global investors. Investment is not colored with sentiment, and looks at the overall situation. What Bibi says is demagoguery. He's done some of the right things, which in a healthy environment would have been pretty good. But before these policies can have an impact, we'll have more violence. In this environment, big companies do okay and little independents do very badly."

But what about all the investment we have seen, even the uptick in the stockmarket? "There is a lot of financial type of investment but little production type of investment—there are investments which can be taken out at will. And in the meantime, we are losing our reputation as a place for global companies to pioneer. It's hard to restart the engine; five years of no investment means ten years of paying the price for no investment. And then what will make our entrepreneurs want to stay in Israel, if they don't have quality of life? There is continuous movement of people, they will want to stay elsewhere. More and more, companies can consult locally and can consult abroad; having more foreign companies here is still important, though in the long run we are going to have start-ups with problems here like everywhere else. But the really critical thing is keeping our people here. I don't need to do a poll to know that 50 percent of the young people would go."

FROHMAN'S IS HARDLY a voice in the wilderness. On the whole, Israel's savviest entrepreneurs know by now that Netanyahu is promoting a small part of truth. David Harman, the former head of education at the Jewish Agency, who has been trying to advance an entrepreneurial educational venture for the past couple of years, puts the matter even more bluntly: "If people think there will be political stability here, they will do business with you. If they don't, they won't. That's why most of the business community—[Nochi] Dankner [the retail magnate], [Dan] Propper [Osem Foods], [Dov] Lautman [Delta Galil], even the venture capitalists like Chemi Peres and Erel Margalit—are left of center. If Bibi is right that Israeli assets are in their heads, then those Israelis will take their heads elsewhere. There was a famous joke about why so many Jews played the violin, and the punchline was 'Try to move a piano.' That hasn't changed."

What about the army? Won't this continue to push the envelope in all kinds of technologies? "Most high-tech entrepreneurs come from certain intelligence units of the army, like *shmone mataim* [the 8/200 unit], just like Bibi says," Harman told me; "but people who know tell me the quality of the new recruits is not what it used to be. If Bibi thinks he can have high-tech geniuses and starve the school system, he's wrong. The universities are getting shafted. Tel Aviv University is on the verge of bankruptcy. Jerusalem's library no longer buys books. We were the beneficiaries of a good Soviet school system, and now the Russian immigrants are founding alternative schools, as in Kiryat Menachem in Jerusalem. But in Jerusalem, the country's largest municipality, 40 percent of the kids are Haredi, 30 percent are Arab, 15 percent are National Religious, and another 15 percent are in secular public schools. Where does Bibi come off bragging about where we get our brainpower?"

Harman might have added that under Netanyahu, the budgets of major Israeli research universities were cut 30 to 40 percent, and many of the funds were redirected to colleges, where standards have dipped appreciably. "My syllabus is shrinking all the time," Haifa University's Rafi Cohen-Almagor complains, "because students are running a kind of auction to get better grades for less work. They don't have to go to university now, they can go to any of the new colleges to get their first degree, and we, the universities can't get public money unless we keep the same number of students, which we cannot. So our budgets keep getting cut—we amalgamate programs and fire people. Haifa has a deficit of 40 million shekels. Everybody is banging on our president's table. Tel Aviv has a deficit of 140 million. No openings for new faculty. We have never had a crisis like this." Something like 4,600 Israelis are now on the faculties of American universities. (Since I spoke with him, Cohen-Almagor has taken a chair in politics at the University of Hull.)

CURIOUSLY, though Israel's entrepreneurial intelligentsia generally assume a connection between peace and wealth, and wealth and globalization, the idea that Israel might join Europe sooner rather than later, or begin with an economic union with Palestine and Jordan, does not come up much in public debate. A number of signal projects have taken shape, like the Jordan Valley development plan, promoted by Shimon Peres, which the Israeli government approved without fanfare in March 2007. (The project, if realized, will include a Red Sea–to–Dead Sea canal, a new airport, a rail link from Jordan to the port of Haifa, hydroelectric generation, desalination, a free-trade zone, new tourist facilities, and more.) But the country's élites are at best divided on the idea of joining anything.

I recall attending a 2003 Herzliya Conference session with EU ambassador Michael Leigh, who carefully laid out the conditions for Israel and its Arab neighbors to deepen ties to Europe. His criteria for a potential Mediterranean member were stringent, dealing with everything from technical standards in a common market to a political dialogue about individual rights and the judiciary. The audience, usually buzzing during the PowerPoint presentations, was attentive. Then the chairman of the session—as it happens, Uzi Arad—decided on a little spot poll. How many, he asked the audience of bankers, generals, government officials, entrepreneurs, professors—the several hundred people in the plenum—would like to see Israel in the European Union? Buttons were duly pressed on voting consoles next to every seat. Roughly half the audience said they were in favor of the idea. Arad was clearly taken aback by the size of the vote. But one might have been equally surprised that *only* half voted for the idea.

The Palestinian entrepreneurial intelligentsia is similarly uncertain about Europe, though more openly positive toward the prospect of federal arrangements with Israel than the Palestinian population as a whole. ("I just take it for granted," Palestinian entrepreneur Sam Bahour told me.) Businesspeople on both sides of the Green Line speak a cooperative language that peace activists on both sides—usually people of the left—cannot appreciate and don't do enough to promote. I have talked to Israeli entrepreneurs in Herzliya one day, then travelled the next day to speak with economists and businesspeople in Ramallah, and I've felt myself in a kind of twilight zone of mutual understanding, where the common task is economic union, both with the wider Arab world and the European community, and the common challenge is to hold on to one's educated middle classes. For both sides, the danger comes from extremists and the politicians who pander to them.

"HARD AS IT IS for us to accept this, we look West," Hisham Awartani insists, "not very far West, very close West." He means that Palestinians look to Israel. "The fantasists say, 'the Arab world,' 'the Islamic world.' 'Let's hook up with hundreds of millions of Muslims.' I say this is rubbish." In the summer of 2005 we were sitting in the Ramallah offices of Khalil Shikaki's Palestinian Center for Policy and Survey Research, surrounded by economic yearbooks, maps, and reports, in a conference room resembling that of a Western consulting firm. Awartani was giving me the elevator pitch—a social entrepreneur talking to yet another foreign writer in Palestine's most beautiful and prosperous town, unlike ruined towns such as Jenin. Awartani exuded the grizzled warmth of a teacher: poised, certain of his views, happy to enlighten me, accustomed to being ahead of his time. But one also detected a certain fatalism in his voice, something one feels particularly in liberal Palestinian circles—people like al-Salqan, Shikaki, and Awartani, people living free in a world of their own making. There is violence all around, and virtually nothing to protect them from assassination by "fantasists" (who, they knew even then, were poised to win the parliamentary elections). Yet there was a certain absolute pleasure to take in truths one can only call scientific. There was also an ironic humor almost any Diaspora Jew would immediately recognize.

"We were the builders, the *halutzim*"—here Awartani smiled at his own twist—"of the Arab world's economies. But we cannot count on Arabs for doing business. We will be happy to take their aid—and if we go down, we will not go down alone. But business is another matter." Can Palestinians not expect Arab investment capital? Awartani had a telling anecdote. "We went to talk to the boss of the Arab Bank, Abdal Majid Shuman—a delegation from the PA, about fifteen years ago—a very difficult man to see, sitting on billions and billions of dollars—a Palestinian from Beit Hanina—and we tried to sell him on development in Palestine. And he said to us, 'You young guys, I don't need lecturing on how to be a good Palestinian. But you say invest in Palestine, so I have to ask questions for which you don't have answers. If you say "charity," my checkbook is ready, just tell me a little more, for whom, what will be done. But when you say "invest," then I say I am custodian of other people's money, I have fiduciary responsibilities to my *own* investors.'"

Awartani internalized the lesson: "This is what I expect from the whole of the Arab world. And, by the way, trade is even more difficult, a big losing battle. Now 90 percent of our exports go to Israel. Before the intifada it was 75 percent! How can we be competitive in Jordan? I say 'West,' because this is where we trade and learn. Don't call it cooperation. That sounds too interactive for the facts on the ground. But okay, call it doing business. People say we have to call each other enemies. Fine, the world is full of examples where enemies do business."

So it is inconceivable, Awartani continued, that the fledgling Palestinian economy will fly without Israeli "complementarity," something that would be good for Israel, too. "We are major customers for Tnuva, Osem, Yakhin; there is no reason for them not to create food-processing plants in Palestine. Israelis cannot just get along on high tech. There are lower-tech businesses in which we can do business and put people on both sides to work—in logistics, coordination, even telecom. Israelis can outsource to Ramallah. And, my God, our oil is tourism. We could be the number-one tourist attraction in the world, hotels from West Jerusalem to Jericho. If the political climate would permit, we'd have tens of millions of Muslims coming to this country, partly out of curiosity, partly to salve their consciences. And health tourism, Arabs coming to Israeli and Palestinian hospitals. How can we do this without cooperation?" This would not just be a one-way street, Awartani insists. Israel could use Palestinian partners to sell to the Gulf states: "Do you want to do this secretly, sneaking in under the table, or close billion-dollar deals with Palestinian partners?"

I pressed the point: Was the implication of all this an economic union, even a single currency? "Very much so," Awartani immediately

broke in, as if waiting for the question. "What I cannot imagine is economic separation, at any level of animosity or bitterness. I cannot imagine that. We could both live comfortably without Jordan, but much
more comfortably with Jordan. Having separation, that would be the
stupidest mistake." And a joint currency? "We have one, a joint currency now. A Palestinian national currency? Very few sane Palestinians
call for a national currency."

I could hear skeptical Israeli friends asking, just whom does Awartani
represent? So I put their doubts to him. "Look, I live in Halabja, a small
kfar eight kilometers east of Tulkarm, twenty east of Netanya, a small
village—I am very close to the grassroots," he said. "Even without
Khalil's [Shikaki] polling, I can tell you 70, 80, even 90 percent would
go for very strong cooperation. Call it what you like—a 'customs
union'—what you like. It means capital flows, labor flows, accommo-
dated trade, tourism. The security issues have to be addressed. But you
Israelis only look at the people who are able to rock the boat. You don't
look at the 90 percent. Of course if we are going to encourage even
Palestinian investors, we have to marginalize the people who are able to
rock the boat. These people in Hamas and so on are not going away.
There will be no 100-percent security. So we have to try to erode their
influence with progress, coopt and contain them."

Later that day, I spoke with Samir Abdullah, the head of the Palestine
Economic Policy Research Institute, who echoed Awartani's view.
"Hamas has a nowhere program," he told me, drawing on a narghile
over lunch. "They flourish when no economic progress is going on.
There will be no obstacle for Israel to be an active partner in the area.
But it will not come the day after striking an agreement, it will take
some time. Anyway, 50 percent of Israelis came from Yeman, Iraq, Mor-
roco, Egypt, Iran—it will be for those people a chance to play a good
role, to advance economic relations, and make Israel a friend for every
country here. But this requires a good-quality peace, a peace that is

durable, and accepted not under pressure, but under international legitimacy, with no time bombs."

He puffed. "Most of the economic problem here is the result of manmade circumstances. The ILO [International Labour Organization] says we have around 26 percent unemployment. The reality is more like 40 percent, and more than 55 percent in Gaza. The cost of capital is the highest in the world, because of the high default rate in our banks, the unreliable court system, and everything else."

Abdullah finally asked himself the most basic question: Is there an economic solution to this political situation? "The answer is no. We will remain on shifting sands. Make the hand lighter, remove one checkpoint, and the economic result will be felt immediately. But it is not sustainable, because the next day, you will have something to make the light hand heavy again. As long as this atmosphere continues, investment will be bad. The private sector will not respond. Even donors will not be able to make investments work."

HAMAS—the fantasists—won the elections in January 2006. They have since taken over Gaza by force, putting Fatah forces to flight. Does this mean people like Awartani and Abdullah are finished? No.

Hamas has taken over a dense, caged, enraged population dependent on international charity. They can spook, but cannot destroy, what's left of the Palestinians' entrepreneurial middle class in the West Bank. Only Israel can do that. Sam Bahour told me that one of the first (and few) things the Hamas government did on the economic front after its election was award a telecom license, through an international competitive bidding process, to a Kuwaiti company, later bought by Qatari interests that do business with Israel. "They also changed the longtime sole Israeli supplier of petroleum products, Dor, to another Israeli company, Paz. Both of these actions were low-lying fruit, given the tremendous corruption in these sectors, much of which is still there. All the plans were in place to make these moves, but all previous governments refused to make them."

So the better question is this: If the outline of a peace plan between Israel and Fatah were agreed to—if a measure of stability could be re-introduced—would there then be Palestinians leading Palestine into economic integration with Israel? If peace came, would there be Palestinians who'd know what to do with it?

I spoke with Shikaki, who has been polling residents of the West Bank and Gaza for over a decade. Born in a Gaza refugee camp in 1953, educated in Beirut during the 1970s, Shikaki has been toughened by the bedlam. But if there was ever bitterness in his soul, it has been incorporated into a larger sense of tragedy. He earned a Columbia University Ph.D. in political science, focusing on statistical methods; he was once a marketing manager for General Motors in the Gulf. He returned to Palestine buoyed by Oslo—a Palestine from which his look-alike brother, Fathi, a founding leader of Islamic Jihad, had been deported. Fathi was eventually assassinated by Israeli forces in Malta in 1995. Shikaki will talk about this as if describing the loss of a loved one in a storm. The key, now, is to protect what reasonable people survived. The future is all calculated risk—better than the catastrophes of the past.

"Our most important divisions are socioeconomic," he said. "What will explode in our faces is *economic* disparities, especially the need to re-build what has become of Gaza. We could make a start on the refugee problem without a peace settlement. If we just built homes and offered long-term mortgages, we could empty the refugee camps here in a few years." The Fatah movement no longer commanded a majority any-where in occupied territory, he said, certainly not in Gaza. Hamas and other hard-line Islamist groups had at least an equal measure of their power. "We need massive construction projects in Gaza. Attitudes change very quickly among people who leave camps. Also more should come here to the West Bank—not by social engineering, but eventually market forces will help bring Gaza refugees here."

The complication for Fatah was the corruption of the PA under Arafat. Fatah came back from Tunis after Oslo and ran the PA as if a personal fiefdom, appointing friends and relatives. They created little in the way of services. Taxes were viewed as nothing but protection paid to bosses, who then formed larger militias. The Islamists, in contrast, made their reputations by flaunting absolute sacrifice, while governance mirrored the purity of the mosque. "If Abu Mazen [Abbas] and the Fatah show themselves able to deliver the goods, international aid, and so forth, this would elevate their reputations somewhat. If Gaza remains an impossible ghetto, who pays the price?"

Was there hope that Palestinian entrepreneurs would meanwhile remain? "The wall has been devastating to some people living in its vicinity, but for the class you are talking about, people who will have to make intelligent decisions about competition, about the family fortune, people upon whom Palestinian growth will depend, the wall has been a tremendous psychological blow. During the last ten years, many of these people came in here, put in time, effort, certainly money. Then all of a sudden, the interim arrangements collapsed. Many left. They have lost confidence in a peace agreement. The wall is telling them there will be no agreement for a long time to come. That political process is doomed, futile. Nothing new for at least ten years. With all of this on their minds, how can you get them to invest?"

But has there not been new activity since Arafat died? "That increased confidence at first. Just the smallest opening toward peace, and we reduced unemployment by 10 percent. We already have housewives investing in the stock market, which has doubled after four years of nothing. But there are limits. If we cannot remove the wall, at least we need to get back into talks. We need to arrange loan guarantees so the banks can turn around and approve loans. Maybe that will help people take some risks. But nothing like this will be sufficient. We need to end the closure regime. This is more important even than the wall. It makes it impossible for Palestinians to move around in the West Bank—it took me an hour to get to you today, a ten-minute trip. But Israelis are unwilling to end it. They say it is security, and they are unwilling to take any of the risks they took ten years ago. But our business class would come back if they could be persuaded that this process is on its way to resolution. We'd get some-body's hundred-thousand investment if there were loan guarantees, an-other hundred thousand if there were an end to closure. Then again, we won't get the million until he believes we are on the way to resolution. Nobody believes that it is, and the wall is their proof."

IT WAS HARD to see where bridges could be built. Could Israeli Arabs help, particularly with Palestinian entrepreneurs? "A significant part of the Palestinians would be willing to see Jewish settlers as part of the Palestinian state, so why would they not accept Israeli Arabs? But this cannot be a part of immediate peacemaking. We might see serious dis-cussion of this once the bilateral issue is resolved, once a decent politi-cal system is in place and economic conditions are not horrible. The issue becomes discussable within a certain context, in which Israel and Palestine have something close to open borders, when there is not a very hard separation. When both sides interact, leading to greater and greater demand for integration. But they cannot have closed borders and say, 'You are now on the other side of the wall.'"

Yet aren't Israeli Arabs Palestinians? "I think for most Palestinians, these are Palestinians like everybody else. But you have to see this in the context of a fragmentation that has either been forced on us, or has sim-ply been the way Palestinians have managed their lives. Jenin is Jenin, not Hebron or Tulkarm—there is a tendency to focus on your own area. National identity joins people together, but that is the limit. For people in border towns, there has been a tendency to see towns on both sides of the Green Line as one, and that has been very positive. But for most Palestinians there has been no interaction—very few have even met Israeli Arabs." And what of the Hebrew language? "Well, some serve in the Israeli army," Shikaki interrupted, "and at the moment, most think they are nationals of an Israeli state, not nationals of a Palestinian state."

Shikaki continued more reflectively. "They inhabit Israeli national institutions, not Palestinian," he said; "I cannot think of one Palestinian institution that includes them. There hasn't been an effort in that direction at all. Where we are focused is on cooperation with Israel, joint ventures—the overwhelming majority of Palestinians think this kind of thing is not only acceptable but desirable. Israeli Arabs make sense to us in that context. Even Jordan has more question marks about it than economic integration with Israel. West Bankers are positive about integration with Jordan, but Gazans like me have had more difficulty with the way Jordan has treated us in the past, so they are afraid of consolidating powers, but this is a perception that can be worked through. Most West Bankers realize there is a special relationship and want to build on it. The current regime is creating a positive environment and Arafat being gone doesn't hurt. Anyway, we've done the polls. Over 80 percent want a common market with Israel and Jordan."

I LEFT SHIKAKI and drove home to West Jerusalem thinking about how the phrase "open borders" simply rolled off his tongue. How could anything so pedestrian and obvious seem so grandiose? Two states, open borders, a common market, partnership with the EU—the works.

Then there were Israeli Arabs, who were caught in the middle, and no longer Palestinians in the ordinary sense. Would they wish to remain, of all things, citizens of a democratic state with an ineradicable Jewish character? Would Israeli Jews, for their part, ever accept them as a part of the Israeli nation?

CHAPTER 6

Hebrew Revolution

And over the years I also learned
to shed my skin.
Like a snake caught
between scissors and paper.
Thus was my fate sealed
in words cut from the roots of pain.
With a tongue forked
in two. One, Arabic
to keep mother's memory alive.
The other, Hebrew—on a winter's night
to love.

—SALMAN MASALHA,
"Sign of Scorpio" (translated by Vivian Eden)

With the important exceptions of nationalist Orthodox and Haredi folk, secluded in their spreading settlements and neighborhoods, nearly everybody in Israel—Ashkenazim, Mizrahim, Russians, and Arabs—is marinated in a popular Hebrew culture whose center is Tel Aviv. The English of international science and business is implanted here, yielding dozens of fertile hybrids. Younger Israelis are now accustomed to shuttling from nuanced Hebrew fiction to subtitled Hollywood movies, to the BBC, or a Lakers game; or from Mizrahi music, to sentimentalized Jewish holidays, to a Thai restaurant—and then to the beach. Israel's Arabs, naturally enough, feel pulled by proximate currents, particularly in the Arab world, and even if the Arab world is skeptical of them. Yet even if they watch Al Jazeera at night, most Israeli Arabs read *Yediot Aharonot,* the popular Israeli tabloid, over lunch. Surrounded as they are by pan-Arab claims, they do not just assimilate into Israel the way former shtetl Jews assimilated into New York City at the turn of the last century. But educated Arab citizens are already acculturated to something very Israeli, different from the old Arab *kfar,* or even their cities of origin. In a condition of peace, Israeli Arabs would be natural partners in developing Israeli enterprises in the Arab world.

Think again of Montréal Jews of my own generation, especially during the Quiet Revolution of the 1960s, connected as we were to the wider American continent, through McGill University, Anglo-American television, etc., but also deeply drawn to the world of *Cité Libre* intellectuals like Pierre Trudeau, not to mention to the hard-skating gods of the old Montréal Forum. Only imagine that Québec culture, not English culture, was our ticket to business and high technology. Hebrew's Jewish character would not, by itself, prevent Arabs from integrating into Israel, if culture were defined, as in Europe and Québec, in linguistic terms wedded to democratic freedoms. Hebrew would certainly not prevent Arabs from becoming genuine, if iconoclastic, citizens of the state. Rather, it would facilitate this.

You can feel the integration most fully in Israeli medical facilities, where Jewish and Arab doctors and nurses deliver treatment, interchangeably, and without discrimination, to any patient. You can feel it in restaurants and tourist facilities, where Jews and Arabs work side by side. When the soccer team from Sakhnin, a team with both Arab and Jewish stars, won the Israel Cup a few years back, Arab youth in the grandstands spontaneously unfurled Israeli flags. Nobody could fully explain the layers of affiliation or spite beneath this act, but nobody doubted its significance.

IRONICALLY, this integration is the inadvertent product of what the original Zionists most intended. They wanted a society of Hebrew-speaking mutts who, in building a national home, would revolutionize the Jewish people. To be sure, they wanted this for themselves, and did not expect Arabs to join. They were swept up by enlightenment ideas and enlightenment heroes, and Zionist writers often saw Arabs as quaint figures on the landscape who, as Sidra has written, were incarnations of their own ancient biblical selves.[1] Pioneers wanted to build a new kind of society, in which Jews would embody socialist realism. But they did not expect the Arabs simply to disappear. They knew the Arab community would, in the words of Ahad Haam, the most original Zionist of all, "not easily give up its position."

I know that most who speak of Zionism these days immediately think, not of cultural revolution, but of anti-Semitism. They assume a movement of Jews who believed they could never quite assimilate in the West, because liberal emancipation was failing there. This Zionist narrative begins, as Israeli television's semiofficial documentary *Pillar of Fire* begins, with images of Alfred Dreyfus being stripped of his epaulets. The narrative ends, as the documentary does, with grim scenes from death camps and stirring footage of Haganah refugee ships dropping their desperate cargo into Tel Aviv's baptizing surf. The not-quite-consistent corollary of this narrative is that while seeking and despairing of emancipation, Europe's Jews were also looking to express their two-thousand-year-old religious pietism. As the narrator of *Pillar of Fire* intones, the "yearning and hope for the return to Zion were the secret to the Jews' survival." They "did not need Herzl to tell them that this was the Jewish state, the Promised Land," since "every page of the Bible bore witness to it."

Actually, when Ahad Haam first visited Jewish colonial Palestine in the early 1890s, he stuck to the farms on the coastal plain and reluctantly visited Jerusalem, which appalled him. "I found many of our brothers," Ahad Haam writes, when he finally visited the Wailing Wall, "residents of Jerusalem, standing and praying with raised voices—also with wan faces, strange movements and clothing—everything befitting the appearance of that terrible wall. I stood and watched them, people and wall, and one thought filled the chambers of my heart: these stones are testaments to the destruction of our land. And these men? The destruction of our people."

AHAD HAAM, whom Weizmann called "our Gandhi," was the pen name for Asher Ginzberg, who lived in the 1880s and '90s in Odessa, the cosmopolitan port from which most desperate Eastern Jews embarked for New York or Hamburg. (Ahad Haam means "one of the people.") His distant hero was, of all people, Herbert Spencer, the intellectual lion of Victorian England, whose sociology of language and Darwinist conception of nations enduring were all in vogue. He took an organic view of the Jewish people, wired together by Hebrew, struggling for existence, competing on sophistication.

Ahad Haam argued for a "spiritual center" in the national home, which would revive the Diaspora. Some take this to mean a big theological seminary, which would send homilies and moral heroes to the West. Critics of Zionism with Orthodox leanings—most recently, former Knesset speaker Avrum Burg—claim that the spiritual center actually valorized Jewish religious values, which are better than, and prior to, anything the Zionists came up with. Western critics sympathetic to Palestinian claims—Jacqueline Rose, again—claim Ahad Haam as the prophet of a transcendent liberal vision, which has been betrayed by Zionist political actions in the land. But these idealized versions of his spiritual center are fairly misguided. Ahad Haam, in the tradition of

Spencer's sociology, was actually a radical activist. Spirit was the product of material efforts: As his disciple, the founder of the kibbutz movement, A. D. Gordon, put it, the spiritual—that is, secular Jewish culture—would rise from Hebrew labor the way butter rose from milk. Zionism, then, entailed science, self-reliance, newness. It also meant, as Ahad Haam wrote in 1897, many generations, "a growing settlement of Jews working without hindrance in every branch of culture, from agriculture and handicrafts to science and literature."

Ahad Haam did not immediately conceive of a state. But he argued strenuously for colonial settlements that would eventually lead to a state. He mentored Weizmann during the negotiations over the 1917 Balfour Declaration. He wanted a "Hebrew national atmosphere"—a congenial space for individual Jews to freely work out custodianship of their past. He inspired the founding of the Bezalel Academy of Art and Design and the Hebrew University. This process of nationalizing Jewish life finally culminated in the 1940s. In Amos Oz's memoir of his Jerusalem childhood, *A Tale of Love and Darkness,* he writes retrospectively about what Ahad Haam wrote prospectively: "Like so many Zionist Jews of our time, my father was . . . embarrassed by the shtetl and everything in it . . . He wanted us all to be born anew, as blond-haired, muscular, suntanned Hebrew Europeans, instead of Jewish Eastern Europeans."

This Zionism meant, finally, a Jewish people in a healthy dialogue with non-Jews. Zionists, unlike Diaspora Jews, would not assimilate into Western nations but would emulate what was best in Western modernism. Ahad Haam projected this future by revisiting the past:

Long before the Hellenists in Palestine tried to substitute Greek culture for Judaism, the Jews in Egypt had come into close contact with the Greeks, with their life, their spirit, and their philosophy: yet we do not find among them any pronounced movement towards assimilation. On the contrary, they employed their Greek knowledge as an instrument for revealing the essential spirit of Judaism, for showing the world its beauty, and vindicating it against the proud philosophy of Greece.

Hebrew was a transcendental instrument. Like Emerson, Ahad Haam edited and mentored a generation of writers and activists who created the new country's DNA: not only Gordon, but Eliezer Ben-Yehuda, the creator of the modern Hebrew dictionary; Weizmann, the national home's first great diplomat; the poet H. N. Bialik; the writer Shmaryahu Levin; even, indirectly, David Ben-Gurion, who founded the Histadrut in the 1920s. Weizmann wrote: "We were the spokesmen of the Russian-Jewish masses, who sought in Zionism self-expression and not merely rescue."[2] It is Zionism's singular tragedy that all of these people are just street names in Israel today, while the term *Zionism* is applied to hilltop settlers with Uzis, flowing forelocks, and visits from Pat Robertson.

"AHAD HAAM WAS a genius, and he is not read properly to this day," a former member of the Knesset told me recently. "He was on to something interesting, really interesting: He understood without too much nationalizing the importance of keeping culture and national identity for the safety of the collective—actually, for self-interest, for the individual development of each member of the collective—that there is no contradiction between liberal values and the collective, that for the individual to develop in the right way, we need the collective. I read most of what he wrote, I am speaking about twenty-five years ago, but I am coming back to it now."

Actually, the Knesset member in question is none other than Azmi Bishara, now in self-imposed exile from Israel. How could his admiration for Ahad Haam's Zionism explain, of all things, that prospects for Arab integration in Israel were dim? His answer brings to mind Gandhi's quip, that while fighting for self-determination from England, he never forgot how he had learned the principle of self-determination *from* England.

"The issue is collective memory," Bishara insisted; "Jews have a nationality here built on the guidelines of language and common Israeli experience—not just language, but uniforms, settlements, history, heroes, whatever. It is a whole collective memory, a feeling of common destiny that unites people together in one nationality. If there is a new Hebrew nationality, distinct from world Jewry—even if this were possible—am I going to be part of it? If we had one nation built on citizenship, like the United States, that's something else, I would be part of that. It would called 'Hebrew-Arab' or 'Israeli' or something. But if you say the Zionist project is done, and the nation is built and could include us—well, the Zionist project was not *meant* to include us."

Obviously, the problem for Israeli Arabs who might otherwise admire original Zionism's psychological subtlety is that it won. Ahad Haam's ideal of rebuilding a broken Jewish people required Hebrew colonial self-segregation. The very institutions that have been excluding Palestinian Arabs since the turn of the twentieth century are what permitted the foundation of a modern, emancipated Hebrew community to take shape in contiguous Jewish settlements—settlements that refused to hire Arabs; settlements created by the Histadrut, the Jewish National Fund, the Jewish Agency.

But what if citizenship could be made more inclusive and a Hebrew-speaking nation could evolve without the activities of Zionist organizations? What if a pluralist Israeli model could develop, in which Zionism remained, to use Bishara's term, "folkloric," but Zionist institutions were retired, a constitution was passed, and Arabs, Russians, and others could integrate in their own ways and at their own pace? Bishara, intrigued, was mostly skeptical. "Some Arab citizens would try to quit their identity and try to become Jews, living individually in the Jewish city," he said; "some would opt for Islamic fundamentalism." But was there no cultural middle ground for Israeli Arabs? In the best of all possible worlds, would there not be a common market and some kind of transnational relationship between Israel and Palestine? Bishara did not condemn the vision. His body language implied that talking about the the best of all possible worlds was a waste of his time. "I can identify with a federative system," he told me; "I see no future without it. But even in the best of all possible worlds, it may be too late for merging two national consciousnesses." Why too late? Because the Naqba destroyed the educated, bourgeois leadership of Arab towns, Bishara insisted. Rebuilding Arab life would require rebuilding them, "with a separate Arab university, or a separate technical facility." The key was to nurture, as old Zionism had, a separate Arab collective.

But *now* who was being Panglossian, I asked him? Was not the retreat of educated Arabs into their towns pretty much impossible? Would not the most ambitious Israeli Arabs be drawn (indeed, like kibbutz children) to cities where Israeli citizenship and Hebrew nationality become pretty much the same thing? To this, Bishara had no answer. Then he grew conciliatory. "People like you and me," Bishara said, "like to see people living together, transcending national differences. We think the act of transcending these differences will make our individual lives richer. We are the people who liked Cassius Clay and didn't know why. But if we go deeper into the details, we have to say only that we *hope* to succeed. Because we don't know, we don't know. At the same time, we can be more realistic here than, say, South Africans, because we know the national differences that are already here. What we can do is transform one side, the state, into Hebrew-speaking and democratic, instead of Jewish, and transform the other into local Arab, instead of pan-Arab." Were not the two transformations just a matter of calling the grass green, I asked? "Don't forget I once ran for Israeli prime minister," he said and winked.

———

SOME YEARS AGO, I attended a seminar at Tel Aviv University celebrating the founding of the journal *Historia*. The American ambassador to Israel, Thomas Pickering, delivered in flawless Hebrew a paper on Jefferson's principles of liberty. Ahad Haam, I suspect, would have wept. Bishara would have smirked. But I cannot think of the prospects for Israeli Arab integration without thinking of that moment, the pride of place, the sense of possibility—Hebrew as the culmination of Jewish modernism.

"When I was a child," Danny Rubinstein, *Haaretz*'s veteran Palestine correspondent, told me, "we used to shout in demonstrations, 'Free immigration, a Hebrew state.' Jewish meant Diaspora. Hebrew meant our thing here. Zionism's real achievement... So Hebrew means 'native' to me, and it conjures up all the old movement politics. Ben-Gurion wasn't sure what to call the state, perhaps Judea, something like that, and he finally landed on Israel, which had a vaguely local connotation, even allowed for such anomalies as Israeli Arab. It could mean citizenship, or at least the concept of citizenship was sunk in it."

Had things changed? "A kind of reactionary Diaspora Jewish cast has taken hold, and it has justified our committing all kinds of terrible discriminatory practices, here and in the West Bank. A settler who is an American citizen—not even Israeli—lives next to an Arab village and gets social insurance. He carries his citizenship with him on his back, it seems, the way Diaspora Jews had carried the homeland. The law says social benefits go to anyone who is Israeli or eligible to become Israeli under the Law of Return."

And yet Hebrew society is still resilient, and Arabs are a part of it, Rubinstein says. "This isn't Canaanist determinism, as some once hoped it would be. Hebrew culture is more conscious of its Jewish roots in a positive way, return to the Tanach, Ben-Gurion's mythology, even as it remains eclectic, full of English. Archaeology was once a cult here among Jews. Come to my daughter's archaeology department, and you find it is half Arab. Arabs once didn't learn this, because they thought they didn't have to. They didn't need to find the evidence of Herod to think this was their place. They're more interested in digging now."

Then there is Tel Aviv. "It is a fantastic place, fantastic," publisher Yehuda Meltzer told me, "in a way, our only place." We were sitting at his favorite diner on Basel Street, Tel Aviv's SoHo, and the smell of the sea was strong over lentil soup. "In America you have a primitive president and a queer fundamentalism, but you also have fantastic culture, fantastic science, fantastic media—my daughter every week plugs herself into the Internet to listen to *This American Life* from Chicago Public Radio. Even if your world is run by Halliburton, you can still live on the margin. Anyway, Tel Aviv is our *only* margin." Meltzer, a Columbia-trained philosopher, runs Sifrai Aliyat Hagag, "Books in the Attic." He was prescient enough to have bought exclusive rights to the Harry Potter series, which has made him something close to rich. So he has made up his mind to translate and publish every Western classic he can. He might live anywhere, and spends a good deal of time in Greece. But nothing compares to his own Hebrew metropolis.

"Israel is superdeveloped," he says, "and we are seeing a transformation in the daily habits of the kids. No paper, only screens. The benign imperialism of America is a real challenge: For kids, life begins with *le-enter*, and goes to *le-delete*. It is hubris to predict what this will do. But the Internet and messaging only reinforce the intimacy of the city. Apart from the fact that Tel Aviv University is stupidly placed out in the periphery of the city, the intimacy leaves you wondering if the makers of the culture are after all not a close-knit club. It seems that everybody's parent was a kibbutznik with an unpublished manuscript in the drawer.

"It's an exciting readership we have," he adds. "When I published a new version of *The Master and Margarita*—and we are way over 30,000 sold—I went to the theater and the usher was reading our translation. I said, 'Aren't you Russian; why read it in Hebrew?' She said, 'I am also

Israeli now and want to see how Bulgakov works in Hebrew.' I hugged her. Another person I met in the market, a Druze Arab, was following our classics series, and he told me, 'You know, of all of the philosophers, I was most impressed by David Hume.' You don't do this for the money! This kind of thing gives life!"

Is so much energy a threat to some? "The openness cuts in all kinds of ways. The Haredi who hate Israeliness had better watch out for child number six, or twelve, or their women, whom they will no longer be able to control any more than Arab families can. You can't subject the Orthodox women to poverty and sexual frustration, generation after generation, and get away with it. The borders are open. *Open.* The only question is how much Hebrew will itself be a border." Does an open border make Israel an easier place for Israeli Arabs, too? "Definitely," Meltzer says. "It is easier to come to a place that promises a bridge to the world of English science and business, and not only to the smaller Jewish world. But it also makes the people who are afraid of this kind of thing more fanatic. The enemy, say the people in the settlements now, is Israeliness. And they are right. The cultural borders are open—they are *open.* For them and for us."

TO MOST ISRAELI Jews, granted, the idea of Arab assimilation into a Hebrew-speaking Israel seems silly. Why would anyone join the club that has you for a member? And many abroad consider the very term *Israeli Arabs* an Orientalist fantasy. "Why," as one irate *Harper's* reader complained about an article of mine in a letter to the editor, "would [Israeli] Palestinians entertain the persistence of Hebrew as a national language when their own language has been historically marginalized?" Was this not more of the "venerable tradition of colonialist thinking"?[3]

I am sitting again in Caffit, the landmark café in the German Colony a few blocks from my home, with the writer Sayed Kashua. It is Friday morning, the beginning of a Jerusalem summer weekend, and the place is buzzing with people catching up with one another. Sayed, for his part, is not having a good day. There are too many sleepless nights with his baby son, too many deadlines, too much Scotch, and now someone is pressing him to speak about the process of acculturation. "Here I am," he says (we are speaking Hebrew), "sitting on Friday morning, drinking coffee I do not like, in a place I have no connection to, but have to pretend I have a connection to, instead of drinking mint tea, or real coffee, and smoking a narghile, with *real* friends." He spies me sharply, to see if his fake confession of fakery has made a dent, pleased with himself.

"We went to a luxury hotel in Tiberius," he tells me, catching me up; "twelve hundred shekels for one night. The woman behind the desk could not have been sweeter. She told us before we left to be a little careful, though, because there were Arabs about. I thanked her. My daughter said, 'Some Jews don't like Arabs and some do, right?' 'Right,' I said. 'And some Arabs don't like Jews and some do.' 'Right,' I said. Then I had a whiskey." He pauses. "Even my daughter," Kashua continues, "will always play a role. You can be friends, like I was in high school, with the children of lawyers and teachers. But you always play this role, you are this anthropological curiosity, something to relax their conscience. It stings. Israeli friends—they don't have a clue, usually. They don't know how to be not 'for' me and Najaf, not 'against' me and Najaf." "You hate *me,* too?" I ask, half-seriously. "A bit," he answers, more than half-seriously.

Fine, I say, isn't it most likely, as between whites and blacks in the U.S., that social integration will happen first among educated Jews so committed to liberal politics that they can't stop thinking about Arabs as means to that end?—"But you don't want these people in your neighborhood," Kashua interrupts—"Yes I *do,*" I interrupt back. "But that's because you just want to live in the country that accepts that most everybody is odd," he says. "That's about right," I say. I had bought Kashua Philip Roth's *The Human Stain,* about a black man passing for white and Jewish. He stayed up all night finishing it. Now he turns serious, warm. "Look, I read all the Israeli writers, Yehoshua Canaan, Sami Michael, Yoram Kaniuk, David Fogel, or the older generation, Aaron Megged, Benjamin Tammuz, writers from the other side, even Amos Oz. But also Jewish writers from outside the country. Then again, I don't always know who is Jewish. *The Metamorphosis* is one of the first things I read. I loved Kafka, a lot, then I found out later he was Jewish. One of the first novels I read was Saul Bellow's *Herzog* in Hebrew translation. Then I bought all his books. I felt that Jews like Bellow understood me, understood what it means when you're a minority. I loved Primo Levi, now I love Zadie Smith—is she Jewish? Arab literature is full of stories of lost empire. The Arabs say, 'We were once great and now have been brought low.' The Jews say, 'Once we were slaves, now we are free.'"

"LOOK, I AM not suffering that much. Sometimes I even enjoy being..." Kashua is thinking. "Enjoy being what?" I ask. He gives up. "Look, I don't have a problem, really. When people really know me. The restaurants, the bars, the friends, the work. But how many Arabs can do the same thing as I'm doing? Maybe a hundred families. They do it for their kids—speaking Hebrew without an accent. I send our daughter to a mixed kindergarten. Not to be Jewish, not to be equal—no way. Just to hide and not be recognized. And save our ass, if there is danger. I always think of her someday stepping in and saving us, with her perfect Ashkenazi accent." Actually, it is a Sephardi accent, I correct him. I demonstrate the Ashkenazi. "Oh, you're right," Kashua says; "if she spoke that way, *we'd* kill her!"

"But you get it," he continues. "I can't lie to her about equality. But you'll find it easier to find your way, find your profession, make friends, we tell her, if you learn their culture. Of course this might all be a big mistake. The great Hebrew accent could be some other reason to get killed, say, if she winds up in some refugee camp in Jordan, and the rest of the people in the camp hear how well she speaks." He is laughing. "I used to have a nightmare of waking up in the Palestinian Authority. I'm over it." Why nightmare? "Come on," he says, getting a little impatient with the devil's advocacy. "The issue, especially for me, obviously for me, is freedom of expression. To write what I want. Even here I don't write everything I want. But over there? Most are also afraid of the economic consequences of this. They are afraid of losing social insurance, and the like. The work. It's not so much the democracy. We don't feel we really live in a democracy. The courts here treat Arabs not so much better than the courts treat everybody in Saudi Arabia. And if Ramallah became a high-tech center, with social insurance, many more Israeli Arabs would be carrying Palestinian flags. But, face it, the Arab world is not so amazing that we want to be a part of it. Be part of Egypt, or Jordan, or Syria? Come on. If a new colonial government like Britain's showed up, to run courts, run things—not grab land, but just run things—it would be easier to get used to than the alternatives."

Actually, I said, I could well imagine Ramallah as a high-tech center a decade from now. "Then a lot of Jews would be marrying Arab girls and moving there," Kashua says. "But for Ramallah to get to the stage Herzliya is today, it would need Zionist vision, and we don't have that!" Then he is serious again: "My daughter could never be a part of a Palestinian state. She'll never even visit there growing up, unless she'll be a journalist—or a leftist. If she'd visit there she'll be seen as coming from Mars, perhaps as the daughter of collaborators. She'll feel that her very walking is strange, that her movement and clothes don't fit the society. She'll feel that she'll never know how people around her think—actually, the same things she'll feel in Israel. Still the nuances of nationalism are all different. Say 'the homeland' in Arabic the way you mean it in Hebrew and, *oy-yoy-yoy.*"

This was my opening. What does it really feel like to flip on that Hebrew switch? Kashua answered more slowly: "Look, on the one hand
this is the language of the enemy, the conqueror. And yet this is the
language that means a kind of freedom for me, more freedom. There
are things I can write about in Hebrew that I cannot write about in
Arabic. I can swear in Hebrew, which are often Arab words, but have an
entirely different nuance in Arabic. I am not sure I could write about relations with women in Arabic, which would give the descriptions an
entirely different status. I need Hebrew to write about freedom. There
are words that are precious to me that I know only in Hebrew. Stories
about sex, or honor—completely different meaning in Arabic. I once
saw a part of my story translated into Arabic on an Internet site. Wow,
I thought, I'm a *bad* boy. Or talk about God and society. Nothing to be
done. It's easier in Hebrew. I don't have an *abba,* a father, as in Hebrew. I
say 'father' in Hebrew and the word loses its sacred quality."

Honor, sex, and freedom, I sum up—"and religion," Kashua com-
pletes the summary. "Religion is not only about dogma and lessons." Is
this sense of personal freedom just for writers, or for Israeli Arabs in
general? "Tell an Arab he's a son of a whore in Hebrew, then tell him in
Arabic, and you'll get your answer."

Kashua's face is suddenly less playful. He is looking over my shoul-
der, through the window, while three Jerusalem police are, as if on cue,
interrogating a couple of obviously intimidated young Arab workers.
"Of course, Hebrew is also a language for apologizing, asking, supplicat-
ing, making nice. You don't debate in Hebrew. You address people bigger than you. This kind of thing warps you. That's one reason why in
Arabic, the word for freedom is a word you learn in demonstrations. It
does not mean the liberty to have a weekend in Tiberius." And yet, day
to day, "most like this country, and can't stand the Arabs from the West
Bank and Gaza—they see them as separate, and have grown up with

this. Sure, there is the discrimination, but not to the point of raising the question, Who am I, and what am I?"

MANY OF KASHUA'S childhood friends, from his hometown of Tira, resent him for his position in Israeli culture. He writes a bad-boy column in *Haaretz*, television screenplays, novels. But then Tira itself is a cultural hybrid, Arab entrepreneurs and Hebrew signs—people speaking Arabic sentences broken by Hebrew phrases, a forty-minute drive from Tel Aviv's nightlife.

Nor is Kashua unique in the Israeli Arab élite—and who knows how far beyond it? Honor, freedom, religion, sex, fathers—again and again, I have spoken with Israeli Arabs for whom these things have been made discussable in Hebrew as never before. They are loath to give up the liberty even as they condemn the bigotry. For Aziz Haidar, a fellow at the Van Leer Jerusalem Institute, the matter is practical: "This language, which has been forced on us, is a tool, with no particular connection to religion, the way Arabic was used by Christians. You learn social work in it. But it has an effect nevertheless on the shape of a person's mind. And Palestinians or Arabs from elsewhere notice this immediately. When Israeli Arabs speak about family, or political parties, or social organizing, or democracy, or human rights, immediately they are seen as Israelis. Israeli Arabs see a difference between Israeliness and Jewishness; indeed, they want to participate in creating this. They see being modern, which they get by means of being Israeli."

There is an irony here, Haidar says. "It is Israeli Arabs who are most strident in their insistence on the liberal democratic state, and so are the guardians, in a way, of classical Zionism. There has been a strong trend toward Israeliness among Arabs since the 1980s. Nothing could be clearer. Not just citizenship, but culture. Israeli Arabs are more Israeli, say, than the new *olim*, the Jewish immigrants from Russia.

"The irony is important, but so is the appreciation of irony itself," Haidar said. "We Israeli Arabs don't have our own Arab literature that celebrates irony. We write as Israelis now, though to do so is very painful. And after Oslo, we began to notice a new tone in the Israeli Arab community. Of irony turning to cynicism. As if there is nothing real, and nothing to hold sacred." There is something ominous about this. "They, Israeli Arab kids, are becoming more and more Tel Avivniks in their manner. Go to a nightclub. So many are Arab kids who are going out to hang out. Go to the sea, or the Kinneret [Sea of Galilee]— they are trying to push the situation away, to forget, no politics. Once we wouldn't miss a newscast. Not today. Too much cynicism."

Danny Rubinstein sees the same trend and wonders how any Arab can cope with it. "In the same way airplanes don't show movies about airplane crashes, the Arab world still cannot play episodes of *Seinfeld*. To watch *Seinfeld* in Saudi Arabia or Kuwait is like watching a movie about a plane crash while riding in a plane. That is the most antifamily program you can find in the world. They make fun of parents. Parents are old. No children. Free sex. No responsibilities. It is the Arab world's nightmare. They don't want this freedom or want to see it. But any young Israeli—Jew or Arab—now laughs along with it."

THE NIGHTMARE, like all nightmares, can be a kind of dream come true. Giath Nasir is a young lawyer who represented the residents of Sheik Sayed who were fighting the wall being erected through their town. "When Arab citizens in Israel hear the term 'Jewish and democratic,' well, it bothers people, but it feels like a fact of life. They interpret this to mean, ideally, a democracy which happens to have a majority of Jews. But if you tell them they live in a state named after the language of one of the sides, it doesn't have a good ring. Then again, 'Jewish state' seems to evoke the religion of one side, so this contradicts the principle of separating religion and state, which they support."

What, I dare, of the phrase *Hebrew republic*? "If this really means republican ideas—well, these are excellent, universal—they mean that we should be a state of real equality, religion, race, sex, orientation, a state of its citizens, just like every other democratic country. The issue of land purchase and residency remains a big incitement. I refuse to be treated worse than a Turk in Berlin. But the vast majority of Arabs are still inclined to go for equality, full equality. Let me preserve my lands and property. And stop allowing people who come here to have more rights than I do the minute they land—chosen people, and all that propaganda. This deeply offends the Arab community."

Nasir is from a minority within a minority—one of 120,000 Arab Christians, who disproportionately earn advanced degrees. How did he make it? "I was born in Kfar Samiyeh, in the north, a mixed town of Druze, Christians, and Muslims, who had been refugees. Then I went to Arab regional high school, mainly with Druze, and focused on study, trying to ignore what was going on around us. Hebrew was the bridge language; if we needed to understand an English word, it was translated in Hebrew, or understand a mathematical concept—again, Hebrew. My Hebrew was good before I got to Hebrew University in 1994."

Did he feel that Hebrew ushered him into a different world? "My father was a poet, a writer, many books on the Arabic language. When you say language is a world of its own, I know this very well. But in the case of Arabic and Hebrew, I don't really feel like the world is so different, not like an Englishman going to France, say. Many of the root words are the same, and the root structure is the same—both from the same Semitic source—even the most basic things. Same letters, same pronunciation. *Boy, mother, father,* the same—it's just easier to take this in than in any other foreign language. *Herut,* freedom, like *horia.* It doesn't feel that foreign. I started listening to the news in this language. So I never felt anti."

Yes, but doesn't *herut* make you think of a peculiarly Jewish and collective form of emancipation? How can Arabs appropriate such nuances, or not be changed by them? "This is complicated, because Arabs are really a fragmented society, which is partly the result of deliberate policy. In the North, we speak Hebrew fluently but speak mainly Arabic, and people are offended when you struggle for words and then settle on a Hebrew word. But the Druze of the North speak Hebrew in their homes. The government cultivated Druze separately, when all they are, really, is a Palestinian Arab group with a distinct religion. But am I changed? When I travel to Amman, through Jordan, I see Palestinians who don't have what to eat, without teeth, whose skin is turned yellow from smoking cigarettes, whose eyes are hollow. Blocks of cement without plaster, let alone electricity. This is 2005. Then you go to Amman and see the villas. You are hard put to find such conditions in the West Bank, and nothing like this in Israel.

"SO WHEN YOU say *liberty* in English, or *herut* in Hebrew," Nasir said, "you are speaking about basic material conditions that Arabs have not attained yet. It has no real meaning to the Arab people. Arab lands have always been conquered—Syria, Lebanon, Turks. My grandfather tells how the Turks conscripted him to fight somewhere near the Black Sea, and he returned with a crippled body. Nobody had the slightest freedom to state their views. Older people still live with paranoia. My grandfather still tells me to keep quiet, he still lives in the era of fear. Does that answer your question?"

It did not, really, but it answered a better one. Did Nasir, then, think that personal freedom is more developed among Israeli Arabs than in other Arab countries? "People are still not quite used to it. Liberty is still hard for them to accept. And it is not easy to demand. In Tel Aviv–Yafo, we still have a problem with street signs not being written in Arabic. So there was a Supreme Court case demanding Arab signs, which was won. But the case quickly became symbolic: Why don't you recognize us, why are we not part of this? I asked the presiding judge involved, why not have laws stipulated in Arabic? Don't we want Arab citizens to embrace the law? An Arab cannot go to the Internet and read the law easily."

So why not become part of a Palestinian state? "Israeli Jews think, You see, things are so much better for them here, so what are *they* complaining about? But these people were born and raised in the state—not just the land, the state. This is *their* country. We are all firmly opposed to being annexed by another Arab country. Why? Because Arab countries are not built on democratic principles. Everything there is 'father and son.' The father is the boss. That's Arab regimes. You get orders from the top, like the father in the family. It is true that we don't have full democracy here—it is not the Garden of Eden. But it is clearly the lesser of two evils. Here we can at least be individuals.

"Palestine is building democracy—a judicial system, elections," Nasir reflected, "but democratic tradition, that takes a few generations. Not something you do in an instant. Look at Iraq—no democratic culture, no sense of the other's view, or of toleration. This means education from the earliest years. We will not give this up, for all of what the state does to us. We cannot forever depend only on the Supreme Court, but at least there is that."

I asked Nasir the inevitable question. Two-thirds of Israeli Arabs were, like him, born in Israel. How many of them thought like him? "Academic people certainly have the same view, and understand their freedoms here very well. They will not give them up. The Arabs of '48, as they are called, were famous for their assimilationist tendencies. Learn the language, show your good intentions. So Palestinians, and the Arab world, see us as traitors: 'Why don't they struggle against the conquest?' Palestinians in the territories generally cannot seem to get over this attitude. 'You are all free, and we have the checkpoints, the curfews.' That's another reason not to join a Palestinian state. Put, say, the people of the triangle into this state and they'll be a new minority, resented, the butt of anger. And why should we contemplate this? Because of the 'demographic problem'? Arabs cannot stand this phrase. We see Haredi families having seven, ten children. Doesn't this eventually mean the imposing of Halakha on others? But they are counting our children. This is a purely racist claim."

Okay, I said, but when Arabs say, "This Hebrew culture is not mine," don't they leave Israeli Jews no choice but to count heads? "Yes, this is true," Nasir said, finally. "We can't say, 'Give us the rights,' and then reject what is in common. But I think that this will change when people start living the same way. Equally. Your rights are my rights. No danger from one another. Look at the Christian community in this country. Much more secular, rights for women, like any normal country. Then we would really have something in common. But culture cannot be imposed. When people feel on the defensive, they will not accept what they would take in freedom."

SOME ISRAELI things would be hard for Arabs to take, no matter what the freedom. Israel will inevitably, understandably accommodate the national holidays and symbols of the Jewish majority. But how could any Arab citizen be expected to sing a national anthem that declares, as "Hatikva" declares, that the Jewish soul has yearned for return during "two thousand years" of exile? Once again, the draft constitution prepared by the Adalah Institute calls for remaking the symbols of the state in legislative committees, where Jews and Arabs would have equal representation. But then, how could any Jewish citizen of the state accept this kind of solution, where four-fifths of the population would agree to award the right of veto over hard-won national distinction to one-fifth?

The issue came to a head of sorts with the appointment of Israel's first Arab minister, the Labor Party's science and technology minister,

Raleb Majadele. In March 2007, Israeli radio, Reshet Bet, reported that Majadele had refused to sing the national anthem at a state occasion. He stood silently and respectfully, but refused to sing the words. Callers to the radio station, and to call-in programs throughout the day, condemned the minister, at times viciously, for refusing to sing the anthem of the state for which he was a high official. (One Middle East expert from the Interdisciplinary Center noted that once, when a Jew was appointed to a ministerial position in Morocco, he sang the anthem, affirming allegiance to the king.) But surely any Arab citizen who is prepared to stand respectfully through "Hatikva" deserves the gratitude of Israeli Jews, not their condescension. Were the Israeli anthem more of an abstract homage to patriotism, like "The Star Spangled Banner," Israeli Arab citizens might be expected to sing it. But asking Arabs to sing "Hatikva" is a good deal more presumptuous than asking Québécois to sing "God Save the Queen." (Imagine the children of Kulaks standing respectfully through a singing of "L'internationale.") Majadele made clear, when he was interviewed on Reshet Bet, that he "salutes the universal values of Israeli democracy." Shouldn't that be enough?

And, again, who is to say that Israel should not alter its symbols, or add to them, to celebrate those more universal values. The changes would not stop Jews from celebrating the songs and symbols of the old Zionist movement whenever they wished. Canada went through just such a process during the 1960s, when the Union Jack was removed from the Canadian flag, much to the dismay of Anglophile conservatives such as former prime minister John Diefenbaker. A process of this kind can be wrenching, but it can also be wonderful. The Union Jack is still on the flag of Ontario, while the fleur-de-lis is ubiquitous in Québec. Why not the Zionist "Hatikva" and, in addition, an anthem of Israel celebrating pluralism?

More and more, it is becoming evident that the borders around Israel's Hebrew world can be defended most successfully by such acts of inclusion. What, if not a spreading Israeli pluralism, will eclipse such documents as the Adalah draft? (What, if not the gradual success of the civil rights movement, discredited Stokely Carmichael's call for black power?) Even people hawkish about hardening the physical borders are seeing the logic of making the cultural ones more permeable. Legal scholar Ruth Gavison, for example, recently published a position paper under the auspices of the Samuel Neaman Institute at the Technion. Under Gavison's system, there would be two levels of legislature—one nationally elected, as the Knesset is today, and a second elected under a regional system.[4] Israel would become a federation of cantons.

Make no mistake, Gavison is a hardliner who sees this federal system extending from the Jordan River to the sea, preempting, it would seem, an independent Palestinian state. And it is hard to see how regional autonomy would translate easily into cultural autonomy, given the mix of populations everywhere. Yet Gavison's projected changes are revealing, for her plan requires, she says, that the official status of the Jewish Agency and the Jewish National Fund be cancelled. These institutions should return to being "private tools" of the Jewish people, and would "settle the claim" that Israel discriminates against its Arab minority. And she calls for amending the Law of Return. The taboos must be broken, she told Haaretz's Shahar Ilan, there must be a balance between the complete ingathering of the exiles and "the state's interest in maintaining the wellbeing of all its citizens." A responsible country should not volunteer to absorb groups of "people with little chances of being absorbed and who are likely to live on the fringes of society in anger and frustration."

Gavison would be appalled, no doubt, to think that her plan, and talk, implicitly endorse Bishara's formulation, that Israel should be the state of its citizens. The point is, formulations like this, like Kashua's cultural ambitions, are in some sense inescapable. Faster or slower, Israel centrists are catching on.

"SAYED KASHUA, whom I don't know, belongs to a very small group of tortured people, tortured souls," Ehud Olmert told me during our breakfast with his wife, Aliza. "In their mentality, in their way of life, they already belong to the Jewish society. They left their villages, they left their tradition—to some degree, the tradition has been a part of their background—but they are modern yuppies, living in an urban society, and for them the urban Jewish society is liberal enough, and open enough, to want to be part of. And yet they don't really feel a part of it because they feel the alienation and the rejection by the majority of the Israelis, and deep down they suffer from the prejudices and the biases and the hatred that they know exist, they feel exist, and"—at which point I could not resist interrupting him:

"Sounds familiar, doesn't it?" I said. "Familiar to what?" he asked. I did not need to supply the answer, for Aliza did. "Jews," she said.

Olmert protested: "Their dominant narrative is the narrative of the Palestinians!" Then he grew more reflective. "In terms of history," he agreed, reflectively, "your question is a relevant question. But it will take perhaps another hundred years for the Arabs to change. And for us to change. And for them to grow used to having a Jewish state, and to become similar enough to us to then start to ask the questions that you are asking me today, about the kind of integration that, in this day, is impossible, because the emotions are so high, the defenses are so obvious, the intensity of the conflict is so predominant"—again, I broke in: "And how would *we* have to change?—and let's forget whether it's a hundred years or not. How would we change to accommodate *their* change?"

"It's funny," Olmert said, "I just gathered all of my advisors and devoted a full day to discussing the problems of the Arabs in this country.

We have so much to do, to change our attitudes toward the Arabs in this country—there is no question about it. It is inconceivable that we'll continue the way we are going, because we are not only a Jewish, we are also a democratic state. We can't run away from it. If we really mean to be democratic then we have to be democratic. And that may create certain challenges to the Jewish nature of the state of Israel. Though there is one thing I'm very happy to defend, and that is the Law of Return."

That's all? "I know that the main challenge to the basis of what Israel is all about is the argument of Azmi Bishara, who demands a country for all of its citizens. Then, if the Arabs become a majority, it'll be a different country from what it is. If the majority of Israelis will not be Jewish, then Israel will not be Jewish. You can't help it because democracy will be stronger. That's why we have to hurry up separation from the territories—we'll miss the time."

But can't we have laws that stipulate, say, that refugees from anti-Semitism have a preference for immigration and naturalization? Isn't the real issue whether one sees the identity of the nation as a blood tie, something a Jew can claim the moment the plane touches down, or whether one has to go through a process of acculturation, the acquisition of the language, the way every other European country does it, the way Canada does it? "You speak about a hundred years from now," I said. "Would there still be a Law of Return a hundred years from now?"

"Most likely the Law of Return will have to adjust itself to the changing circumstances," Olmert said. "Anyway a hundred years is not really such a long time. You and I can look back fifty years. We won't live to see these changes. A hundred years is symbolic. It can be fifty years. It can be something else."

After her husband left, I confessed to Aliza Olmert that I feared we might not have fifty years. In any case, I said, Yehuda Amichai's poetry, not the Law of Return, embodies the Zionist project for me. She looked at me softly. "Hebrew is my homeland," she said.

_____

HOW COULD Israelis think otherwise: think that the Jewish identity of Israelis is something fixed, exclusive—not learned? "It all started at Sinai—that's when the problems started," the writer A. B. Yehoshua assured me, digging into this very question. "Something immoral happened. Moses found a wretched people—without a territory, without a language, a mob of slaves—promised them a land, and welded religion into them. So you got this alloy of nationalism and religion. But this is unnatural. The nation, in this view, is a kind of biological fact, but also a territory, a common experience, like a family. You can't tell your son, 'Believe this or that or you are not my son.' Or tell the members of a nation, because you believe differently, 'You are not part of this thing.' But neither can religious faith stop at national boundaries. Salvation, beauty, the rest. If you are Thai and want to become Jewish, can you be told, fine, but you have to stop being Thai and become a part of the Jewish nation? It's like being told that if you want to be a Kantian you have to be German."

I was sitting with Yehoshua in his Tel Aviv apartment, the table laden with fruit, the pictures of his grandchildren everywhere. Bulli, as his many friends call him, challenged Zionists' dogma before Zionists admitted to having dogma. Who, if not Bulli, was in a position to reflect on how penetrable the borders of Hebrew culture were? Who better exemplified how public attitudes might change? Bulli's early story, "Facing the Forests," struggled bravely with the moral pain of a young Israeli Jew coming to grips with how the JNF had covered over with greenery an Arab town razed during the 1948 war. His novel, _The Lover_, caused a storm in the late 1970s when it imagined, Styron-like, the sexual passion of an Israeli boy for a Jewish woman, a book that subsequently became a part of the high school canon. In 1986, however, Bulli found himself drawn into a vexed debate with Anton Shammas, whom he had counted as a friend. Shammas was the first prominent Israeli

Arab writer to publish in Hebrew, a man who had married an Israeli Jewish woman from a northern kibbutz, and whose fictionalized memoir, *Arabesques,* would make him famous. He argued—implicitly in his work, and in many public appearances—for a version of Israeliness spacious enough to include his alloyed Palestinian consciousness. In claiming Hebrew as his own, did Shamas wish to preclude the possibility of an Israeli identity, rooted in Jewish national experience, and thus turn being Israeli into nothing more than formal citizenship?

Bulli was distressed. Interviewed by the journal *Revue Politika,* he unexpectedly erupted: "I say to Anton Shammas—if you want your full identity, if you want to live in a country that has an independent Palestinian personality, that possesses an original Palestinian culture, then rise up, take your belongings and move 100 meters to the east, to the independent Palestinian state that will lie beside Israel." The dispute soon got out of hand. Since he was a longtime peace advocate, Bulli's words were taken by some on the left to mean an endorsement of expelling Arabs, which they clearly were not. If anything, Bulli intended to imply that Israeli Arabs should hope to become a recognized national minority ("like the Kurds in Turkey," he later told me). Yet Bulli was not just knocking down a straw man, either. Phrases like "full identity" and "independent personality" suggested a state that might be something like a Jewish person, the projection of an integral Jewish people—a state that could be joined by others, but not without sacrificing other identities. The writer David Grossman eventually tried to mediate. "For me," Bulli told Shammas at a meeting arranged by Grossman, "Israeli is the authentic, complete, and consummate word for the concept 'Jewish'!" Shammas replied: "You see Israeliness as total Jewishness, and I don't see where you fit me, the Arab, into that Israeliness. Under the rug?"[5]

Anyway, this public dispute ended a decade ago, when the Oslo Agreements seemed about to conjure away old contradictions. Yet the questions raised then remain. So I asked Bulli, was it not time to clarify what he really meant to say to Shammas? Why *not* welcome the Arab minority into the Hebrew culture? His complex answer suggested not so much a change of heart, but that his dispute was never really with Shammas in the first place.

"THE PROBLEM WAS that Anton was telling me that he wanted this place to be some kind of completely neutral entity, like America, to which people from all over the world come. But the French did not, for the sake of the Polish Jews, give up on their story of the Gauls, or kings named Louis, their traditions. Anton wanted us to give this up—" "But a Hebrew entity," I interrupted, "cannot give this up in any case, and Shammas was willing to live in Hebrew." "Yes," Bulli continued, "Hebrew is crucial. But Hebrew is attached to a people with a history, the people who brought it here had a history, which they wanted to see perpetuated, memorialized. Was Anton Shammas prepared to forgo his Palestinism and adopt this history? He was not. Basically, he saw us as a minority in an Arab majority."

The language, in other words, is the product of a people who still have a history to make. "I am French, say. I have decisions to make, now. Okay, I want to refer to the past. But do I go back to the feudal codes?" Bulli was getting excited: "Now I am here. I want to know what do I do if I catch a terrorist, a Hamas person, who is suspected of having information about the next bomb? To what extent, if at all, may I torture him? We do not have a long history of sovereignty. Are we going to go back to King David for answers? So we might go to some texts and find out what Maimonides may have said about something. But our references are not great. I always tell my rabbinic interlocutors, how come you people never have anything to say about national insurance or welfare? I want to hear your religious reference to Netanyahu's abandonment of the poor. Where is it?"

This slide from his dispute with Shamas to his running battle with rabbis is not as quirky as it might seem. Bulli may fear the added demands of Arabs who claim Hebrew and Israel as their own, but his real impatience is with Diaspora Jews who, knowing little or no Hebrew, have presumed the modern Jewish nation to be nothing more than the historical People of the Book. He's also impatient with Israeli rabbis who've depicted Jewish law as having all the social answers, while they themselves are really focused on pietistic rituals. He wants, in other words, Israel's Hebrew culture to be, as Ahad Haam had hoped, the vessel for Jewish communitarian experience. Shammas's demand for inclusion, in this context, is not impossible but has been something of a diversion. Diaspora Jews and cloistered yeshiva students, neither of whom fully participate in the national life, presume to have something like a full Jewish identity merely by steeping themselves in the Talmud or referring back to classical rabbinic texts. This seemed absurd to him. They have no pragmatic sense of Judaism—what Jewish ideas become in practice. They don't know the Hebrew language, the land, the anxieties. In a way, they are even further from Jewish life in full than Shammas is.

"You look at the texts—the Talmud, etc.—and what they purport to be about are hypothetical situations in which moral decisions have to be made. Not theology, not big ideas like Plato. We have texts about realities. But in fact, we have more texts than realities, since the realities were in the hands of the goyim at the time. So the connection between these texts and the material realities today is hard to see; and the religious groups aren't working to make the connection, anyway. True, these texts may have a certain greater weight than others. But the problem is what we do today. We make Judaism today. Are we going to guiltily make it according to texts? Did the Americans go into Iraq by looking for a saying or rule derived from Jefferson's administration? If someone can do that, fine. But we are making Judaism today, what we *do* is Judaism!" (In fact, we could do with a Jeffersonian constitution, I thought, but let it go.)

WE NEEDED a simple yes or no. Could Bulli's practical nationalism open itself to Sakhnin? "Of course," Bulli said. "We created a spiritual center here in the larger sense, and Sayed Kashua can write in it. I want an Israel in which Arabs or anybody else can be Israelis in the sense of internalizing the anxiety and splendor of Jewish history and not convert. The path to this moment will pass though many anomalies. I saw on TV some time ago a debate between Marwan Barghouti and a Palestinian collaborator, both of them speaking Hebrew. It was fantastic. Look," he was winding up, "we have all kinds of religious variations here, too. It is not for me to be some Vatican telling people what is or is not appropriate Judaism. And I am speaking about the need in Israel to let into the national life the principle that we may have another religion here. The way Americans had to deal with the prospect of Senator Lieberman as vice president. The religious here are not just fighting over the Land of Israel. They are really fighting over legitimacy, sovereignty, in this country. Do you think they care simply about this or that settlement, or whether to dig under this or that graveyard? They care about who will determine the purpose of this people.

"Our democracy is going to be subtly different from any other. Every people is a variation on something more universal. There is much in common, but also variations which make for distinctions, which make for real humanness. Sure, there are influences of Jews on Christians, or Christians on Muslims, but we still want to know what is different— like American and French democracy, but the differences make things specific. And our specific nation is strong enough. Like the structure of America after the revolution."

One matter was especially unoriginal. "We have to separate religion from the nation, the state," Bulli insisted. "It is the key to our surviving here for the next hundred years." Nor, today, would Bulli invite Shammas to leave. Anybody who wants to find out should test to see what

Jewish culture is made of. For Shammas, alas, the point is moot. He is a professor at the University of Michigan, and does not see himself living in Israel again. "We have tried to raise the children in Arabic and Hebrew," he told Sidra and me a few years back, "but you know you have become an American when in the middle of the night your children call for water in English." More recently, Shammas told me of his fear that even if Bulli's clarification suddenly became national policy, it may be too late for most Israeli Arab youth, for whom Palestinian identity has become stronger than Israeli. Perhaps he is right.

THEN AGAIN, perhaps not. I paid a call, finally, on my neighbor, Mordechai "Morale" Baron, once Dayan's aide, the commander of IDF education during the time of the Six-Day War. During the early 1970s, when I first met him, he was the director of the Zionist Organization's youth and pioneering department, whose job it was to recruit excitable young people like myself. One side of Baron's family had been Polish Catholic, so he always exuded a strong liberal sensibility. But over the years he drifted steadily from Dayan's orbit into a stately nonconformism, heading for a while the leftish nonprofit alternative to the United Jewish Appeal, the New Israel Fund. And most important to his political consciousness is his blended family. One of his daughters married an Israeli Arab a few years back, another married an Orthodox man. Baron recently allowed a film to be made about his relations with his children, which he hoped would prove a kind of guide to Israeli pluralism.

"A daughter of mine is married to a native of Nazareth, an Arab fellow, who was educated in this country. A second daughter is married to an Orthodox fellow, born in Morocco, who came here with a Ph.D. from Paris, in a field quite like mine, the sociology of education." Baron paused, measured me, then went on. "They are both fine people and I love them both—that is not the issue. But as I have said many times, publicly, the Palestinian fellow is immediately closer to me than the fellow from Paris, who goes to the synagogue and puts on *tfilin*. When I sit with the former son, I sense the Land of Israel, and a clear secular orientation, like mine. When I sit with the latter, I sense Paris, and a world apart."

Does he see a future for both in the same land? "I have spent much of the past twenty years on the issue of Arabs in this country. When I sit with my Palestinian son-in-law, I cannot see him saying, 'Now I am a citizen of a Hebrew republic,' period. What I do see is two possibilities, both theoretical, for the long term—and I assume we are not speaking about maintaining the status quo, which is horrible. The first is a kind of new Hebrew melting pot, into which the Palestinians will come. I don't see this as completely impossible. After all," Baron continued quietly, "their kids in North Tel Aviv are more or less the products of the American TV culture, and they are Jews and Arabs on the margin.

"Yet I think the more realistic scenario is a second one, a kind of bi-national federation for two nations here, not a state in which both nations have exactly equal status. This will still be a predominantly Jewish state. But Arabs would have rights both as individuals and even as nationals. This seems to me more reasonable. Anyway, either scenario might prove itself. But if the new state will only hide a new form of oppression, then I have failed."

Conclusion:
Closing the Circle

What the mind alone cannot achieve, life, nature, and work achieve. While the hands learn to work—the ears to hear, the eyes to see—the heart to realize what is here—so the soul learns to soar over mountains, skip over hills, exalt itself—stretching itself into infinite distance, embracing the land around, the world, and its inhabitants, and seeing itself embraced in the arms of the whole world.

—A. D. GORDON,
Letters (c. 1915)

In April 2005, the RAND Corporation issued a study on the future of Palestine that captured the imaginations of Middle East experts around the world. Its policy suggestions (on security, health, water, etc.) were unexceptional; what catapulted its lead authors, Steven N. Simon and C. Ross Anthony, into a momentary spotlight was their vivid idea of the "arc." According to the study, major towns and cities of Palestine—including Nablus, Ramallah, Jerusalem, Hebron, and Gaza City—would be linked by a high speed train—an arc of rails and overpasses, making it possible to travel from southern Gaza to the northern West Bank in less than ninety minutes. "Each rail station, located several miles from existing historic urban cores," the study said, "would create a focal point for new development and would connect to a historic core via a new boulevard and an advanced form of rapid bus transit." Along the path of the train new commercial and residential neighborhoods would be developed, to accommodate population growth—as many as 6.6 million Palestinians by 2020, assuming natural population growth and immigration. The transportation arc would "pump economic activity into the historic centers of Palestinian cities" and assure their preservation and revitalization, creating "a ladder of linear cities along the defining mountain ridge of the West Bank, and preserving open land for agriculture, forests, parks and nature reserves."

The RAND plan was lovely. What almost nobody seemed to notice, however, was that the Palestine envisioned by the plan was actually an almost perfect mirror of contemporary Israel within the Green Line. Israel, too, is a ladder of linear cities and suburbs, wired to the global economy, settled along the coastal plain—a growing megalopolis, from Beer Sheba to Haifa, swinging around to the Valley of Jezreel and the Galilee, and tied together by a band of rail and roads. Indeed, if you superimposed the area of the wretched Gaza Strip on coastal Israel, from the north of Bat Yam to Netanya, you'd pretty much include the entirety of Tel Aviv, Ramat Gan, and Herzliya, where something more than half the Jewish population of the country lives—and by far the greatest part of its GDP is earned. The very word *country* seems something of an exaggeration in this context. Israel's coastal plain has a small hinterland, some very pretty mountains in the Galilee, where Jews and Arabs are about equal in number, and some desert ranges in the Negev, inhabited mainly by bedouins. Israel, it is true, also includes the corridor to Ben-Gurion Airport and up to Jerusalem and back, as Palestine has a corridor to Amman. But such east-west movement is more anomalous than natural.

One often hears the complaint that the Palestinian state envisioned by various peace plans is being left "a mere 22 percent of original Mandatory Palestine." The fact is, the real Israel lives on not much more of the historical territory. The Jewish arc faces an Arab one. If they want to survive as independent states, both Israel and Palestine will have to close the circle, while Israeli Arabs shuttle between both arc lengths. A border will of course be necessary, to establish residency for taxes, voting, and so forth. But with peace, and in time, how many will care where the border is? Israelis and Palestinians will have to work out how to share state jurisdictions that cannot be divided. Families in Tulkarm will not go to the beach in Gaza; software designers in Herzliya will not overlook technical talent in Ramallah and go first to Bangalore. Nor will Hebrew culture be endangered by the prospect of these mingling populations. Like Singapore Chinese, the Hebrew entrepreneurs, technologists, scholars, artists, and designers will establish the region's liveliest political economy. They will create cultural forces to be reckoned with. Who cares how many square miles Singapore is?

Israel will then remain the place where Jewish literary, artistic, and technological masterpieces, created in Hebrew, are open to the currents of the developed world. It would be, by any common measure, a Jewish state. But it would also be a state of its citizens—and global partners. The challenge, as *Haaretz* columnist Aluf Benn writes, is to "determine the borders of Israel in the east, with the Palestinians and the Syrians, and to hasten Israel's joining the international community as a normal member; to reabsorb the settlers who will be evacuated from the West Bank, without exacerbating the tension between Jews and Arabs within the Green Line; to establish a more stable and effective regime, and perhaps even a constitution; and to offer an attractive economic and social future to young people in order to combat the temptation of (brain-draining) globalization."[1]

BUT IS A POLITICAL border really imaginable? This book cannot stay current with the peacemaking—or the new rounds of violence—but a recent conference suggests that on this front, at least, the more things change, the more they'll remain the same:

In November 2006, I visited the campus of Al-Quds University in Abu Dis, an eastern suburb of Jerusalem, to attend an international conference on Palestinian refugees. Numbers are hard to validate, but it is widely accepted that five million survivors and descendants of the 750,000 Arabs who fled (or were chased out of) Israel during the 1948 war, as well as the 500,000 who were displaced in 1967, remain refugees. Of those living outside the Palestinian Authority, about two-thirds of registered refugees are in Jordan, where most qualify for citizenship, and 30 percent are evenly divided between Syria and Lebanon, where they generally do not. As many as 40 percent of the refugee families still live in squalid camps, in leaking houses of cracked concrete and tin roofs. Only about 20 percent of camp dwellers—so the American University of Beirut sociologist Sari Hanafi claims—marry people from the outside; the camps, he argues, using a fashionable term, are "heterotopic places," like bones misplaced in muscle, with no "connective tissue" to the urban centers where real life happens.[2]

Israelis, speaking more *dugri,* will tell you the refugee camps are just breeding grounds for Palestinian revanchist fantasies, and should have been cleaned up by the Arab states two generations ago, the way Israel cleaned up camps of Jewish refugees from Iraq, Morocco, and Yemen.[3] Palestinians tell you that their right of return is sacred ("No one can abolish it," Yasir Arafat told *Al Hayat* in 2002, reviewing why the Camp David Summit of 2000 had collapsed[4]). Israelis respond that return is inconceivable, even veteran Israeli peace activists like the writer Amos Oz.[5] Sari Nusseibah, the founding president of Al-Quds University, once argued that the Palestinians should renounce the right of return and focus their national energies on building one state, not populating two. But that was before Hamas won any election. It was hard to see what, if anything, a conference could accomplish.

———

THE DRIVE TO Al-Quds University should take no more than fifteen minutes from my home in the German Colony, since it is just a few miles past the Hebrew University on Mount Scopus, as the crow flies. Abu Dis is located on the next scatter of hills beyond the Augusta Victoria Hospital, where Arab residents of this part of Jerusalem typically go for medical treatment. But my driver took almost fifty-five minutes in light traffic, since Abu Dis is now formally dispatched to the territory of the PA, just behind the security wall, which snakes through Jerusalem, as through the rest of the West Bank.

To get to Abu Dis, to find a checkpoint through the wall instead of proceeding from Mount Scopus directly, we had to drive around the burgeoning Jewish suburb of Maale Adumim, formally on our side, but actually leapfrogging Adu Dis several miles to the north.[6] Imagine going from Wall Street to NYU via the Upper West Side, looping east around Central Park. Imagine making the trip to the hospital from Abu Dis, when the traffic is heavy, your identity card says you are no longer a resident of Jerusalem, the checkpoint guard got up on the wrong side of the bed, and your wife is in labor. It gives a whole new meaning to the phrase *right of return.*

I finally got to the conference building—as it happens, a stone's throw from the wall and its defiant graffiti. But the ambience was edgy only in the way of university gatherings. There were students in jeans, tees, and tank tops milling around outside. There was a frantic but gracious administrator seeing to name tags and earphones for simultaneous translation, while a skinny young man tested PowerPoint slides on the beamer—all for scholars and journalists and politicians at registration tables, chatting over coffee cups or fingering worry beads, looking over one another's shoulders to see if there were anyone more important to chat with. The only hint that we were not quite ready for globalization was that the conference kit came in a faux leather case, handsome as these things go, but smelling vaguely of diesel fuel. (Sadly, one wondered if the supplier's factory had any windows.)

THE TWO FEATURED speakers of the morning were Saeb Erekat, the intense, perennial Palestinian chief negotiator, still close to (and bringing greetings from) PA President Mahmoud Abbas; and Nabil Sha'ath, perhaps the most affable diplomat of the old brain trust around Yasir Arafat. Sha'ath had managed the Palestinian negotiating team on refugees at the peace summit at Taba, the Egyptian resort town on the Red Sea, in January 2001. That summit, undertaken while the Al-Aqsa Intifada burned in the background, was the last time Israelis and Palestinians formally tried to come to a final status agreement within the framework of the 1993 Oslo Accords. At the time, Bill Clinton had just left office, but his bridging parameters, negotiated in Washington in December 2000 and meant to close the gap that had emerged between Ehud Barak and Arafat at the failed Camp David talks six months before, served as the agenda.

Israeli negotiators had reported progress, but the summit was rushed because of an impending Israeli election, in which Ehud Barak was widely expected to take a beating from Ariel Sharon. Now, five years later, Erekat still spoke passionately. Using Arafat's marquee phrase, he called for the "peace of the brave," the release of prisoners on both sides: "a comprehensive calm—no Palestinian missiles, no Israeli shells." He did not really deal with the refugees but rebuked "forces that sow division"—namely Hamas, which had accused Abbas's Fatah party of having forgotten the refugees. Erekat acknowledged that Hamas had been democratically elected but warned the party not to bypass the PLO, the national umbrella organization, which Fatah still controlled.

After almost a year of Hamas trying to consolidate power in the PA—prompting Western sanctions, political isolation, and so on—the

PA was now stuck with tens of thousands of unpaid teachers, police, and other civil servants. Fatah was rising steadily in the polls and now seemed assured a majority in any new election. But no election seemed imminent. The air was buzzing with talk of a unity government, led by Fatah's own Abbas, and of the urgency of his meeting with Hamas's Khaled Meshal to avoid civil war. But it was hardly clear even then whether any unity terms could end Western sanctions or, indeed, pre-empt armed violence between middle-class Fatah leaders, who were strong in most West Bank towns, and Hamas, which controlled the ruins of Gaza. (Hamas finally threw Fatah forces out of Gaza in June.)

When Sha'ath's turn to speak came, his real mission at the conference became clear. He was to encourage new negotiations by claiming that the past negotiations at Taba had almost succeeded—also by implying that Hamas was only making a bad situation worse. The refugee negotiations at Camp David had gone nowhere, Sha'ath said, because the Israelis had been stalling. But at Taba, the refugees were not shunted aside, and their troubles would have been resolved according to a number of "modalities." He roared them out in bullet form: There would be financial compensation for lost property. There would be paid relocation to the Palestinian state. There would be contributions by donor countries, and even by Israel, to that state. (One economist present cheerfully put the amount of reparations at $137 billion.) There would even be a program of limited family reunification in Israel, up to a number "acceptable to the Israeli government," say, ten thousand a year over five years.

One might have expected a certain excitement when Sha'ath finished his speech, but the applause was merely polite. It was as if everybody had heard it all before. And, of course, we had. For these "modalities" were entirely familiar, virtually identical with the principles subsequently incorporated into the Geneva Initiative, a document signed by a team of Israeli and Palestinian politicians, writers (including Oz), and public intellectuals, in December 2003.[7] The organizers of what has come to be known simply as Geneva—Yossi Beilin, the former Israeli justice minister, and PA Information Minister Yasir Abed Rabbo—had both been at Taba and wanted to complete its work. Their Geneva document amounted to a comprehensive peace deal.

THE OUTLINES OF Geneva seemed self-evident the moment they were committed to paper: There would be a Palestinian state established in the West Bank and Gaza, joined by a highway or train, and using the 1967 borders as the starting point. Land swaps (for example, from the Negev to Gaza) would allow densely populated Jewish settlements around Jerusalem and Hebron, some 150,000 people, to be annexed to Israel, but Israel would evacuate Jewish settlements on the hills around major Palestinian cities. (Of all major urban settlements, only Ariel in the north and Qiryat Arba in the south would be evacuated, since access to them required long fingers of land, jutting into Palestine, and making a contiguous state impossible.)

Arab neighborhoods of Jerusalem, including those in the Old City, would be absorbed into the Palestinian state, with the Haram al-Sharif and its mosques coming under Palestinian sovereignty. The Jewish Quarter, the Wailing Wall, and excavations adjacent to the Temple Mount, would stay under Israeli sovereignty. International forces, mainly under UN auspices, would help police the Old City and the shared border. Israel would maintain a three-year security presence in the Jordan Valley, and security cooperation under U.S. mediation would continue beyond that date.

That was the deal—that will always be the deal, more or less—and Sha'ath, it seems, could only restate it. Nothing Hamas or the settlers do can change its terms. The refugee problem, which was supposed to prompt Palestinian declarations of steadfastness, and strike fear in the hearts of Israelis, was actually resolved four years ago. Indeed, the border was resolved. Jerusalem was resolved. The placement of international forces was resolved. As King Abdullah of Jordan put it recently, "You have the road map, you have Taba, you have the Geneva Accord. So, we don't have to go back to the drawing board."

According to a spring 2007 poll, moreover, over half of Israelis and about half of Palestinians already accept the terms of this agreement. And Abdullah might have added that we also have the Saudi plan, adopted by the Arab League summit in March 2002, declaring that all regional states will simultaneously recognize Israel in return for the 1967 border, which the Geneva plan calls for. I put the matter point-blank to Sha'ath. Had the Palestinian Authority formally accepted the terms of the Geneva Initiative? "Well, that depends who we're talking to," he told me. "If I were talking to current Israeli negotiators and I said I accepted Geneva, they would say, 'Great, let's start from there and negotiate a compromise.' If I were talking to Yossi Beilin, our attitude would be different. It would be a short negotiation."

I AM RECALLING this conference because it raises a vexing question. If the framework for a full peace has been negotiated, why are we still killing each other? The short answer is the logic of violence itself. The Oslo process was supposed to yield, first, a period of confidence building, and second, final status talks to produce an agreement. What we actually have since 2000 is, first, a final status agreement, and second, the calamitous erosion of any confidence to implement it: prosettler provocations, suicide bombings, assassinations, missiles, shells, hollow ultimatums—and then Lebanon.

So the logic is cruel but easy to penetrate. Even with the failure of Oslo, the Palestinian majority—over 71 percent, according to polls conducted by Shikaki's Palestinian Center for Policy and Survey Research—wants the violence to end, and will settle for a Palestinian state alongside Israel. In a poll conducted in March 2006, Shikaki found that 47 percent of the 1270 respondents in the West Bank and Gaza Strip said they would bring Hamas to power again if elections were held a second time, but 75 percent said they want Hamas to hold negotiations with Israel. What other polls, including Shikaki's, have demonstrated again and again since the outbreak of violence in the fall of 2000 is that although significant majorities on both sides want to advance to peace, approximately 90 percent on each side believes the other side does not.

The *New Yorker*'s David Remnick has reported affectingly on Hamas's anti-Semitic attitudes—"the notion of worldwide conspiracies and Jews sparking everything from the French Revolution to the First World War."[8] Sermons from Gaza mosques describing Jews as "poison" and "vermin" have circulated widely on the Web, leaving even Arab commentators disgusted.[9] It will take a generation of relative peace for such attitudes to dissipate, as in post-war Europe. But are these attitudes the cause of the violence or its byproduct? Can people with democratic imagination really doubt the answer?

Consider, in this context, the 2003 Israeli documentary film *Arna's Children*, to my mind, the most compelling testament to the nemesis of revenge since Hamlet. The film begins in 1993 with the effort of the Israeli antioccupation activist and psychologist Arna Mer to work with a small circle of neglected teens in a Jenin refugee camp. Mer had fought in the Palmach in 1948, then joined the Israeli Communist Party and married a Palestinian. In 1996, having won a Scandinavian peace prize, she and her son, the filmmaker and actor Julio Mer Khamis, began a theater group with "her children" in Jenin; acting, she believed, would provide the children a nonviolent way to channel their rage. The enemy was nihilism. With great sympathy and subtlety, Julio chronicled these events, and the subsequent lives of the little actors, during Arna's last years and after her death. He then went back to Jenin after Operation Defensive Shield and wound up telling the heartbreaking story of the transformation of these magical little boys into terrorists.

Nobody who has raised sons, or just mentored young men, could fail to be moved by what *Arna's Children* reveals. One youth showcased in the film, a lean kibitzer named Yusuf Switat, was thrilled about the play, which he performed in 1996. He spoke to Julio on camera, with sweet sincerity, about slowly learning to trust him and his mother—"Jews were supposed to be our enemies!" He wondered out loud why "Arabs had never done this kind of thing" for him and his friends. When Israeli television came to report on the play, Yusuf introduced himself with lean poise: "Call me Yossi," he insisted. He was wearing an army jacket—did he imagine himself playing a soldier? He answered that he loved the Syrian army, as if he were speaking of a favorite football team. And why did he love the theater? "I can tell people what I feel. What I want and don't want. Whether I love life or not. That sort of thing."

Just six years later, at the height of the Al-Aqsa Intifada, Yossi found himself cradling a dying schoolgirl in his arms after she had been hit by stray Israeli tank fire. Within days, he led a suicide attack in Hadera, murdering four Israeli women in cold blood and severely wounding many others. He was shot dead in the street.

It is nearly impossible to recall this now, but a pervasive goodwill was still evident as late as the Christmas before the turn of the millennium. During those chilly, brilliant nights, Sidra and I frequently drove the ten minutes from our home in southeast Jerusalem to Bethlehem's Manger Square, just to hang out with the hopeful young Palestinian entrepreneurs who had invested their life savings in stores selling olive wood carvings and elegant glass dishware. The border checkpoint was manned by Israeli soldiers who cheerfully confiscated your loose chocolate. Palestinian soldiers then waved you through with a bashful nod.

Hamas was, to be sure, gaining ground during those days. Some Palestinian schools and camps emphasized struggle until victory. Meanwhile, the number of Israel's settlers doubled, while per capita Palestinian incomes halved. Still, the shopkeepers complained—not about Israelis, but about hysterical stories in the world press about Y2K failures and millennial sects, both of which were defeating tourism. They were looking forward to the pope's visit, scheduled for the spring, to put things back on track. A Palestinian company had just invested over a million dollars to refurbish the adjacent hotel. An Israeli technical firm was working on the satellite uplink to send the Palestinian Christmas service and millennium celebration to the world's cable stations. "This," said Sidra, "is as close to heaven as we are likely to get."

The University of Toronto sociologist Robert Brym carefully studied all 138 suicide bombings between September 2000 and mid-July 2005. He concluded that in the vast majority of cases the suicide bombers themselves—whatever their ideological predispositions, or the groups that claimed responsibility—had lost a friend or close relative to Israeli fire. They acted, he wrote, "out of revenge."[10]

BUT THERE IS a longer answer, which is that nothing stands in the way of an agreement except for the reciprocal reluctance of the Israeli prime minister and Palestinian president, both openly committed to a two-state peace, to act boldly in the face of self-righteous, potentially violent domestic opposition. Fatah's erratic exploitation of international promises, to try to gain the upper hand against Hamas in Gaza, has failed for now, though it is hard to see what Hamas will do with its coup in the absence of donor funds. But Fatah is only one side of the equation.

The Israeli center has its own doubts, which the rightist opposition plays on. Peace, after all, is not just the absence of violence but the presence of justice. How will Israel, arguably Jewish and democratic, outlast a peace process, where concessions to Arab power seem to invite both attack and existential repudiation? Islamist groups like Hamas reject Israel, or at least reject the vague mix of Israel's occupation and Zionism's revolutionary career. Israeli Arabs insist on equality. Iran poses a nuclear threat. Syria protects Hezbollah. Even Labor leaders in the peace camp, like former deputy defense minister Ephraim Sneh, have conjured nightmare scenarios reminiscent of RAND studies early in the Cold War. Why not tough things out and wait for better timing?

The answer, of course, is that time is not working for Israel, and certainly not for Israel's toughness. The IDF will never again have the power to impose its will on Israel's neighbors—not with guerilla groups getting missiles, Israeli entrepreneurs trying to make meetings in London, and CNN waiting around for new footage of apartments turned to rubble. Meanwhile, settlers create new facts, and new Palestinian Hamlets join gangs and take up weapons. Curiously, some centrist leaders oppose peace initiatives because of the so-called war on terror, arguing that a life-and-death fight is inevitable with the Arab world, and concessions of any kind will be interpreted as a victory for terrorists. One expert I know put the matter this way: "How can Israeli soldiers fight a ten-year-old boy who wants to die? Or a teenager at the wheel of an exploding truck, smiling because he knows that in ten seconds he will be in heaven? This is the generation I am afraid of!"

Actually, these are not the words of an Israeli security professional. They were spoken by Leila Sharaf, Jordan's onetime information minister, whom I interviewed back in 1984.[11] She warned that the occupation would inflame the whole region. My point is that the hard line has not exactly worked, and whatever its neighbors think of Israel's legitimacy, most Arabs (including most Palestinians) take its existence for granted. They fear eruptions of violence would seem to justify Islamist extremism, threatening the very regimes Israel could make peace with. Key Arab neighbors—Jordan, Egypt, Qatar—already have either diplomatic relations or trade ties with Israel and do not seek its elimination. Élites in these states are as appalled (and threatened) by jihadism as Israelis are; they worry that the occupation, the bombing of Lebanon, the cruelties of battle—all of these—have made anti-Israel feeling rampant in the Arab world, making jihadism harder to contain than it would otherwise be. This is what gives teeth to the Saudi proposal.

Inertia is not a new problem. But in the absence of a clear peace strategy—an endgame for everybody's chessboard—the contradictions of the situation remain, and then leaders on both sides become hostage to every Islamist radical and fanatic settler who wants to blow up whatever residual goodwill there is. This very point was made, paradoxically, by Ehud Barak back in 1993, when he resisted the Oslo framework. It largely accounted for his headstrong effort to force the outlines of an agreement when he became prime minister in 1999. It was divisive enough when Sharon removed eight thousand settlers from Gaza. Should any centrist prime minister now start down a path to remove at least 75,000 more from the West Bank, many of them armed and entrenched, for the sake of Palestinians who—so my dry cleaner says— "only *yefei nefesh* [pretty souls] like Beilin could trust"? What prime minister could survive that, unless there was something far worse to fear?

THIS IS WHERE America and the rest of the world comes in—or not. As I write, all parties are justifiably focused on the Saudi plan, which the Olmert government seems intent on pursuing in some form. The parties are gearing up for the Annapolis summit, which Secretary Rice is promising to mediate. But is mediation enough, and are international players projecting enough power? The Saudi plan makes only vague references to the 1967 borders, refugees, Jerusalem, and so forth. How to get to what Secretary Rice calls a "political horizon" without getting into details? For their part, can Israeli and Palestinian leaders be trusted to endorse the Saudi plan without endorsing something like the details of Geneva? Everybody knows Abbas would prefer not to disappoint radical Palestinian refugees in Lebanese camps. Everybody knows that Sharon and the people close to him, including Olmert, favored pulling out of Gaza mainly because they thought this would make it easier to unilaterally annex large parts of Jerusalem and the West Bank.

And in this context, the focus on Iran's nuclear threat is a potentially lethal diversion. It could invite preemptive strikes against Iran that would make a peace process all but impossible, and widen the gulf between Israel, America, and the Islamic world as a whole. Sure, America, Europe, and the Gulf States should act to mitigate an Iranian bomb through all diplomatic and economic means. But Israel's barely concealed nuclear deterrent, against any future Iranian bomb, is as good as any deterrent America ever had against Moscow's threat. And it is not exactly sane to assume Iranian leaders themselves all suffer from a peculiar suicidal madness—that there is a short Islamist hop from Iran's enriched uranium to an incinerated Tel Aviv, willingly paid for with an incinerated Tehran. (Some Middle East scholars— Daniel Pipes, for instance—claim that fanatic Iranian mullahs are so used to losing martyrs, as in the Iran-Iraq War, that they'd be willing to see much of Iran's population die in order to wipe out Israel. This psychological insight brings to mind certain Soviet experts during the 1970s—indeed, like Daniel's father, Richard Pipes, then plumping for the MX missile—who argued that Russia's communist leaders would be willing to launch a first strike and accept the losses from an American retaliation, since Russians had lost tens of millions of civilians during World War II and are therefore more cavalier about human life than Americans.[12])

No, the great challenge for American foreign policy—and the European Union's, for that matter—is to get each side to trust in something without having to trust the other. And what the Israeli prime minister needs is not more encouragement to fight terror, but a bigger dose of what the Palestinian president has been getting: the sense that great powers are forcing the issue, bringing the sides to a deal that leaders and majorities will ultimately accept but do not have the courage to sow division over. Sooner or later, this will start with American leaders openly endorsing Geneva-like principles and planning international forces to displace the Israeli occupation. They will also have to stop settlements, period. The sorest part of the West's problems in the Middle East is the Israeli-Palestinian conflict, and the sorest part of that conflict is settlements.

In July 2007, it is true, President Bush warned Israel about expanding settlements. Friendly declarations were never enough. When Bush's father tried to use real political force to end settlements in 1991, empowering then secretary of state James Baker to deduct expenditures on settlements from American loan guarantees to Israel, most Israelis, even liberal *Haaretz* writers, rushed in to question their friendship toward Israel. American Jewish organizations rallied congressional allies, especially allies in the Democratic Party, to protect Israel's freedom of action. Paradoxically, a majority of Israelis have always believed what official U.S. policy always insisted, that settlements are an obstacle to peace. Settlements are actually an unmitigated disaster, yet they have increased tenfold under the continuing friendship of Ronald Reagan and George Shultz, Bill Clinton and Dennis Ross. Granted, Baker has Saudi business connections. (He once said privately—or so it has been widely reported—"Fuck the Jews, they didn't vote for us, anyway.") Still, calling Baker anti-Israel for trying to end settlements was a little like calling your friend disloyal for trying to take away your cocaine.

Nor have times really changed with leading Democrats. What electable Democratic presidential candidate in 2004 even raised the question of West Bank settlements? American Jews are more dependable contributors to the Democratic Party than almost any other demographic, and elections are still fought largely by brand managers. What consultant will allow a candidate to prejudge the outcome of Israel's negotiations or limit Israel's freedom of action? By the time this book is published, will we have seen, say, Hillary Clinton's endorsement even for "bridging parameters" that carry her own name? Think of the reaction to Jimmy Carter's recent book.

Nevertheless, the last thing Israel will need in the months ahead is just what Israeli prime ministers typically ask for: the gradualism of the roadmap without pressure, a free hand to deal with terror, more confidence-building measures, more time. For the only thing that will build confidence today is a clear commitment of Americans and Europeans to a definite plan like Geneva. In its absence, Israeli centrists and Palestinian moderates become hostages to every Islamist terrorist or hard-line Israeli officer who makes the decision to pursue militants. The Israeli leader needs to be able to say what Abbas has been brought to say to his rejectionists: "You are alienating America and the world; we have to choose between the old dreams and our future needs; it's not me, it's reality."

THESE DIPLOMATIC SOLUTIONS still seem just beyond reach, though I suspect that once a peace process is restarted, the pace of diplomacy will prove surprisingly quick. In 1993, before they were soured by indecision and assassination, the Oslo Accords produced an overnight change in the climate; hope—that "thing with feathers," in Emily Dickinson's words—was released. I concluded, therefore, that the present period of indecision, so pregnant with the future, prompts a final conversation. Israel's twentysomethings are by definition the realization of the old dreams. It is their futures Israeli leaders are presumably trying to secure. What do they think about their prospects in the region, indeed, about a Jewish and democratic state? Is there optimism of the will? I decided to ask.

I assembled a group of my former business students at the Interdisciplinary Center—not a scientific sample, but not a monolithic group, either: all in their late twenties, some married, some still messing around. They all live in the Tel Aviv area now, digging in—young Israelis at their best, talkative, hopeful, diligent, liking things their own way. They had lived in other places, New York, London, Miami, India. They were determined to make their lives right where they were. There was Milly, the sparky niece of a former Likud minister, always hating the practice of law, always sticking with it; Yaacov, the religiously observant son of a Mizrahi immigrant in Kiryat Gat, already carrying himself like the family scion; Assaf, the serene former fighter pilot still living on his parents' moshav, now flying for El Al and teaching yoga; and finally Yaron, the Tel Aviv entrepreneur with a brother in New York and a genius for punchlines. They knew something of my views and that I wanted to know theirs. What kept them in Israel? Milly, as usual, jumped in first.

"When I was five," she said, starting with the basics, "we moved to Long Island for a while, and my father, who was from a religious home—you know, knitted yarmulkes—sent me to a yeshiva so that I'd learn Hebrew. Those Jews were so hostile to Israelis who were obviously not religious. My brother, who was twelve, had a little ponytail from Israel, and the rabbi came up to him while he was waiting for the bus and just cut it off—which was, like, illegal. We went to synagogue on Yom

Kippur and sat in some empty seats, and the woman there started yelling at us that seats were supposed to be paid for. The energy was awful, all about being fashionable, Jappy—you know, Jewish American Princess—I couldn't wait to get back home."

"That's why I want to raise my children here," Yaron broke in. (Speaking about raising children comes naturally to young Israelis, in a way it doesn't to Americans.) Did everybody make the same decision? I asked. Yes, they said. "That, and not to make decisions," Yaron said.

But what exactly does *here* mean, I pressed them. "Last weekend, my husband's family, a very leftist family, got into a discussion. The idea of a Hebrew republic"—Milly had read an article of mine—"kicked off a two-hour discussion. We started to really get into the details—what does it mean to earn Israeli citizenship, is it to be Israeli or Jewish, what it means for Arabs here. I don't think a lot of people here want to hear that Israel should be Israeli the way France is French." Why not? I asked. "Because most want Judaism. They want it without repression, they want the holidays, that sort of thing. Norms, not laws. They want Kashrut along with the right, which is widely exercised, not to be kosher in restaurants and hotels. It's a joy not to have to travel on Yom Kippur, but make it a law and everyone will drive. Norms, not laws."

Norms, not laws. I wasn't sure why this Israel was not like France. But before I could push back, Yaacov took things in a different direction: "I've gone through a change. The country used to be more united; people had more in common. But in the past ten years—call it globalization—we have become more developed, we have wanted to see more, experience more—Jews always want to jump to the head of the line. And we've become more like the outside world—we've developed and advanced. And this is affecting what we mean by 'Jewish and democratic.' Religion reflects more primitive—well, not primitive, ancient—values, more historical consciousness, which has to keep up. Fine, I have all kinds of ideas about how Judaism might accommodate modernization. But here comes the disintegration. Seculars will say, 'Okay, I'll circumcise my son, but I don't want a rabbi, I am in the center. Everybody for himself'—"

"Or perhaps they can come together to support the legal conditions that make a secular society possible," Milly broke in, obviously concerned by Yaacov's direction, not appreciating what a profound point she had just made; "coming together to support a society of choices is also social consciousness—"

"Yes, true," Yaacov replied, "but I still think we are too focused on ourselves, on what's good for us, and not on the community that is all around us. My folks are from Libya and Morocco," he says. "My grandmother tells me about how she gave up everything to make it here, and it breaks her heart that any of us would leave. They came here for a Jewish state, Jewish values, connection, safety. Now this is all weakened. How this affects 'Jewish and democratic,' *walla*, who knows, since we'll always want to be Jewish, but *democratic* is a sacred word, we'll never want a totalitarian country, so we'll always continue the tension, a secular majority against an Orthodox minority."

"But the Arabs have to be taken into account," Milly replied. "The demographic trends will bring us a growing Arab minority that will confront a growing Haredi minority. There will be an explosion here. It hurts me, too, to think about everything there was here, the kibbutzim, and the pioneering hats, but the question is now how to get through the twenty-first century. How are we going to have a state that fits with the people who are living in it today—Haredi, secular, whatever? What will solve the social divisions, which reflect us younger people, who see things differently? We need to keep an open mind toward immigration and education, to preserving a Jewish character, but find a formula to bring people together, without repression, secular and *dati*, Jews and Arabs. Ten years from now, I don't want to see an Arab majority or a Haredi majority. We can start by finding a way to

give Russian immigrants the citizenship they deserve but can't get because their Jewishness is not pure. Our tests for citizenship should
become more sophisticated, and include, at least, language and knowledge of our history, like in America."

ASSAF, THE PILOT, serene as a buddha, now took over the controls,
homing in on his conclusions as if on a landing strip. "I think there is a
trend in the Western world as a whole, of which we are a small part, toward a kind of spirituality, a fatigue with the 'me.' At the same time,
Jews have tried to return to sources and there is a fatigue with the
sources. We don't want Judaism as such, *dat*. We want religious values,
spiritual values, but don't want hatred of goyim, or war over land, or
the keeping of commandments over the lives of human beings. This
trend creates a vacuum, which has to be filled by an all-encompassing
frame—one that answers the individual, fullness, happiness, what
religion sometimes gives you. But it has to be complete, inclusive, of
Arabs, and of all the complex reality we face. And we are very, very far
from this.

"We, the people who believe this, are a minority," Assaf continued,
apparently including his interlocutors, "but an influential minority.
People with political, economic, and social leverage. Small numbers,
and getting smaller—but this does not mean the future is not in our
hands. The vision is very far, and it doesn't matter how vague, or resented, or mocked we are. Maybe not for this generation. But you
see people working toward this vision, and you have something to
hope for.

"And I mean the vision of a constitution," Assaf continued, "based on
what is most beautiful about Judaism. We have to engender this constitution on a temporary Jewish majority, since the numbers and identities are changing all the time. Partly because of assimilation, partly

because of Arabs. The responsibility of this Jewish majority generation, nevertheless, is to bring our society forward as far as we possibly can, and then perhaps evaporate. No funds for synagogues. But funds for schools that teach all students the best values of the historical Jewish people. We can't assume a permanent majority of Jews, but we can still bring the state to the highest possible stage of humanism, social consciousness, liberal democracy, as Jews—leave something structured and more permanent, do our job, and let go."

Assaf seemed to understand that he was saying something that had been left curiously unsaid. So he moved quickly to fill in the white space: "Let's look at what is happening elsewhere in the world, after all—there are societies more enlightened than ours, other countries originally founded on religion—" at which point Milly broke in: "But you are already conceding the loss of a Jewish state!" Assaf had thought this through: "Look, in the not-too-distant future, there will not be states in this sense—little by little, things are melting. If you just look at the big trend, the long years ahead, you see the direction—European integration, globalization, a human being as a human being. Religion gets you apparent solidarity, while secularism gets you pluralism, a different kind of solidarity, perhaps, but not as fierce. Anyway, I choose pluralism."

Assaf had finished, simplicity following complexity. This was such a fresh voice, yet sounding uncannily like the reasonable idealism of Chanan's parents' generation. Religious imagination was assured in this vision, but not state-supported religious institutions. National and ethnic feelings were assured, but not nation-states or ethnocracies. Yaron took this all in and found his opening:

"I don't think we have a real democracy here, or that Israelis know what this is. Either you have democracy or you don't, sort of like sex— Bill Clinton notwithstanding. And perhaps we shouldn't strive for a democracy if the people here aren't ready for it. I grew up largely in America, which is a democracy, though since Iraq they've been doing not very democratic things for many years. But as long as we have this religion in the background, we have this optical illusion called 'democracy.' I agree with most of what Assaf said. You look at Europe, and the Treaty of Rome is the top thing. But we have to be patient. Ireland, say, which was founded on a religious distinction, still tries to avoid issues that will inflame Catholics. We'll have to do the same here."

THE DEBATE was suddenly joined from all sides, point upon point, things we had all heard before, but could not be said too often. Why secularize? Did that really mean repressing religion? No, that meant giving freedom to religion; it is Orthodox religious authority that represses freedom. Does democracy mean majority rule? No, it means much more. Were we not all proud to be Jews, and yet was not the Jewish religion racist? But could not racialism be retired by focusing Jewish identity on national life—the language and culture of the new Jewish nation? Always, the logic circles back to ordinary freedoms.

"Clinton said a wise thing," Assaf began, summing things up. "He said, 'The things that are good in America are able to fix the things that are bad in America.' I think the same can be said of Judaism, which is ultimately about the hunger for justice, knowledge, the truth. Freedom is very much a part of this—it, too, is truth. It works on people over time, and plays into our hopes. So all we can do is work to create the conditions for freedom to evolve."

Milly had to leave and was growing impatient. She had a dream and was itching to share it: "'Jewish and democratic' is a cliché. Okay, there is a Jewish majority and majority rule, but also all of the contradictions—inequalities for some citizens since they are not Jews, laws that privilege rabbinic things, which bother us more or less, and the anger from people who push off religion because of radical rabbinic power plays. But if I could shut my eyes and open them to a Jewish and democratic society, this is what it would be like a year from now.

"First," she said, as if drawing conclusions for all the assembled, "everybody should celebrate their holidays, the Sabbath, commandments, as they please. I don't eat milk with meat and shrimp, but I drive on Shabbat. My husband doesn't agree to the diet. Whatever is good for whomever. Each in his or her own way, Jews and non-Jews. But on Yom Kippur, there should not be cars in the streets, not because it is forbidden, but because that's the custom. Two, I want a country in which young people would not have to think about going abroad for freedom or money. Three, I want a country with a lot of immigration from all over the world, not only Jews, but people who feel connected to our Jewish history and struggle—because of the Holocaust, or the Bible. People who won't have to convert to acculturate. Four, we have to preserve the Jewish character without assuming Jewish force, through education, experience. I want to see a country where people say they are Israeli. When I was in America, I didn't say I was Jewish; I said I was Israeli—*Israeli*. It is based in Judaism, but that is not its essence. In fact, maybe we should punt this 'Jewish and democratic' designation and just say 'Israeli.' "

THIS MIGHT HAVE been the last word, but it was not. Their conversation went on for hours more, though I listened less and less to their specific points, and sank back into a loving admiration just for the way they made them, the way parents do with their grown-up children more often than they'd care to admit. But I also felt a rising disquiet, thinking what a misfortune Israel would suffer if, after all, more of these remarkable young people would get caught up in futile escalations or just left the country to pursue their freedom. This was not a hypothetical fear. I thought again about that poll, that nearly half of

Israel's young people do not feel connected to the state, while a quarter of them do not see their future here.

Israeli leaders, centrists all, will tell you how appalled they are by that poll. Some question the willingness of young people to sacrifice, blaming themselves for tolerating hedonism. Some will publicly lament how the Jewish state was supposed to be a "light unto the nations." Perhaps they could just learn from the nations for a while.

ACKNOWLEDGMENTS

The Israeli writer David Grossman once told me that he writes political journalism when he can no longer absorb, or stand, the way other people put things—not the arguments, exactly, but the words and phrases that determine the arc of arguments. This book grew out of countless moments like that, with dozens of people who have inspired or provoked me, in America and Israel, over what already seems to me a reasonably long life. I cannot acknowledge them all here and I cannot thank them enough. I hope they know who they are: I am keenly aware of having been blessed with many good conversations.

Some fifty people, more recently, agreed to be recorded and quoted. I have identified all but one in the manuscript and it would be tedious to list them all here again. To them I owe a special debt.

It is customary to thank one's spouse last, usually for intimacies or support not quite related to the job at hand. The custom in this case would be ridiculous. When it comes to Israeli politics and culture, Sidra DeKoven Ezrahi is the most important conversation partner (and impresario) I have. She revived my devotion to Israelis and their fate. She urged me back into the public conversation. She opens Hebrew literature to me. She defends Jewish enlightenment. She's also read and criticized many drafts, and eventually put her skills as an English professor to work, line by line. Then she praised me. My conversation with Sidra is what Aristotle would have called this book's final cause.

As to its efficient cause, or causes, again I have been blessed. The chain went something like this. Lewis Lapham called me in December 2004 to write a 3,000-word "letter" from Jerusalem for *Harper's* magazine; a 9,000-word essay gushed out. "Talk to Ellen," Lewis said—and the Ellen in question was Ellen Rosenbush, the magazine's managing editor. She suggested a strategy for rewriting, then secured the cover. When I thought I might want to expand the argument into a book, Ellen put me in touch with Jim Rutman at Sterling Lord. Jim, it was immediately clear, was a rare man: an agent whose humility, intellectual gifts and moral taste editors genuinely respected. He brought the book to Andrea Schulz at Harcourt. He became my first reader.

Which brings me to the luckiest break of all. Andrea demonstrated enthusiasm, patience, and mastery of the process, including page editing of the kind editors are not supposed to do anymore. Phone calls and e-mails were always answered. There was never a time I did not feel grateful for her professionalism—and growing friendship. I am also grateful to the copyediting staff at Harcourt, especially David Hough, for every fact checked and every nit picked.

A number of friends and colleagues read the manuscript, whole or in part, at various stages. I would like to acknowledge them for their time and tough love, especially Amos Elon, Howard Sachar, and Sara Noble. My oldest friend, Shelly Schreter, wrote a thirty-three-page critique. Yehuda Melzer, Nelson Aldrich, David Harman, Yoram Peri, Yaron Carni, Jim Carroll, Alvaro de Soto, Hendrik Hertzberg, and Christopher Lydon read the book when it was near completion and added their advice and encouragement. I could say, as authors mostly do, that the book's failures are mine alone, but this implies too much that its virtues are. So let me just say that without such readers my book would not be what it is. I am grateful to my old friend and mentor, Rabbi Ben-Zion Gold (the former director of Harvard Hillel), who read the piece in *Harper's* and suggested to—actually, instructed—me to turn the article into a book. Finally, my children, Ben, Ellie, and Tamar, each read the manuscript as it was taking shape; when I am not too distracted by the gratitude I feel that they are adult professionals, quite capable of reading critically as colleagues do, I learn more from them than they know.

A Note on Transliteration

Many Hebrew words (names, etc.) in this book illustrate well-known problems of how to transliterate them into English. For example, the Hebrew letter *het,* as in Yitzhak, is often written *chet,* as in Menachem. Also, the article *ha,* which is *the* in Hebrew, is sometimes separated from its noun by a hyphen (as in *ha-mazon*) and sometimes not (as in the newspaper *Haaretz*). Consistency would mean that some Hebrew words familiar in American media would be transliterated in ways that seem affected (writing Menachem Begin would require my writing Chasidim, not Hasidim, for example). So I have decided against consistency per se. My practice throughout has been to present the word in a way least likely to stop the reader, or if a stop is inevitable, most likely to aid in pronunciation.

ENDNOTES

Prologue: The Situation

1. The commission's interim report, published April 30, 2007, said in part: "The decision to respond with an immediate, intensive military strike was not based on a detailed, comprehensive and authorized military plan, based on careful study of the complex characteristics of the Lebanon arena. A meticulous examination of these characteristics would have revealed the following: the ability to achieve military gains having significant political-international weight was limited; an Israeli military strike would inevitably lead to missiles fired at the Israeli civilian north; there was not another effective military response to such missile attacks than an extensive and prolonged ground operation to capture the areas from which the missiles were fired—which would have a high 'cost' and which did not enjoy broad support. These difficulties were not explicitly raised with the political leaders before the decision to strike was taken."

2. *Haaretz*, May 1, 2007.

3. See Yaron Ezrahi's extended essay, *Rubber Bullets: Power and Conscience in Modern Israel*, New York: Farrar, Straus & Giroux, 1997.

Chapter One: Basic Laws

1. President's Conference, *Democracy Index*, Israel Democracy Institute, May 2003.

2. Interview with Ahuva Oren-Pines, former Israel Broadcasting Authority board member, July 25, 2005: "Most of the general managers [of the IBA] are until our day the 'yes-men' of the politicians; put in a professional manager, and it will be hard for him to function."

3. Dan Rabinovtz, "A Lesson in Citizenship," *Haaretz*, December 20, 2005.

4. http://www.knesset.gov.il/description/eng/eng_mimshal_yesod2.htm#2

5. See Meron Benvenisti's article, "The Blue Box," *Haaretz*, May 29, 2007.

6. Howard Sachar, *A History of Israel*, New York: Knopf, 1976, p. 438.

7. *Jewish Weekly*, February 4, 2005.

8. Interview, January 25, 2004.

9.   "Only four out of 104 communities covered by Galilee development plan are Arab," by Jack Khoury and Yoav Tren, *Haaretz*, November 9, 2005.

10.   Conversation with *Haaretz* correspondent Danny Rubinstein.

11.   *Haaretz*, August 24, 2006.

12.   Geocartagraphia poll, reported in *Haaretz*, March 22, 2006.

13.   *Haaretz*, February 27, 2006.

14.   See Uli Schmetzer's article, "Jews-only bill roils Israel Cabinet; endorses land legislation that foes call racist," *Chicago Tribune*, July 10, 2002.

15.   The state prosecutor's office said, "The attorney general's opinion, as it was presented to the JNF, is that the Israel Lands Authority must adhere to the principles of equality, and is forbidden from discriminating against people based on their nationality, even when the land in question is owned by the JNF." *Haaretz*, May 20, 2007.

16.   See Amiram Barkat's and Yoval Yaoz's article, "Rightist MK: Fire AG for Letting Non-Jews Buy JNF Land," January 28, 2005.

17.   See Amiram Barkat's article, "70 percent of Israeli Jews oppose selling JNF lands to Arabs," *Haaretz*, January 10, 2005.

18.   *Haaretz*, July 24, 2007.

19.   This summary account taken from reports of the Anti-Defamation League, http://www.adl.org/Israel/Conversion/testing-principles.asp.

20.   *Mabat*, Israel Broadcasting Authority, November 27, 2005.

21.   *Haaretz*, September 20, 2005.

22.   *Journal of Educational Sociology*, Vol. 27, No. 8, Israel (April 1954), pp. 369–379.

23.   See Paul Eidelberg's paper presented to the American Political Science Association annual conference in Washington, D.C. on August 31, 1997.

24.   Tom Segev, *1949: The First Israelis*, New York: Free Press, 1986, pp. 45–6.

25.   *Haaretz*, November 9, 2006.

26.   This data is available from the Sikkuy site, "Employment, income and poverty."

27.   Interview, August 4, 2005.

28.   Sikkuy report, "Education, 2003–4."

29.   See Tamar Rotem's report, *Haaretz*, November 5, 2006.

30.   The poll was conducted by Haifa University professor Sammy Smoocha, and was published in *Haaretz*, March 13, 2007.

31.   *Haaretz*, September 19, 2005.

32.   *Yediot Aharonot*, December 18, 2005.

33.   These observations from the Palestine Center Annual Conference in Washington, D.C., November 2005.

34.   *Haaretz*, October 23, 2005.

35.   *New York Times*, January 21, 1972.

36.   "The High Court's Doomsday Weapon," *Haaretz*, May 15, 2006.

37.   See her article, "A Country for Some of Its Citizens," *Haaretz*, February 23, 2007.

Chapter Two: West Bank Settler

1. A version of this story appears in the prologue of the first edition of *The Tragedy of Zionism*, New York: Farrar, Straus, Giroux, 1985.

2. Interview, August 8, 2005.

3. *New York Review*, April 18, 1974.

4. See Sidra DeKoven Ezrahi, *Booking Passage: Exile and Homecoming in the Modern Jewish Imagination*, Berkeley: University of California Press, 2000.

5. http://www.knesset.gov.il/description/eng/eng_mimshal_yesod2.htm.

6. *The Accidental Empire: Israel and the Birth of the Settlements, 1967–1977*, New York: Times Books, 2006.

7. Townhall.com, January 30, 2006.

8. See Maxime Rodinson's *Israel: A Colonial Settler State?* New York: Monrad Press, 1973, pp. 41–55.

9. See Sa'id B. Himadeh's *The Economic Organization of Palestine*, American University of Beirut, 1938, p. 290.

10. I first discussed this matter at length in "Zionist Colonialism: Myth and Dilemma," *Dissent*, Spring 1975; see also *The Tragedy of Zionism*, chapter 5, "Independence or Colonialism."

Chapter Three: "A Spade to Dig With"

1. Reported by Hilary Appelman, Associated Press, December 31, 1997.

2. Israel Policy Forum, Weekly News Analysis, Washington, D.C., Volume 4.03.

3. Quoted from Jeffrey Goldberg's *New Yorker* article, "Among the Settlers," May 31, 2004.

4. "What Kind of Life Should We Create in Eretz Yisrael?" in *The Zionist Idea* (Hertzberg, ed.), New York, 1970, p. 546; see also the second edition of my book *The Tragedy of Zionism*, p. 96; I took the liberty of translating the word *Torah* to "Holy Law."

5. *Haaretz*, October 25, 2005.

6. Howard Sachar, *A History of Israel*, New York: Knopf, 1976, p. 380.

7. See Nehemia Strasler's "The Artful Dodgers," *Haaretz*, December 22, 2005.

8. *Haaretz*, November 17, 2006.

9. *Haaretz*, July 8, 2007.

10. November 4, 2005.

11. See Gerald M. Steinberg's report, Jerusalem Center for Public Affairs, October 2, 2000.

12. Jewish Telegraphic Agency, July 12, 1996.

13. *Trial and Error*, New York: Schocken, 1966, p. 464.

14. Reported in *Haaretz*, October 6, 2005.

15. See my article, "The Old West," *The American Scholar*, Spring 2003.

16. The Hebrew University's Menachem Brinker once told me that philosopher Isaiah Berlin once took him to a plaque over a cafeteria at Oxford's Balliol College, where these words were inscribed in Latin—"the harshest lie in the world," Berlin said.

17. Interview with the author, July 27, 2005.

18. December 26, 1926; see *Acts of Religion,* by Jacques Derrida, London: Routledge, 2002, p. 226.

19. I have myself in *the Tragedy of Zionism.* I followed Koestler's line of thought, expressing the fear that modern Hebrew, even with all its neologisms, lacked the word for *freedom* in Orwell's sense; that a child growing up in the most sheltered neighborhoods of Israel, with little higher education, and without exposure to the Western influences of, say, students at the Hebrew University, might be constrained to see *democratia* as vaguely inauthentic. I noted that the most common political word for freedom, *herut,* was immediately associated with the tradition of the Passover Haggadah, implying collective freedom from national domination; while the nuances of the term *chofesh haprat,* which did imply something like personal freedom, were actually given meaning by, precisely, a universe of imported and artificial-sounding terms, like *democratia* itself, or from British common law left over from the Mandate. The Hebrew University philosopher Avishai Margalit mocked my claim in *The Tragedy of Zionism,* suggesting that I was something of a Victorian snob who would elevate, not Hebrew, but English to "the divine language of God." (Children might learn the meaning of *hofesh,* he said, simply from the fact that this was their word for summer vacation, "the opportunity to do as you please and in your own good time and in places other than the usual.") He argued that Israel was becoming, if anything, a more democratic country, at least in the populist sense of "participation." I certainly did not mean to imply that Western-educated Israelis like Margalit are, by virtue of their Hebrew, less competent as democrats than Americans are; and if I was (and remain) in the thrall of a "liberal theology," Margalit has since shown then that he can be one of its most effective proselytizers.

20. Interview with the author, August 4, 2005.

21. Yehuda Amichai, *Shirei Yehuda Amichai,* Vol. 1, p. 86, Jerusalem: Schocken, 2002.

Chapter Four: The Center's Liberal Demography

1. See my article, "The Lost Tribes of Israel," *Prospect,* June 2001.

2. *Yediot Aharonot,* "The Barak Effect," June 14, 2007.

3. See Lilly Galili's article, "A Jewish Demographic State," *Haaretz,* June 27, 2002; and also *Haaretz,* February 25, 2003.

4. The interview was given to M. J. Rosenberg of the Israel Policy Forum, January 16, 2004.

5. See Judt's article, "Israel: The Alternative," *New York Review of Books*, October 23, 2003.

6. See my review of his book, *Peace in the Middle East?* and his response, *New York Review of Books*, January 23, 1974, and July 17, 1975. This exchange is still circulating widely on the Web.

7. *Haaretz*, December 17, 2006.

8. "The Inseparables," *New Yorker*, April 24, 1995.

9. "Letter to an American Friend: Soured Promise," *Jerusalem Post*, March 10, 1987.

10. See Yair Sheleg's excellent report on these matters, "Judaism First—Democracy Can Wait," *Haaretz*, April 16, 2002.

11. Uzi Arad, Uzi Dayan, and Yehezkel Dror, "Zionist Manifesto for the State of Israel" (Hebrew), Jerusalem, 2004.

12. "Swap Meet," *New Republic*, November 28, 2005.

13. Interview with Ari Shavit, *Haaretz*, January 9, 2004.

14. *Haaretz*, December 3, 2002.

15. "Camp David: The Tragedy of Errors," *New York Review of Books*, August 9, 2001.

Chapter Five: The Business of Integration

1. See his article in *Haaretz*, January 4, 2000.

2. See her article in *Haaretz*, February 26, 2007.

3. "Export Labels Split Israel," *Christian Science Monitor*, December 3, 2003.

4. See my article, "Why Israel's High-tech Boom Is in Danger," *Fortune*, May 11, 1998.

5. "Don't Bank on It," *Haaretz*, January 11, 2007.

6. See my article, "The Victory of the New Israel," *New York Review*, August 13, 1981; and "Israel's Future: Brainpower, High-Tech—and Peace," *Harvard Business Review*, November 1991.

7. *Mabat*, Israel Broadcasting Authority, December 7, 2005.

8. See his interview, *Haaretz*, March 3, 2007.

9. BBC report, June 7, 2004.

10. December 26, 2005.

11. The data has been collected by Meretz MK Avshalom Vilan.

12. April 24, 2006.

13. See Ruth Sinai's report, *Haaretz*, December 25, 2005.

14. *Jerusalem Post*, May 6, 2006.

15. Institute for Economic and Social Policy at the Shalem Center in Jerusalem, headed by Professor Omer Moav and Dr. Arik Gold, *Haaretz*, June 11, 2007.

Chapter Six: Hebrew Revolution

1. "On Brothers and Others," G.T. Reimer and J. Kates, eds., *Beginning Anew: A Woman's Companion to the High Holy Days*, New York: Simon and Schuster, 1997.

2.   *Trial and Error*, p. 54.

3.   *Harper's*, April 2005; my original article, "Saving Israel from Itself," appeared in the January 2005 issue.

4.   See Shachar Ilan's full report in *Haaretz*, January 11, 2007.

5.   *Sleeping on a Wire*, Chaim Watzman, trans., originally published in 1994; Picador edition, 2003, pp. 252–4.

Conclusion: Closing the Circle

1.   *Haaretz*, January 26, 2006.

2.   Conference notes. See his publications.

3.   http://www.jewishvirtuallibrary.org/jsource/History/jewref.html.

4.   http://memri.org/bin/articles.cgi?Page=archives&Area=sd&ID=SP42802.

5.   http://www.guardian.co.uk/comment/story/0,3604,417958,00.html.

6.   http://www.fallingrain.com/world/WE/0/Abu_Dis.html.

7.   http://www.geneva-accord.org/HomePage.aspx?FolderID=11&lang=en.

8.   *New Yorker*, February 27, 2006.

9.   See Nazir Majali, "Philosophy of Death," *Haaretz*, April 23, 2006.

10.   *Toronto Star*, June 14, 2006.

11.   *New York Review*, "Jordan: Looking for an Opening," September 27, 1984.

12.   See Daniel Pipe's "Iran's Final Solution Plan," *New York Sun*, November 1, 2005; see also my analysis of Richard Pipe's nuclear views in "Breaking Faith: Commentary and American Jews," *Dissent*, Spring 1981.

Index